SOCIAL HOUSING, DISADVANTAGE AND NEIGHBOURHOOD LIVEABILITY

In a groundbreaking study carried out in the late 1990s, researchers studied seven similar social housing neighbourhoods in Ireland to determine what factors affected their liveability. In this collection of essays, the same researchers return to these neighbourhoods ten years later to see what's changed. Are these neighbourhoods now more liveable or leaveable?

Social Housing, Disadvantage and Neighbourhood Liveability examines the major national and local developments that affected these neighbourhoods: the Celtic Tiger boom, area-based interventions, and reforms in social housing management. Additionally, the book examines changes in the culture of social housing through studies of crime within social housing, changes in public service delivery, and media reporting on social housing.

Michelle Norris is a Senior Lecturer in social policy at the School of Applied Social Science, University College Dublin. In 2010 she was appointed to the National Economic and Social Council, which advises the Irish government on social and economic policy, and in 2011 she was appointed as chair of the board of the Housing Finance Agency, which finances housing for low-income households in Ireland. She also convenes the Comparative Housing Working Group of the European Network for Housing Research (ENHR).

Housing and society series
Edited by Ray Forrest, School for Policy Studies,
University of Bristol

This series aims to situate housing within its wider social, political and economic context at both national and international level. In doing so it will draw on the full range of social science disciplines and on mainstream debate on the nature of contemporary social change. The books are intended to appeal to an international academic audience as well as to practitioners and policymakers – to be theoretically informed and policy relevant.

Housing Young People
Edited by Ray Forrest and Ngai-Ming Yip

Beyond Home Ownership
Edited by Richard Ronald and Marja Elsinga

Housing Disadvantaged People?
Jane Ball

Women and Housing
Edited by Patricia Kennett and Chan Kam Wah

Affluence, Mobility and Second Home Ownership
Chris Paris

Housing, Markets and Policy
Peter Malpass and Rob Rowlands

Housing and Health in Europe
Edited by David Ormandy

The Hidden Millions
Graham Tipple and Suzanne Speak

Housing, Care and Inheritance
Misa Izuhara

Housing and Social Transition in Japan
Edited by Yosuke Hirayama and Richard Ronald

Housing Transformations
Shaping the space of 21st century living
Bridget Franklin

Housing and Social Policy
Contemporary themes and critical perspectives
Edited by Peter Somerville with Nigel Sprigings

Housing and Social Change
East–West perspectives
Edited by Ray Forrest and James Lee

Urban Poverty, Housing and Social Change in China
Ya Ping Wang

Gentrification in a Global Context
Edited by Rowland Atkinson and Gary Bridge

SOCIAL HOUSING, DISADVANTAGE AND NEIGHBOURHOOD LIVEABILITY

Ten years of change in social housing neighbourhoods

Edited by Michelle Norris

Routledge
Taylor & Francis Group

NEW YORK AND LONDON

First edition published 2014
by Routledge
711 Third Avenue, New York, NY 10017

and by Routledge
2 Park Square, Milton Park, Abingdon, Oxon OX14 4RN

Routledge is an imprint of the Taylor & Francis Group, an informa business

British Library Cataloguing in Publication Data
A catalogue record for this book is available from the British Library

Library of Congress Cataloging-in-Publication Data
Social housing, disadvantage, and neighbourhood liveability : ten years of change in social housing neighbourhoods / edited by Michelle Norris.
    pages cm.—(Housing and society series)
  Includes bibliographical references and index.
  1. Public housing—Ireland. 2. Housing policy—Ireland. 3. Crime in public housing—Ireland. 4. Ireland—Social policy. I. Norris, Michelle.
  HD7288.78.I73S658 2014
  363.5'8509416—dc23
  2013018106

ISBN13: 978-0-415-81639-7 (hbk)
ISBN13: 978-0-415-81640-3 (pbk)
ISBN13: 978-0-203-44085-8 (ebk)

Typeset in Bembo
by RefineCatch Limited, Bungay, Suffolk

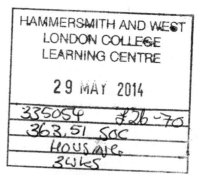

MIX
Paper from
responsible sources
FSC
www.fsc.org   FSC® C013056

Printed and bound in Great Britain by
TJ International Ltd, Padstow, Cornwall

CONTENTS

FIGURES, IMAGES AND TABLES

Figures

Images

Tables

ACKNOWLEDGEMENTS

This book is the result of contributions made by numerous people over a long period. These contributors are too many to name individually but the authors would like to collectively thank all of the residents and service providers in the seven case study neighbourhoods who were interviewed during the 1997–8 and 2007–9 rounds of fieldwork and were so open and honest in your views and generous with your time. We hope that we have represented your views accurately in the book and painted a fair and balanced picture of life in the neighbourhoods where you live.

The authors would like to thank the following people who made a central contribution to the completion of the fieldwork on which the book draws:

1 Catherine Anne Field (University College Dublin) conducted fieldwork in Fettercairn and Fatima Mansions, Dublin and acted as project coordinator during the 2007–9 phase of the study; Jackie O'Toole (Institute of Technology, Sligo) conducted most of the fieldwork on Cranmore, Sligo; and Alan Egan conducted the fieldwork in Deanrock, Cork during this phase.

2 Kathleen O'Higgins (formerly of the Economic and Social Research Institute), Ruiraí McAuliffe and Séamus Ó'Cinnéide (both formerly of NUI Maynooth) and Dónal Guerin (Cork City Council) who contributed to the fieldwork and write up of phase one of the study in 1997–8.

3 Joe Donoghue (Fatima Groups United) and John Whyte (Fatima Regeneration Board and F2 Centre) who provided us with information on Fatima Mansions during both phases of the study and helped us access interviewees in that neighbourhood during both rounds of fieldwork.

4 Paddy Flannery and Martin Sinnott (Moyross Community Enterprise Centre), Chris Sheridan (Health Service Executive), Anne Kavanagh and Helen Fitzgerald (Paul Partnership), and Kieran Lehane (Limerick City Council)

who provided us with information on Moyross and helped us access interviews there in 2007–9.
5 The following people who took the photos included in the book: Matt Kavanagh (3.1, 3.3), Brenda Fitzsimons (3.2), and Chris Maguire (3.5). Thanks also to Clúid Housing Association, which contributed Image 3.4.

In addition, we would like to acknowledge the contribution of the organisations that funded the research. The first phase of the research was undertaken on the initiative of the Katherine Howard Foundation, which also provided substantial funding. The Department of the Environment, Community and Local Government, the Combat Poverty Agency and Area Development Management also contributed funding for the first phase. By 2007–9 the Combat Poverty Agency had been amalgamated into the Department of Social Protection and Area Development Management had been renamed Pobal, but both organisations repeated their funding for the second phase of the research in their new guises, as did the Department of the Environment, Community and Local Government.

Parts of Chapter 4 were originally published in M. Norris and C. O'Connell (2010) 'Social Housing Management, Governance and Delivery in Ireland: Ten Years of Reform on Seven Estates', *Housing Studies*, 25 (3).

CONTRIBUTORS

Mary P. Corcoran is Professor of Sociology at the National University of Ireland, Maynooth, where she is also a research associate at the National Institute for Regional and Spatial Analysis (NIRSA). She is a graduate of Trinity College, Dublin and Columbia University, New York. Her research and teaching interests lie primarily in the fields of urban sociology, public culture, and the sociology of migration. The author of numerous scholarly articles and reports, in recent years she has co-authored *A Sociology of Ireland* (fourth edition, 2012, with Perry Share and Brian Conway) and *Suburban Affiliations: Social Relations in the Greater Dublin Area* (2010, co-author with Jane Gray and Michel Peillon) and co-edited *Reflections on crisis: the role of the public intellectual* (2012, with Kevin Lalor) and *Ireland of the Illusions: a sociological chronicle 2007–2008* (2010 with Perry Share).

Eoin Devereux is Senior Lecturer in Sociology at the University of Limerick. With research and teaching interests in both economic and cultural sociology, Eoin's work has focused on the theme of media representations of class and other social inequalities. He is the author of the academic bestseller *Understanding the Media* (second edition) and the editor of *Media studies: Key issues and debates*, both published by Sage in 2007. Other publications include the co-edited book *Morrissey: Fandom, representations and identities* (2011, co-authored with A. Dillane and M. Power) and 'Behind The Headlines: Media Coverage of Social Exclusion in Limerick city – The Case of Moyross' in N. Hourigan (ed.) *Understanding Limerick: Social Exclusion and Change* (2011, co-authored with A. Haynes and M. Power).

Tony Fahey is Professor of Social Policy at University College Dublin. His research deals with a range of issues connected to social policy in Ireland and the European Union, including family dynamics, housing, poverty, and spatial aspects of disadvantage and of policy responses to disadvantage. Current projects include a detailed analysis of family well-being in Ireland based on the data from the Growing Up in Ireland survey and an international study on the impact of social inequalities on family patterns in European countries.

Catherine Anne Field is a Lecturer in public health in the National University of Ireland, Galway. She co-ordinated the 2007–2009 phase of this study and also conducted the fieldwork on a number of the case study neighbourhoods.

Trutz Haase has been an independent social and economic consultant since 1995. Previously, he worked for the Northern Ireland Economic Research Centre (Belfast), the Combat Poverty Agency (Dublin) and the Educational Research Centre at St. Patrick's College (Dublin). Throughout his work as a consultant, he has been responsible for the design and implementation of monitoring and evaluation frameworks for government programmes aimed at alleviating poverty, as well as developing resource allocation models to target social expenditure on the basis of objective need criteria. In this capacity, he has worked for a number of Irish government ministries, municipalities, and non-governmental agencies. He is best known for his work on the development of the Pobal HP Deprivation Index, which features in the National Spatial Strategy and the current Regional and Local Development Plans. Work outside the Republic of Ireland includes studies for the Northern Ireland Statistics and Research Agency, Special EU Programmes Body, International Fund for Ireland, OECD and European Monitoring Centre for Drugs and Drug Addiction.

Amanda Haynes is a Lecturer in sociology at the University of Limerick. Her research interests centre on the analysis of discursive constructions as processes of exclusion and strategies for inclusion and include a particular interest in their relationship to inequalities in status, treatment, and material conditions on the basis of ethnicity, racism, citizenship, and social class. Her publications include 'Class Invisibility and Stigmatisation: Irish Media Coverage of a Public Housing Project in Limerick' in C. Pascale (ed.) *Social Inequality and the Politics of Representation: A Global Landscape* (2012, co-authored with M. Power and E. Devereux); 'Why Bother Seeing the World for Real? Google Street View and the Representation of a Stigmatised Neighbourhood' in *New Media and Society* (2013, co-authored with M.J. Power, P. Neville, E. Devereux, and C. Barnes); 'At the edge: Media constructions of a stigmatised Irish housing estate' in *Journal of Housing and the Built Environment* (2011, co-authored with E. Devereux and M.J. Power); and 'Mass Media Re-Presentations of the Social World: Ethnicity and "Race"' in E. Devereux (ed.) *Media Studies: Key Issues and Debates* (2007).

Eileen Humphreys is a Postdoctoral Fellow at the Institute for the Study of Knowledge in Society (ISKS) at the University of Limerick. She has worked in public policy research or consultancy since 1986 on social capital in local communities of place (urban and rural); social aspects of urban regeneration (education, labour market); and health inequalities. Working within a neighbourhood-based analytical framework, current or recent research includes: outcomes for children and families; health inequalities in ageing populations in urban neighbourhoods; evaluation of area-based regeneration. She has worked extensively on programmes supported by EU Structural Funds, which adopt a local development approach.

Des McCafferty is Professor and Head of the Department of Geography in Mary Immaculate College, University of Limerick, and a research associate of the National Institute for Regional and Spatial Analysis. His research interests lie in urban geography, with a particular focus on issues of residential segregation, urban poverty and disadvantage, and area-based measures to combat exclusion, and he has participated in both Irish and European research projects in these areas. Recent work includes a report (co-authored with Eileen Humphreys and Ann Higgins) on children and families in Limerick's regeneration estates, which was commissioned by Limerick city Children's Services Committee. He has served, on election, as President of the Geographical Society of Ireland and as Chairman of the Irish Branch of the Regional Studies Association.

Michelle Norris is a Senior Lecturer in social policy at the School of Applied Social Science, University College Dublin. Her research interests centre on social housing management and finance, urban regeneration in Ireland, and also on comparative analysis of these policy fields across the European Union. She has led over 20 research projects on these issues since 2000 and produced 50 publications on the results and her work had a significant impact on housing policy in Ireland. In 2010 she was appointed to the National Economic and Social Council, which advises the Irish government on social and economic policy, and in 2011 she was appointed as chair of the board of the Housing Finance Agency, which finances housing for low-income households in Ireland. She also convenes the Comparative Housing Working Group of the European Network for Housing Research (ENHR) with Professor Mark Stephens of Herriot Watt University, Edinburgh.

Cathal O'Connell is a Senior Lecturer in social policy at the School of Applied Social Studies, University College Cork. His research and teaching interests centre on the development of Irish social policy, housing policy, and social housing management. His recent publications include: *The State and Housing in Ireland* (2007, Nova Press); 'Citizenship and Social Exclusion in Limerick', in N. Hourigan (ed.) *Understanding Limerick: Social Exclusion and Change* (Cork University Press, 2011); and 'Social Housing Management, Governance and Delivery in Ireland: Ten Years of Reform on Seven Estates', *Housing Studies*, 25(10), 317–34 (with M. Norris).

Aileen O'Gorman is a Postdoctoral Research Fellow in the School of Applied Social Science, University College Dublin. Her research interests include drug use, drug markets, and drugs policy; inequality and spatialised social exclusion; community development and community activism; the interplay between social, crime, drug, and urban policies; area-based initiatives and regeneration; research methodologies and community/participatory research. She is author of a number of commissioned research studies, has published in international journals and presented her work at national and international conferences. She has worked as a researcher in a variety of university, government, media, and community settings including the National Advisory Committee on Drugs, Ireland; the Centre for Urban and Community Research, Goldsmiths College, University of London; the Drug Indicators Project, Birkbeck College, University of London; *the Daily Telegraph*, London; and Fatima Mansions, Dublin. She is a member of the European Society for Social Drugs Research; has provided drugs research training programmes in Ireland and Europe; has participated in a number of expert working groups for the European Monitoring Centre for Drugs and Drug Addiction; and is a member of the editorial board of the international journal *Drugs, Education, Prevention and Policy*.

Martin J. Power is a Lecturer in sociology at the University of Limerick, Ireland. With a specific focus on the sociology of urban regeneration, his research interests include social class, inequality and social exclusion, and neo-liberalism and the retraction of the welfare state. His publications include 'Tarring everyone with the same shorthand? Journalists, stigmatization & social exclusion' in *Journalism: Theory, Practice and Criticism* (2012, co-authored with E. Devereux and A. Haynes); 'Exploring the "learning careers" of Irish undergraduate Sociology students through the establishment of a Sociology Student Journal' in *Teaching Sociology* (2012, co-authored with P. Neville, A. Haynes, E. Devereux, and C. Barnes); and 'Internalising Discourses of Parental Blame: Voices from the Field' in *Studies in the Maternal – Special Edition on Austerity Parenting* (2012, co-authored with C. Barnes).

GLOSSARY

ABIs	Area-based interventions – publicly funded programmes aimed at combating disadvantage in neighbourhoods that are targeted on the basis that they are identified as disadvantaged.
ALMP	Active labour market programmes – measures to enable long-term benefit claimants to gain skills and network with potential employers, which will help them make the transition back into the mainstream labour market.
CCTV	Closed-circuit television.
CE	Community Employment – the principal ALMP in the seven case study neighbourhoods at the time of writing. It pays a small additional stipend to benefit recipients in return for part-time work on social projects and also provides training.
CLÁR	Ceantair Laga Árd-Riachtanais – Gaelic title, which translates as 'impaired high-need areas', this programme directs public expenditure to the most disadvantaged rural areas of Ireland.
DEIS	Delivering Equality of Opportunity in Schools – a public programme that aims to overcome educational disadvantage by additional investment in schools selected on the basis that they have a disadvantaged student body.
ED	Electoral Division – small areas into which census data can be disaggregated.
EOCP	Equal Opportunities Childcare Programme – a public programme to provide childcare to enable parents to return to education or employment. The programme ran from 2000 to 2006.

Garda (plural Gardaí)	Irish police force.
GDP	Gross Domestic Product.
GNI	Gross National Income.
Guards	Informal name for the Irish police force.
GYDP	Garda Youth Diversion Projects – community-based projects run by the Gardaí that aim to help young people move away from behaviour that might get them into trouble with the law.
LDSIP	Local Development and Social Inclusion Programme – funding programme for area-based initiatives in Ireland.
LDTFs	Local Drug Task Forces – area-based initiatives established in neighbourhoods where heroin use is most prevalent.
LES	Local Employment Service – area-based intervention that aims to promote the reintegration of long-term unemployed people into the workforce.
MABS	Money Advice and Budgeting Service – a state-funded debt and financial management advice service.
NDS	National Drugs Strategy – national strategy statement on illegal drug use first introduced to cover the period 2001–8 and renewed for 2009–16.
NESC	National Economic and Social Council – a national corporatist body that advises the Irish government on economic and social policy issues.
PHDI	Pobal Haase–Pratschke Deprivation Index – created by Trutz Haase and Jonathan Pratschke (Haase and Pratschke 2008).
POBAL	A not-for-profit company with charitable status set up by government for the purpose of managing programmes for government and the EU.
RAPID	Revitalising Areas by Planning, Investment and Development – a local development programme, targeting deprived urban neighbourhoods.
RDTFs	Regional Drug Task Forces – programmes with a similar structure and remit to the LDTFs, but covering larger areas (regions, rather than city neighbourhoods or towns).
RTÉ	Radio Telefís Éireann – Ireland's national television and radio broadcaster.
Social Partnership	The corporatist system of policy making that was influential in Ireland during the period under examination in this book.
Taoiseach	Irish prime minister.

1

INTRODUCTION

Tony Fahey, Michelle Norris and Catherine Anne Field

Introduction

This book provides an analysis of over a decade of social change and public policy intervention in seven social housing neighbourhoods in Ireland, viewed in the context of national and European trends in urban neighbourhood disadvantage and renewal. It emerges from a research project on the seven neighbourhoods carried out between late 2007 and early 2009, which extended an earlier study of the same neighbourhoods carried out by more or less the same group of researchers in 1997–8 (see Fahey, 1999, for an account of the earlier study). The more recent study thus took the form of a ten-year follow-up to that original work. Although there were some differences in the questions asked and research methods employed in the original and follow-up phases, the project as a whole offers a quasi-longitudinal perspective on the trajectory of seven social housing neighbourhoods during a ten-year period in Ireland, when the economy boomed and the state greatly expanded its policy responses to the problems of poor urban neighbourhoods. The interest of the study thus lies in the decade-wide then-and-now character of the analysis it provides and its detailed examination of how national trends and policies are reflected in the circumstances of particular neighbourhoods.

In this book, the researchers who conducted the study draw on the knowledge they accumulated from the initial and follow-up phases to present and analyse aspects of the life of the neighbourhoods and their development over the ten years encompassed by the study. The chapters in the book are separately authored. The topic each contributing author deals with and the approach adopted, in part, reflect his or her individual expertise and perspective but together the contributions seek to build what we hope is an inclusive and coherent picture. Most of the analyses focus on what happened over the ten-year period in the seven neighbourhoods, taking account of initial conditions as reported in the original study and attempting to trace the trajectories that led to outcomes that could be observed ten years later. The book thus expands on the original study primarily by adding a ten-year time dimension but also by reflecting further on the lessons to be learned from the experiences of the seven neighbourhoods over the whole period and what these might mean for policy.

Themes

As part of that further reflection, we develop the concept of 'social liveability' in the present book and use it as a framework within which to restate key insights from the original study and focus the findings of the follow-up (see below for an outline of the origins of this concept). This concept is intended to draw attention to the attractiveness of neighbourhoods in residential terms as a feature that is analytically distinct from their level of social disadvantage and warrants attention in its own right from academic analysis and policy intervention. It emerged early on in our study of the seven neighbourhoods that wide variation between and within them in their attractiveness to residents was one of their most evident and striking features. One only had to walk into the neighbourhoods to see that some were physically neat, orderly and little different in appearance from surrounding middle-class neighbourhoods (save perhaps for the sometimes smaller size of dwellings), while others were dilapidated, rubbish strewn, defaced with graffiti, bare of foliage and sometimes pock-marked with empty, boarded-up units. In some cases, that contrast leaped out within a two-minute walk in the same neighbourhood as one turned from a well-settled and thriving street or road or block of flats in a particular housing development to its twin around the corner that could be a depressing picture of shabbiness. Interviews with residents and analysis of housing allocations backed up these visible contrasts in that areas that looked well typically were in high demand – they had waiting lists of prospective tenants who wanted to get in or, in the case of social housing that had been purchased by tenants, commanded reasonable prices in the housing market. Areas that looked distressed, by contrast, had waiting lists of tenants seeking to transfer elsewhere or had experienced a collapse in prices for privatised dwellings. The differing levels of attractiveness of a neighbourhood to residents were thus evident not only in sharp differences in visual appeal but also through residents' revealed preferences as expressed either by actual movement into or out of the neighbourhood or by waiting lists in the case of social housing tenants or house prices in the case of private purchasers (see further below on the concept of liveability).

In light of their origins in broadly similar socioeconomic contexts and physical design configurations, that variation between and within social housing neighbourhoods, in our view, was a puzzle. Why did neighbourhoods – or parts of neighbourhoods – that fundamentally were so similar turn out so differently? Why did some tip over into spirals of decline, while the majority settled and evolved into unremarkable and broadly well-integrated residential environments? Why was it necessary to mount massive programmes of 'regeneration' in some areas (which often involved extensive demolition of sometimes relatively new housing) and not in similar areas nearby?

It seemed important to try to answer these questions, in part because of the harm that was caused to residents in areas where failures of liveability occurred – whatever disadvantage those residents may have experienced as low-income households could be made worse by the sharp deterioration in the quality of the local environment that neighbourhood failure entailed. A better understanding of how such deterioration happened and how it might be averted thus seemed worthwhile. There was also a concern about the waste of public resources that occurred when the decline of a neighbourhood caused what was often expensive and well-built social housing to fall into ruination. In addition, it seemed important to highlight these wide contrasts and the exceptional nature of truly bad outcomes in order to combat the negative stereotyping of social housing that often cropped up in public discourse and provided an ill-informed influence on housing policy decisions.

From the outset, then, our approach focused on *differentiation* as a key feature of social housing neighbourhoods. That approach acknowledges the general risk factors that affect most social housing – high concentrations of low-income households, low educational levels in the resident population, high unemployment rates, insufficient local amenities and facilities, urban design features that are not always suitable, and so on. When it comes to accounting for the fate of neighbourhoods, these risk factors have some explanatory purchase, not least because they indicate why failures of liveability typically occur in social housing rather than in areas of private middle-class housing. These factors are also important in their own right because they point to limitations in the life chances of those affected that warrant being tackled by public policy.

Important as these risk factors are in themselves, however, they do not account for the differentiation that occurs *within* social housing, particularly when we recall the micro-level on which that differentiation can sometimes occur. The usually cited risk factors are distributed too widely and uniformly in the social housing sector and are too inconsistently linked to the circumstances of particular neighbourhoods to explain their contrasting outcomes. In fact, from our survey of the largely successful history of social housing in Ireland in the original study (Fahey, 1999), it emerged that urban areas with concentrations of socially disadvantaged tenant households succeeded more often than they failed. The most common outcome was that they created settled, liveable neighbourhoods that merged seamlessly into the general urban housing fabric. With the passage of time and the operation of tenant purchase schemes, those areas often blended into the private housing sector and their original social housing neighbourhoods were largely forgotten.

Another way of stating this outcome is that while all problematic neighbourhoods had relatively disadvantaged resident populations, only a minority of disadvantaged population clusters generated unliveable neighbourhoods. Sometimes, indeed, it seemed that the link between the social profile of the resident population and the social quality of the neighbourhood environment contained an element of reverse causality: the emergence of the first signs of deterioration in a social housing complex or neighbourhood could prompt a flight of better-functioning households and set in train a downward local spiral of weakening social composition and worsening liveability in the locality.

This perspective, therefore, considers neighbourhood liveability and the social profile of the resident population as analytically distinct issues, while also recognising that they are closely interlinked. In the original study, as we sought to disentangle these two elements and focus more closely on liveability, we concluded that physical factors – the location, build quality, housing type, and size of neighbourhoods – could be important influences but usually were of secondary significance. Social factors, rather, were the primary proximate influence. As a general rule, people were willing to live in poor buildings if the quality of community and neighbourhood life was good, but they were unwilling to live in good buildings if they considered the quality of community/neighbourhood life to be poor (Norris, 1999).

Examining what the crucial social influences were, we pointed to the central role of highly contingent micro-level factors that in their most proximate and visible form turned on aspects of local social order or what is now often referred to as community safety. These factors undoubtedly were rooted in macro-social conditions but at local level were uneven and unpredictable in their pattern of occurrence. They usually emanated from small numbers of troubled and disruptive households or individuals whose 'acting out' behaviour in public spaces in particular areas lay at the core of the more damaging forms of neighbourhood liveability problems. These problems could manifest themselves in the form of noisy or unruly neighbours, vandalism, joy-riding, harassment, or levels of criminality ranging from petty burglary and local drug dealing through to serious organised gang violence. In some (though not all) of the neighbourhoods in our study, illegal drugs were at the centre of many social order problems, though the nature of the activities involved varied and changed over time, ranging from drug dealing and drug taking in public spaces to violent conflict between drug-dealing gangs (see Chapter 8). The typical view of residents in locations most affected by factors such as these was that while community was strong and supportive in the area, the social quality of the locality was undermined by small groups of neighbours who behaved in these disruptive ways and blighted the lives of those around them (for a similar picture of micro-variation in disadvantaged communities in Ireland and its links with social order problems see Hourigan's account of 'micro-social systems' in disadvantaged areas in Limerick city – Hourigan, 2011, pp. 60–73).

Residents considered that they suffered doubly from the disruptive minorities – first because they were often the direct victims of their actions, and second because the disruptive few undermined the reputation of neighbourhoods and gave rise to a stigma that affected all residents equally. The distinction drawn by residents between the 'sound' majority and the few disruptive troublemakers undoubtedly oversimplified reality, but it nevertheless seemed to capture an important part of the dynamic of decline in unsuccessful neighbourhoods (O'Higgins, 1999).

While the majority of residents often considered themselves the victims of troublemaking minorities within neighbourhoods, those troublemakers, viewed from a different perspective, often emerged as victims themselves. They typically came from dysfunctional family backgrounds or suffered from problems such as mental illness, personality disorders, drug or alcohol dependence, or a persistent history of personal failure and low self-esteem. Many thus had difficulties and rights that needed to be taken into account in devising remedies for troubled neighbourhoods, though in instances where disruptive behaviour had escalated into criminality, the urgent primary requirement from a neighbourhood pro-tection point of view was effective policing to remove or contain the threat the behaviour represented.

Furthermore, when it came to services, the inability of particular relevant services to deal with the needs and problems of these small segments of the population could be identified as a central problem in its own right, over and above any general limitations in services as a means to address wider patterns of social disadvantage. General improvements in service quality thus needed to include measures to reach out to the most marginalised families and individuals – what Hourigan (2011) calls the 'disadvantaged of the disadvantaged'. The study concurred with criticisms of the historically poor estate management record of local authorities but also found that moves towards a more hands-on responsive management approach had been in place since the early 1990s. The impact of that development had not become evident by the time the study was carried out (Guerin, 1999).

The conclusions and recommendations of the original study highlighted the need for social housing policy and practice to focus on social order issues and move them to the top of the agenda as a necessary first step in regenerating problem neighbourhoods. It pointed in particular to the need to put in place both preventive and treatment measures that would target those who were the cause of disruption and provide them with the supports and controls that would enable them to integrate more effectively into the community. However, it also emphasised the importance of not overstating the prevalence or severity of social problems in local authority housing, in view of the large segments of the social housing sector where these problems were absent or slight (Fahey, 1999).

From original study to follow-up

Social housing is intended to alleviate social deprivation, yet by the 1980s and 1990s, in Ireland as in many other countries in Europe, it was often blamed for worsening the plight of the poor. The most common criticism was that it concen-trated deprived people into large, unattractive, poorly serviced neighbourhoods and so fomented social problems – poverty, crime, drug addiction, vandalism, and alienation – and provided a poor physical and social environment for personal well-being and family life (Emms, 1990). The 1997–8 study sought to test this view in the Irish case by examining seven social housing neighbourhoods in detail and locating them within the broader picture of social housing in Ireland. As outlined in the previous section, it found that the negative portrayal of the failures of social housing was excessively bleak and undiscriminating. It argued for a more nuanced analysis that recognised differentiation of outcomes as a key feature and sought to pinpoint more precisely how differentiation occurred and what were the causes of the extreme high-profile instances of failure that did so much to colour the overall perception of social housing.

In the ten years after the original study was carried out two major strands of social change emerged in Ireland that were likely to have affected the seven neighbourhoods. One was the boom in the economy that took off around 1994–5 and was only beginning to affect the neighbourhoods when the original study began in 1997. During this boom, Ireland had among the fastest growth rates in the developed world – Irish GNP per head more than doubled between 1994 and 2007. The numbers at work rose from 1.2 million in 1994 to 2.1 million in 2007, and the unemployment rate fell from 16 per cent in 1994 to 4 per cent in 2000, at which level it remained until 2007. The long-term unemployment rate fell from almost 11 per cent in the late 1980s to just over 1 per cent in 2001 (Central Statistics Office, various years b). Some analyses of the boom concluded that it effected a marked decline in consistent poverty (the official government definition of poverty, which incorporates both income and lifestyle deprivation) and that increased public spending improved the quality of public services (Layte, Nolan, and Nolan, 2008; Russell, Maître, and Nolan, 2010). Others emphasised the negligible decline in income inequality over the period of the Celtic Tiger (e.g. Nolan and Maître, 2008), the unequal distribution of the benefits between capital and labour (Allen, 2000; O'Hearn, 1998), and the large portion of public expenditure increases accounted for by higher public sector salaries and employee numbers rather than service expansion (Kelly, McGuinness, and O'Connell, 2009). In the light of debates about what the social impact of the boom was (Fahey, Russell, and Whelan, 2008), the question arose whether the benefits of the boom filtered into poorer urban neighbourhoods, including our study neighbourhoods, and what could be learned from their experience about the effects of rising national prosperity on deprived urban areas generally.

The second key development was the growing reliance in public policy on area-based interventions (ABIs) as a means to alleviate disadvantage and promote social and economic progress in deprived areas. This development was common to many countries and reflected a widespread international view that characteristics of poor places as well as poor people needed to be taken into account and tackled by anti-poverty policy. The standard focus of the welfare state on policies for people rather than places seemed insufficient to deal with poverty black-spots and so add-on ABIs that intensified the efforts of the welfare state, in particular high-need neighbourhoods, were developed in a wide variety of forms, particularly since the early 1990s (Lupton and Turok, 2004; Modarres, 2002; O'Connor, 1999; Smith, 1999). These measures arose in many different areas of social provision, including active labour market programmes (ALMPs), educational initiatives, and criminal justice measures (OECD, 1999; McLaughlin, 2005). They had in common that they utilised some means of identifying relatively small areas – 'neighbourhoods', loosely defined – that could be construed as multiply disadvantaged and sought to construct

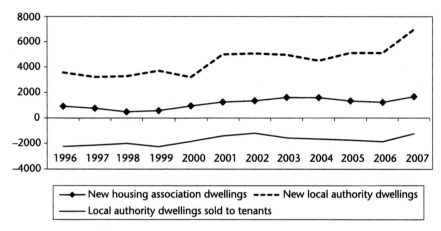

FIGURE 1.1 Social housing output and sales to tenants in Ireland, 1996–2007

Source: Department of the Environment, Community and Local Government (various years)

either single-sector or multi-sector interventions that worked through local communities and public agencies over limited periods of time (usually months or small numbers of years) in order to bring about one-off uplift in local social conditions in those neighbourhoods (Madanipour, Cars, and Allen, 2002).

In Ireland, interest in area-based initiatives first emerged in the 1980s in response to high concentrations of unemployment in particular areas. That interest expanded from the early 1990s and gave rise to a large and diverse range of programmes originating in a number of government departments and agencies, targeting a number of forms of disadvantage, and, in most cases, operating through quite elaborate local partnership structures (Geoghegan and Powell, 2006; Haase and McKeown, 2003; Walsh, 1999). While their core objective was to improve living conditions and employment prospects in poor neighbourhoods, these programmes were also championed by some as having broader significance – for example, as a means to empower local communities, improve the quality of local democracy and stimulate innovation in social and political as well as economic life (Sabel, 1996).

By the mid-1990s, all the seven neighbourhoods in the present study were the target of such interventions, in many instances multiply so (O'Cinnéide, 1999). Over the following decade, the number and scope of programmes increased to the point where at least some of the neighbourhoods were densely supplied by activities that, in most cases, were largely separate and uncoordinated and were difficult to list and count much less view in an integrated way. Ireland as a whole, and the seven neighbourhoods in the present study in particular, thus presented an instance of intensive development of the area-based approach – but in an unfocused, uncoordinated way. The programmes mounted within this approach have generally been closely monitored from a rule compliance viewpoint and some have been subjected to outcome assessment. But the usual practice in monitoring, at national and even more at local level, has been to focus on inputs and processes rather than outcomes and to look at programmes individually rather than at their collective scale and impact (Fitzpatrick and Associates, 2007; Bamber *et al.*, 2010). Thus part of the rationale for the present study was the desire to fill a gap in our understanding of this area first by providing a bird's eye view at the national level of the scale and nature of area-based anti-poverty programmes in Ireland and, against that background, to provide a local perspective on what these programmes amounted to on the ground in the seven neighbourhoods in the study.

Prompted by interest in these issues, the core members of the same team that had carried out the original study re-assembled in 2007 in order to design and carry out a ten-year follow-up study of the same seven neighbourhoods. The broad purpose was to examine how the liveability of the neighbourhoods had developed over the ten-year period, particularly in light of the two main developments in the national context just outlined. The study therefore adopted a two-stranded approach − a *social strand* focusing on socioeconomic change in the neighbourhoods and a *policy strand* that aimed to document and analyse state interventions in the neighbourhoods, particularly those that could be classified as area-based interventions.

The objective of the social strand was to document change in social conditions in the study neighbourhoods under a number of headings − employment, unemployment and living standards, housing standards and the built environment, social order, neighbourhood and community, and relationships with state agencies − and to locate these changes within broader social and economic trends in urban areas in Ireland. The policy strand of the study sought to outline the growth of international interest in area-based anti-poverty initiatives since the 1960s, provide a national overview of these initiatives in Ireland and their expansion since the early 1990s, trace their presence and significance in the study neighbourhoods, and draw conclusions on their value for combating social disadvantage. In the present book, as we outline further later on, we present a section of each of these two strands, but we also take selected topics that warranted closer attention and gather them together in a third section where social change and policy development are treated in combination.

International research context: differentiation and liveability

The study is located at the intersection of a number of traditions of research on urban social disadvantage found in developed countries, particularly in Western Europe. One relates to the nature and trajectory of social conditions in urban social housing neighbourhoods and their levels of what we refer to as 'social liveability'.

During its 'golden age' in Europe, in the decades after the Second World War, the social housing sector grew rapidly and was widely viewed as a solution to slum living, housing shortages, and unaffordable rents (Harloe, 1995). However, as that era came to an end in the 1970s, perceptions of social housing changed and many observers began to see it as a cause rather than a solution to urban poverty (Dunleavy, 1981). The sector entered what was perceived as a new era of 'slummification'

(Vestergaard, 1998, p. 115) as it became increasingly focused on housing the poorest households. Some social housing neighbourhoods entered a spiral of social decline that prompted better-functioning households to leave and left the residents who remained behind living in unpopular, difficult-to-manage neighbourhoods (Emms, 1990; Elander, 1994; Power, 1997).

This declinist, problem-focused view of European social housing proved influential and contributed to a shift in emphasis in social housing policy away from the provision of new dwellings to the regeneration of those difficult-to-manage neighbourhoods where social housing was already a major presence (Kintrea, 2007). In some European countries this analysis also prompted radical reforms in social housing management (such as an increased focus on combating anti-social behaviour) and governance (privatisation, transfer of dwellings to alternative social landlords and the provision of social housing in mixed tenure neighbourhoods) (Atkinson, 2007; Forrest and Murie, 1988; Pawson, 2006; Scanlon and Whitehead, 2007).

Some recent research has argued that the declinist view of social housing is excessively negative and sweeping and takes too little notice of the diversity of social conditions found in disadvantaged urban neighbourhoods in European cities. For example, a multi-country European study reported on in Rowlands, Musterd and Van Kempen (2009) placed a new emphasis on differentiation as a key feature of social housing: it found that although most social housing tenants are disadvantaged and some social housing neighbourhoods failed, others with apparently identical characteristics functioned well and even the worst neighbourhoods often had clusters of residents who were satisfied with their neighbourhoods. Similarly, Lupton's (2003) longitudinal study of the trajectories of 12 disadvantaged neighbourhoods (nine of which were mainly social rented) in Britain found that their fortunes 'pulled apart' as economic growth impacted unevenly on different neighbourhoods, households, and occupations. These authors emphasised the need to appreciate and understand this differentiation in order to get a proper grasp of how social housing has functioned in Europe.

As outlined earlier, the approach adopted in the present study falls squarely into this differentiation perspective. It too highlights the contrasts that can emerge between neighbourhoods that originated in similar conditions of disadvantage. It also points to the different levels at which variation can be observed, particularly in regard to the quite sharp contrasts that often emerge at the micro-level. The study can thus be considered as an attempt to contribute to an understanding of the dynamics of differentiation within and between low-income neighbourhoods in modern urban contexts. As such, it links to the extensive literature on neighbourhood change and failure, or more specifically to the authors within this genre who focus on micro(or within neighbourhood)-differentiation and drivers of failure (see: Lupton and Power, 2004; Van Beckhoven, Bolt, and Van Kempen, 2009, for reviews of this literature). These include: Hoyt (1939) and Hoover and Vernon (1959), who focus on neighbourhood lifecycle and population instability; Taylor (2000) and Innes' (2004) research on social order and crime; Putnam (2000) and

Dekker and Bolt (2005), who examine community cohesion; Hastings' (2004) work on reputation and stigma and Newman (1972), who examines the role of the built environment.

Liveability

As part of our contribution to this literature, we suggest here that it is conceptually useful to distinguish between social disadvantage or deprivation in a neighbourhood and its *liveability*. The concept of liveability dates back to the 1950s, at which time it was used in rural and urban sociology in analyses of the decline of small rural communities in the face of rapid urbanisation (Kaal, 2011). In those cases, the imbalance in job opportunities and living standards between scattered rural areas and growing urban centres led to an exodus of rural populations that tended to undermine the foundations of rural social and economic life and weaken the liveability of rural settlements. The concept was soon appropriated by the urban design and town planning fields, and in recent decades has underpinned research, urban renewal, and land-use policies and political campaigns in cities in Western Europe, Australia, Canada, and the United States (Evans, 2002; Harm, 2011; The Cities Alliance, 2007; Wheeler, 2004). Despite its widespread use, liveability lacks a uniform definition and established theoretical framework (Woolcock, 2009). Harrop (2005, p. 2) suggests that it is generally used to refer to 'the degree to which a person can function, feel comfortable in and enjoy the place in which they live'. Current usage is rooted in the town planning concept of amenity (which incorporates public health and safety, visual amenity, and cultural heritage) but recently has expanded to take account of analyses of peoples' experiences of place contained in the environmental psychology and well-being literature and the urban design literature that links liveability to the built environment. Reflecting its lack of a clear definition and diverse roots, the indicators employed to measure liveability also vary. According to Harrop (2005, p. 2):

> . . . over time the idea of liveability has expanded from a concrete concern for public health and safety to a diverse and seemingly unconnected set of aspects to make up a mixed bag of concrete and subjective but none the less valued set of concerns and desires.

The concept of liveability used in the present study is adapted from this back-ground but is directed towards a distinctive focus – the social scientific analysis of neighbourhood dynamics in low-income urban areas. In the current dominant usage in town planning and urban design, much of the interest liveability is driven by the aim to enhance the experience of urban living in conditions of affluence where the functional basics of city living – employment, housing, transport, public services, and so on – are already catered for, albeit imperfectly. That approach is about progressive striving to overcome the downsides of highly evolved city living and define and achieve the most liveable urban environments possible – an advanced form of urban consumerism. It is matched by the growth of 'place ratings' businesses that seek to identify the best cities and neighbourhoods to live in (Hovey, 2008).

Here, however, we are concerned with the other end of the scale – low-income neighbourhoods faced with the struggle to maintain minimum sustainable standards of urban living in the face of internal and external pressures on their resources and capabilities. In an urban counterpart of the concerns of rural sociology in the 1950s referred to earlier, the problem in this context is the viability of fragile communities existing in the lower reaches of the urban socioeconomic scale. These communities can and often do settle and thrive, but they also sometimes enter a spiral of decline that prompts exodus of residents who can manage to escape, and entrapment in socially and physically blighted neighbourhoods among those who cannot. These cases of neighbourhood failure thus perform poorly on what some analysts regard as the fundamental test of liveability – the trend of net population migration, or, in other words, whether the neighbourhood is able to attract and retain residents (Hovey, 2008; Kaal, 2011). The concern here, then, is with lower thresholds of liveability, how vulnerable communities stay above those thresholds, and what might cause others to fall below them.

The concept of liveability used in these terms is not intended to identify a precisely defined set of neighbourhood features that can be measured on an overall liveability scale. Such a scale may well have its uses and may eventually be produced but we do not attempt to create one here. Our purpose, rather, is to explore and establish liveability as a dimension of urban spatial organisation that is often thought of as more or less co-terminous with other dimensions (particularly neighbourhood deprivation or disadvantage) but that we wish to suggest is sufficiently distinct so as to be capable of some degree of independent variation. The import of this distinction is that, having identified liveability as a distinct dimension, we can highlight differentiation in liveability *per se* as the central focus of our study and as an aspect of neighbourhood dynamics that we believe warrants more attention in research in this field.

A key aspect of liveability understood in this way turns on the contrast between social disadvantage and liveability: the former, when applied to neighbourhoods, can be thought of as an aggregated variable based on household data whereas the latter is a collective-level variable. The social disadvantage of a neighbourhood is typically measured by reference to summing or averaging household characteristics such as incomes, employment and unemployment, educational attainment, family composition, and so on. A socially disadvantaged neighbourhood in this sense is one that contains large numbers of households or individuals that score poorly on these variables (for an analysis of a neighbourhood based on a variant of such an approach, see Chapter 2 in this volume). Liveability, by contrast, can be thought of as a property of the neighbourhood itself, as evidenced to some degree by the externally observable quality of public spaces but more importantly by how resident households perceive or react to the neighbourhood (see Chapter 3 in this volume, also Chapters 8 to 10). Thus, one easily observed sign of poor liveability is an uncared-for or dilapidated appearance in an area (judged by standards prevailing in low-income housing generally), while another and more fundamental one is that housing is in low demand among households that normally would be expected to live in such areas.

A second aspect of what we seek to capture in our concept of liveability relates to our focus on *social* liveability and concerns those collective features of the neighbourhood that have most bearing on its attractiveness to residents. Part of the problem in defining liveability, noted earlier, derives from the multiplicity and variety of factors that can be influential not only as between one city or neighbourhood and the next but also as between the perceptions and experiences of one individual and the next in the same area. In low-income neighbourhoods where the focus is on low levels of liveability, influences that are often identified include the level of services and amenities available in the locality – schools, medical services, public transport, shops, entertainment outlets, or other amenities such as playgrounds, sports fields, parks, etc. Poor architectural or urban design features may also play a role, relating, for example, to the design and build quality of dwellings, the layout of streets and residential blocks, the size of neighbourhoods (either in population or spatial terms), and their location in the larger urban space. We recognise that all these factors can and do have a bearing on liveability and many of them come into play in the seven estates in our study (see Chapter 3). However, we suggest here as a matter of empirical observation that, as outlined earlier, their influence is rarely dominant, particularly when it comes to those factors that have a severe detrimental effect on the quality of neighbourhoods. The important proximate factors in the latter cases, rather, typically have to do with aspects of social order and the social tensions and threats to the residents' sense of safety and security they give rise to. Residents in all social housing neighbourhoods, and indeed in all neighbourhoods in modern cities, may have concerns along these lines. However, our contention is that problems ranging from disruptive anti-social behaviour by young people through to serious criminality by organised gangs can be particularly severe in troubled low-income areas and are the most common catalyst of the sharp declines in liveability that give rise to neighbourhood failure. The negative consequences of such behaviours derive in part from direct effects on residents and the quality of the social environment and in part from the reputational damage that also causes the residential appeal of neighbourhoods to be downgraded. It is the essentially social nature of these processes – their origin in people's behaviour and the resulting social construction of neighbourhood – that cause us to refer to *social* liveability as a critical dimension of neighbourhood dynamics.

A further point that can be made concerning social liveability in this sense is that, again as we observe on the ground in our study estates, the social environment in neighbourhoods is itself a complex and many-sided thing and can show contradictory features. In particular, the presence of serious problems of social order leading to severe pressure on social liveability can co-exist with strong social bonds and a lively sense of community. This may particularly be the case in Irish social housing complexes since these were generally small in size, had relatively good build quality, and had very low numbers of ethnic minority households among their residents. They thus contrast with the large, low-quality, mass-housing neighbourhoods containing large ethnic minority populations that are usually seen as typical of 'problem estates' in other European countries (Rowlands *et al.*, 2009). In any event, poor social liveability does not necessarily imply absence of community (see especially Chapter 3; also Fahey, 1999). Residents in troubled neighbourhoods often speak of having great neighbours and a strong local community life while at the same time bemoaning the impact of a troublesome few on the local social atmosphere. In some instances, tensions and divisions arising from responses to anti-social behaviour can weaken community or lead to spatial stratification of micro-areas within neighbourhoods, while in other instances community mobilisation against anti-social behaviour can have a binding effect among active neighbours. Thus, while we identify social order problems as the most common source of low social liveability in troubled neighbourhoods, the processes involved can vary a great deal and are central to the social life.

Research design

Case study neighbourhoods: details of the locations and characteristics of the seven neighbourhoods examined in the study are set out in Image 1.1 and Table 1.1 below. These neighbourhoods were not selected according to a rigorous sampling

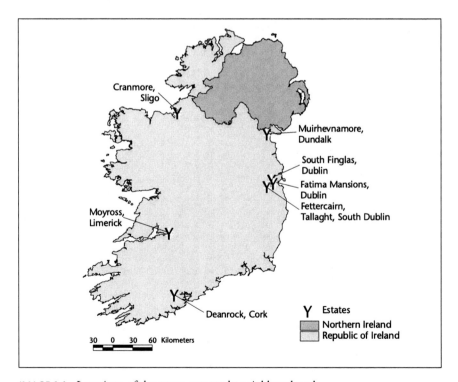

IMAGE 1.1 Locations of the seven case study neighbourhoods

TABLE 1.1 Characteristics of the seven case study neighbourhoods

Name and date of construction	Number and type of dwellings	Tenure	Dwellings and public space	Location
Cranmore (1970–85)	499 standard 2-storey terraced and semi-detached houses laid out in 14 cul-de-sacs	Originally all local authority (Sligo Town Council) rented. 52 houses were transferred to Cluid Housing Association in the 1990s. 50% of units were sold to tenants by 2006/7.	Good build quality and design in cul-de-sacs with amble green space. Housing association dwellings were refurbished as part of transfer of ownership.	Central, well-serviced location in the centre of a large provincial town. Shopping centre and schools are within easy walking distance.
Deanrock (1968–70)	Originally 210 terraced houses and 108 flats. All flats were demolished in 2006. Most houses are 3-bed.	Originally all local authority (Cork City Council) rented. Approximately half had been sold to tenants by 2006/7.	Poor initial build quality (system built), but extensively refurbished in the 1990s. Contains large open green, functionless space. Houses are laid out in monotonous grid.	Good inner-suburban location in a middle-class neighbourhood in a large provincial city. Good local services and public transport to the city centre but beside a busy road.
Fatima Mansions (1949–51)	Originally 320 flats in 4-storey blocks. Rebuilt in 2007 to include 180 social rented flats and houses, 70 'affordable' dwellings for sale at below market value and 396 private flats for sale on the open market.	Originally all local authority (Dublin City Council) rented and not eligible for purchase by tenants. Social rented dwellings were reduced in 2007 and the tenure was diversified to include private housing.	Initial poor build quality and flats were surrounded by open functionless space; the flats are accessed by stairwells and decks that are unsecured and provide havens for drug users. Following rebuilding the build quality and quality of open space is now good.	Good location, surrounded by settled middle-class housing with easy access to local services and to Dublin city centre.

Estate	Dwellings	Tenure	Build quality and layout	Location and services
Fettercairn (1980–3)	692 houses in three sub-estates. All of the houses are standard 2-storey, 3-bedroom units.	Local authority (South Dublin County Council). Tenant purchase was 18% in 1996. Now 50%.	Initial good build quality and dwellings were upgraded during the early 2000s to improve windows, central heating, etc. Reasonably well laid out in cul-de-sacs, but with large amounts of open functionless green space.	Peripheral location on the edge of Dublin, part of a large concentration of local authority housing. Landlord, social, and commercial services were poor in 1997 but improved significantly by 2007.
Finglas South (1970–7)	2,060 standard houses mainly 2-storey terraced and semi-detached, organised into several sub-estates.	Originally all constructed by the local authority (Dublin City Council). Some for sale to low-income households. 75% were owner occupied in 1996, and 84% by 2005.	Varied layout in cul-de-sacs. Houses in some parts of the neighbourhood front onto alleyways and this design is unpopular with residents. Extensive featureless green space.	In the inner suburbs of Dublin. Reasonably good access to services in Finglas village and surrounds. Reasonably good public transport to the city centre.
Moyross (1973–87)	1,190 standard houses, mainly 2-storey terraced and semi-detached. Most are 3-bedroom, 2-storey dwellings.	Originally local authority (Limerick City Council) but 34 dwellings were transferred to Respond! housing association in 1994. Tenant purchase was 25% in 1996 and 31% in 2006.	Good build quality and well laid out in cul-de-sacs, low-density design. Large amounts of open green space that is functionless but well maintained.	Peripheral location on the edge of a provincial city, poor access to shopping facilities but a church, community centre, and small shops are located in the neighbourhood.
Muirhevnamore (1973–87)	627 standard houses mainly 2-storey terraced and semi-detached. 86 reserved for older people.	Originally all local authority rented (Dundalk Town Council). 25% of dwellings were tenant purchased in 1996. 50% in 2006.	Well laid out in cul-de-sacs, low-density design alleyways running at the back of houses has created some problems.	On the edge of a provincial town. Relatively well serviced – schools, two shops, a small health centre, and a community centre are located in the area.

Source: Information supplied by social landlords, researchers' own observations

procedure in the statistical sense (see Corcoran and Fahey, 1999, for a fuller discussion), but nevertheless they are broadly representative of the key characteristics of the Irish social housing sector (Norris, 2005). Three of the case study neighbourhoods are in Dublin – Ireland's capital and largest city – and are distributed between the inner city (Fatima Mansions), the inner suburbs (Finglas South), and the outer suburbs (Fettercairn). A further two neighbourhoods (Deanrock and Moyross) are in the suburbs of Cork and Limerick – respectively the second and fourth largest cities in the country. The two other neighbourhoods are located in provincial towns – Muirhevnamore in Dundalk and Cranmore in Sligo. These towns and cities cover the majority of Irish regions and their selection reflects the predominately urban location of social housing.

The choice of case study neighbourhoods also reflects the predominant build form of the social rented tenure in Ireland, which is standard houses rather than multi-family dwellings (generally called flats in Ireland). Among the neighbourhoods under examination only Fatima Mansions contains flats currently and, at four storeys in height, by international standards these would be considered low-rise (Ireland's only high-rise social housing neighbourhood, at Ballymun, Dublin, was recently largely demolished). Deanrock did include some flats when we first visited in the mid-1990s but because of their poor build quality these had been demolished by the time of our second visit (a common intervention in regeneration projects in Ireland) (Treadwell Shine and Norris, 2006). Most of the seven neighbourhoods are relatively modest in size – only two (Moyross and Finglas South) contain more than 1,000 dwellings – which reflects the rarity of 'mass' social housing neighbourhoods common elsewhere in Europe (see Power, 1997; Rowlands et al., 2009).

As mentioned above, in contrast to the norm elsewhere, in Ireland the state (in the form of local authorities) continues to directly own and manage the majority of the social housing stock in Ireland (80 per cent nationally at the time of writing) and this is reflected in the seven neighbourhoods (see Table 1.1). The remainder is managed by non-profit housing associations and co-operatives. This sector has expanded significantly in recent years, principally due to new building rather than the transfer of social rented dwellings from the local authorities. However, in two of the seven study neighbourhoods (Cranmore and Moyross) a number of local authority rented dwellings were transferred to housing associations during the decade under examination (see Table 1.1). Urban local authority tenants in Ireland have enjoyed the right to buy their dwellings (at a substantial discount from the market value) since the mid-1960s, so large sections of most social housing neighbourhoods, including the neighbourhoods under examination here, have been sold to tenants and some of these dwellings are now owned by for-profit landlords (Norris, 2005; see Table 1.1). For this reason and also because private sector housing output has significantly outpaced social house building in recent decades, the percentage of Irish households accommodated by local authorities fell from 9.7 in 1991 to 7.2 in 2006 (comparable data for housing associations are not available) (Central Statistics Office, various years a).

As is explained in Chapter 3 of this volume, the seven neighbourhoods also include a mix of high-demand and low-demand housing. The social rented sector in Ireland is strongly residualised so case study neighbourhood residents are predominately disadvantaged (see Chapter 2 of this volume) and in keeping with the norm in the country at large until recently their population was largely mono-ethnic (white, born in Ireland or the UK, and of Catholic religious background) (Norris, 2005). Among the seven neighbourhoods, only the Electoral Division (ED – census small area) where Fatima Mansions is located had a substantial proportion of non-Irish or UK nationals in 2005 (20 per cent of residents), whereas in all of the other seven neighbourhoods non-Irish or UK nationals accounted for less than 8 per cent of the population in 2006 (Central Statistics Office, various years a).

Fieldwork and secondary data analysis: the methods used to examine the neighbourhoods were varied and consisted of a somewhat different mix in the follow-up phase carried out in 2007–9 than in the initial study of ten years earlier. In terms of primary research, both phases of the study were implemented via in-depth interviews and analysis of survey data and local management data where available. However, the focus of the study shifted between phases and the methodology was amended accordingly.

Phase one dealt mainly with the experiences of tenants, particularly in regard to the influence of the local social and physical environment on the liveability of their neighbourhoods and their relationships with their social landlords. It relied primarily on in-depth, semi-structured individual interviews (70) and focus group interviews (26 interviews with 78 individuals) with residents to gather information. During this phase 55 interviews with local service providers and community leaders (housing managers, police, teachers, etc.) were also conducted. By 2007, a greater quantity of relevant survey and management data were available (e.g. evaluations of estate regeneration or community development schemes, community consultations regarding regeneration schemes, local surveys of tenant satisfaction, health and well-being, etc.) so this was incorporated into the analysis. The follow-up study also made more use of quantitative indicators to track social change in the neighbourhoods – particularly of an index of social disadvantage called the Pobal HP Deprivation Index (PHDI), which was devised by Trutz Haase and Jonathan Pratschke using Small Area Population Statistics (SAPS) data from censuses from 1991 to 2006 (Chapter 2). It also drew from interviews with service providers and community leaders (100 in total) involved in the neighbourhoods and residents (ten group interviews with 35 individuals, and 30 individual interviews).

The policy strand of the study sought to outline the growth of international interest in area-based anti-poverty initiatives since the 1960s, provide a national overview of these initiatives in Ireland and their expansion since the early 1990s, trace their presence and significance in the study neighbourhoods, and draw conclusions on their value for combating social disadvantage. At the national level in Ireland, the challenge this objective posed was to delimit what could be counted as area-based anti-poverty initiatives, and quantify their total scale. To that end, the study took the year 2006 as the reference year and sought to assemble information on the design and expenditure of all national programmes that could be counted as area-based and as having an anti-poverty focus. It thereby sought to arrive at a 'bird's-eye' view of this whole field of activity in Ireland in the year 2006. In the counterpart examination of the study neighbourhoods, the goal was to provide a local view of the same field of activity in the same year, though as we shall see below, the impact of certain regional and local programmes, along with contributions from private philanthropy, meant that what happened on the ground in neighbourhoods was not simply a local reflection of national programmes.

The complexity of neighbourhood-level activity and the difficulty in assembling comprehensive, accurate information on relevant schemes were such that the team decided to focus intensively on four of the seven neighbourhoods – two that clearly had high levels of intervention (Fatima Mansions and Moyross), and two where relevant initiatives were fewer in number (Deanrock and Cranmore). The analysis of programmes in these neighbourhoods then proceeded through four steps:

1. Compile a detailed inventory of interventions – i.e. identify and classify every substantial area-based programme that was in any way related to alleviating disadvantage, that was implemented in the study neighbourhoods, or that reached significant populations within the neighbourhoods. The main focus was on programmes that received at least some public funding. Programmes funded by private philanthropy also proved to be significant in some neigh-bourhoods and account was taken of these, but as the accuracy and complete-ness of information on philanthropic supports were uncertain, they are only partly integrated into the analysis.
2. Quantify the inputs associated with each programme, particularly expenditure, and sum them to arrive at an estimate of total inputs per neighbourhood and per household in each neighbourhood. This proved a particularly challenging exercise and these challenges and the strategies employed to overcome them are outlined in Chapter 7.
3. Examine the outputs of the programmes and insofar as the data allow, quantify and analyse these.
4. Insofar as possible, examine the question of programme impact. In view of the number and variety of activities involved, the study could not apply the controls or rigorous before-and-after measures that would be required to provide formal impact assessment. Nevertheless, it was possible to offer some comment on the impact of all initiatives viewed together, if only by assessing their overall scale and fit with the kinds of problems in the neighbourhoods they sought to address and the opinions of those involved in their implementation in the case study neighbourhoods.

Operationalising the analytical framework: The various data sources drawn on in this study are used to explore the trajectories of liveability that occurred in the study neighbourhoods during the decade under examination. They also enable us to assess the significance of social policies and services, particularly area-based interventions, for these trajectories. Liveability is assessed here in terms of demand for dwellings among potential occupants, satisfaction of existing occupants, quality of the social environment, reputation and stigma, and quality of the built environment. On this basis, Chapter 3 categorizes the neighbourhoods along a trajectory that ranges from high to low liveability and classifies change along a continuum of improvement, stability, and decline.

Structure of the book

A key theme in this study is the relationship between social disadvantage and liveability at the neighbourhood level. Neighbourhood disadvantage is examined by Trutz Haase in Chapter 2. This reveals that all but one of the seven neighbourhoods were significantly more disadvantaged than the national average in 1996, and despite a marked absolute improvement during the economic boom, they continued to be disadvantaged relative to the national average in 2006. However, Chapter 3 (by Mary Corcoran) reveals marked differences in the liveability of the case study neighbourhoods despite similar levels of disadvantage. Furthermore liveability did not always change in line with changes in disadvantage over the decade.

Chapters 4 to 7 report on the core of the policy strand of the study, which is mainly concerned with ABIs (though a range of policy issues also crop up in other chapters). Chapter 4 (by Michelle Norris and Cathal O'Connell) sets an important part of the context by examining change in social housing management. Chapters 5, 6, and 7 turn to ABIs proper. Chapter 5 (by Eileen Humphreys and Des McCafferty) examines the rationales for ABIs, while Chapter 6 (by Michelle Norris) presents a national-level overview of the contemporary development of ABIs in Ireland. Chapter 7 (also by McCafferty and Humphreys) profiles ABIs in four of the seven case study neighbourhoods, in terms of spending and the extent and focus of activities undertaken. They do not attempt a formal evaluation of the impact of ABIs but nevertheless, by providing a detailed analysis of their scale and variety, provide valuable new insights into the significance of ABIs in the neighbourhoods they examine.

Chapters 8 and 9 (both by Aileen O'Gorman) turn to issues connected with social order that we identify as central to liveability throughout the study. Chapter 8 focuses on drugs and drug markets, while Chapter 9 provides a broader account of social order and community safety. Chapter 10 (by Amanda Haynes, Eoin Devereux, and Martin J. Power) turns to another aspect of the same issues by examining the reputational consequences of local disorder. They use a case study method that focuses on media reporting of some high-profile episodes in Moyross and the stigma it creates. Chapter 11 (by Michelle Norris and Tony Fahey) sums up and presents conclusions to the study.

References

Allen, K. (2000) *The Celtic Tiger: The myth of social partnership in Ireland*, Manchester: Manchester University Press.

Atkinson, R. (2007) Spaces of discipline and control: the compounded citizenship of social renting. In J. Flint (ed.), *Housing, urban governance and anti-social behaviour: Perspectives, policy and practice* (pp. 99–116), Bristol: Policy Press.

Bamber, J., Owens, S., Schonfeld, H., Ghate, D., and Fullerton, D. (2010) *Effective community development programmes: A review of the international evidence base*, Dublin: Centre for Effective Services.

Central Statistics Office (various years a) *Census of population of Ireland*, Dublin: Central Statistics Office.

— (various years b) *Measuring Ireland's Progress*, Dublin: Central Statistics Office.

Corcoran, M. and Fahey, T. (1999) Methodology and overview of estates. In T. Fahey (ed.), *Social housing in Ireland: A study of success, failure and lessons learned* (pp. 84–100), Dublin: Oak Tree Press.

Dekker, K. and Bolt, G. (2005) Social cohesion in post-war estates in the Netherlands: Differences between socioeconomic and ethnic groups, *Urban Studies*, 42(13), 2447–70.

Department of the Environment, Community and Local Government (various years) *Housing statistics bulletin*, Dublin: Department of the Environment, Community and Local Government.

Dunleavy, P. (1981) *The politics of mass housing in Britain 1945–1975: A study of corporate power and professional influence on the welfare state*, Oxford: Clarendon Press.

Elander, I. (1994) Paradise lost? Desubsidization and social housing in Sweden. In B. Danemark and I. Elander (eds.), *Social rented housing in Europe: Policy, tenure and design* (pp. 95–122), Delft: Delft University Press.

Emms, P. (1990) *Social housing. A European dilemma?* Bristol: School for Advanced Urban Studies.

Evans, P. (ed.) (2002) *Livable cities? Urban struggles for livelihood and sustainability*, Berkley: University of California Press.

Fahey, T. (ed.) (1999) *Social housing in Ireland: A study of success, failures and lessons learned*, Dublin: Oak Tree Press.

Fahey, T., Russell, H., and Whelan, C.T. (eds.) (2008) *Quality of life in Ireland: The impact of economic boom*, Dordrecht: Springer.

Fitzpatrick and Associates (2007) *Value-for-money review of the Local Development Social Inclusion Programme 2000–06. Final Report*, Dublin: Department of Community, Rural and Gaeltacht Affairs.

Forrest, R. and Murie, A. (1988) *Selling the welfare state: The privatisation of public housing*, London: Routledge.

Geoghegan, M. and Powell, F. (2006) Community development, partnership governance and dilemmas of professionalization: Profiling and assessing the case of Ireland, *British Journal of Social Work*, 36(4), 845–61.

Guerin, D. (1999) Relationships with Local Authorities. In T. Fahey (ed.), *Social housing in Ireland: A study of success, failure and lessons learned* (pp. 191–210), Dublin: Oak Tree Press.

Haase, T. and McKeown, K. (2003) *Developing disadvantaged areas through area-based initiatives*, Dublin: Area Development Management Ltd.

Harloe, M. (1995) *The people's home. Social rented housing in Europe and America*, Oxford: Basil Blackwell.

Harm, K. (2011) A conceptual history of livability, *City: analysis of urban trends, culture, theory, policy, action*, 15(5), 532–47.

Harrop, L. (2005) Tests for liveability: Keeping pace with change, paper presented at the State of Australian Cities Conference, www.griffith.edu.au/conference/state-australian-cities-2005/papers (accessed 7 October 2012).

Hastings, A. (2004) Stigma and social housing estates: Beyond pathological explanations, *Journal of Housing and the Built Environment*, 19(3), 233–54.

Hoover, E. and Vernon, R. (1959) *Anatomy of a metropolis*, Cambridge, MA: Harvard University Press.

Hourigan, N. (2011) *Understanding Limerick: Social exclusion and change*, Cork: Cork University Press.

Hovey, B. (2008) Review essay: In search of urban livability, *Journal of Urban History*, 34(2), 552–61.

Hoyt, H. (1939) *The structure and growth of residential neighborhoods in American cities*, Washington: Federal Housing Administration.

Innes, M. (2004) Signal crimes and signal disorders: notes on deviance as communicative action, *British Journal of Sociology*, 55(3), 335–55.

Kaal, H. (2011) A conceptual history of livability, *City*, 15(5), 532–47.

Kelly, E., McGuinness, S. and O'Connell, P. (2009) Benchmarking, social partnership and higher remuneration: Wage setting institutions and the public-private wage gap in Ireland, *Economic and Social Review*, 40 (3), 339–70.

Kintrea, K. (2007) Policies and programmes for disadvantaged neighbourhoods: Recent English experience, *Housing Studies*, 22(2), 261–82.

Layte, R., Nolan, A., and Nolan, B. (2008) Health and health care. In T. Fahey, H. Russell, and C. Whelan (eds), *Quality of life in Ireland: Social impact of economic boom* (pp. 105–22), Dordrect: Springer.

Lupton, R. (2003) *Poverty street: The dynamics of neighbourhood decline and renewal*, Bristol: Policy Press.

Lupton, R. and Power, A. (2004) *What we know about neighbourhood change: A literature review*, London: London School of Economics.

Lupton, R. and Turok, I. (2004) Anti-poverty policies in Britain: Area-based and people-based approaches. In U-J. Walther and K. Mensch (eds), *Armut und Ausgrenzung in der 'Sozialen Stadt'* (pp. 188–208), Darmstadt: Schader Stiftung.

Madanipour, A., Cars, G., and Allen, J. (2002) *Social exclusion in European cities: Processes, experiences and responses,* London: Routledge.

McLaughlin, E. (2005) Forcing the issue: New Labour, new localism and the democratic renewal of police accountability, *Howard Journal of Criminal Justice*, 44(5), 473–89.

Modarres, A. (2002) Persistent poverty and the failure of area-based initiatives in the U.S., *Local Economy*, 17(4), 2447–70.

Newman, O. (1972) *Defensible space: People and design in the violent city*, London: Architectural Press.

Nolan, B. and Maître, B. (2008) Economic growth and income inequality: Setting the context. In T. Fahey, H. Russell, and C. T. Whelan (eds), *Quality of life in Ireland: Social impact of economic boom* (pp. 27–42), Dordrect: Springer.

Norris, M. (1999) The impact of the built environment. In T. Fahey (ed.), *Social housing in Ireland: A study of success, failure and lessons learned* (pp. 101–24), Dublin: Oak Tree Press.

— (2005) Social housing. In M. Norris and D. Redmond (eds), *Housing contemporary Ireland: Policy, society and shelter* (pp. 160–82), Dublin: Institute of Public Administration.

O'Cinnéide, S. (1999) Local development agencies. In T. Fahey (ed.), *Social housing in Ireland: A study of success, failure and lessons learned* (pp. 211–32), Dublin: Oak Tree Press.

O'Connor, A. (1999) Swimming against the tide: A brief history of federal policy in poor communities. In R. Ferguson and W. Dickens (eds), *Urban problems and community development* (pp. 77–138), Washington, DC: Brookings Institute Press.

O'Hearn, D. (1998) *Inside the Celtic Tiger: The Irish economy and the Asian model*, London: Pluto Press.

O'Higgins, K. (1999) Social order problems. In T. Fahey (ed.), *Social housing in Ireland: A study of success, failure and lessons learned* (pp. 149–72), Dublin: Oak Tree Press.

OECD (1999) *The local dimension of welfare-to-work: An international survey*, Paris: OECD.

Pawson, H. (2006) Restructuring England's social housing sector since 1989: Undermining or underpinning the fundamentals of public housing? *Housing Studies*, 21(5), 767–83.

Power, A. (1997) *Estates on the edge. The social consequences of mass housing in Northern Europe*, Basingstoke: Macmillan Press.

Putnam, R. (2000) *Bowling alone: The collapse and revival of American community*, New York: Simon and Schuster.

Rowlands, R., Musterd, S., and Van Kempen, R. (eds) (2009) *Mass housing in Europe: Multiple faces of development, change and response*, Basingstoke: Palgrave Macmillan.

Russell, H., Maître, B., and Nolan, B. (eds) (2010) *Monitoring poverty trends in Ireland 2004–2007: Key issues for children, people of working age and older people*, Dublin: Economic and Social Research Institute.

Sabel, C. (1996) *Ireland – local partnerships and social innovation*, Paris: OECD.

Scanlon, K. and Whitehead, C. (2007) Social housing in Europe. In K. Scanlon and C. Whitehead (eds), *Social housing in Europe* (pp. 8–34), London: London School of Economics.

Smith, G. (1999) *Area-based initiatives: The rationale and options for area targeting* (CASE paper 25), London: Centre for the Analysis of Social Exclusion, London School of Economics.

Taylor, R. (2000) *Breaking away from broken windows*, Boulder, CO: Westview Press.

The Cities Alliance (2007) *Liveable cities: The benefits of urban environmental planning*, Washington, DC: The Cities Alliance.

Treadwell Shine, K. and Norris, M. (2006) *Housing policy discussion series: Regenerating local authority estates – review of policy and practice*, Dublin: Centre for Housing Research.

Van Beckhoven, E., Bolt, G., and Van Kempen, R. (2009) Theories of neighbourhood change and decline. In R. Rowlands, S. Musterd, and R. Van Kempen (eds), *Mass housing in Europe: Multiple faces of development, change and response* (pp. 20–52), London: Palgrave.

Vestergaard, H. (1998) Troubled housing estates in Denmark. In A. Madanipour, G. Cars, and J. Allen (eds), *Social exclusion in European cities* (pp. 115–30), London and Philadelphia: Jessica Kingsley Publishers.

Walsh, J. (1999) The role of area-based programmes in tackling poverty. In D. Pringle, J. Walsh, and M. Hennessy (eds), *Poor people, poor place: A geography of poverty and deprivation in Ireland*, Dublin: Oak Tree Press.

Wheeler, S. (2004) *Planning for sustainability: Creating livable, equitable and ecological communities*, London: Routledge.

Woolcock, G. (2009) Measuring up? Assessing the liveability of Australian cities, paper presented to the State of Australian Cities Conference, http://soac.fbe.unsw.edu.au/2009 (accessed 7 October 2012).

2

CHANGING DISADVANTAGE IN SOCIAL HOUSING

A multi-level analysis

Trutz Haase

Introduction

The decade between the 1996 and 2006 censuses was a period of unprecedented economic growth. After decades of comparatively poor economic performance, the country experienced its first ever true economic boom (Kennedy, Giblin, and McHugh, 1988; Nolan, O'Connell, and Whelan 2000). This boom transcended people's perception of what might economically and socially be possible; it also shaped their future expectations. If the boom of the late 1990s and early 2000s was unprecedented, so was the suddenness of its collapse towards the end of 2007. However, the post-boom experience lies outside the timeframe covered in the present study so the present chapter takes the story only up to 2006. For the decade prior to 2006, one cannot meaningfully interpret what has happened at local level unless one does so with reference to the developments in Irish society as a whole.

This chapter examines social change and disadvantage in the seven case study neighbourhoods and compares developments in this regard to the national context. This analysis draws on work carried out by the author as part of the continuing development of the Pobal HP Deprivation Index – an instrument for measuring the spatial distribution of affluence and disadvantage in Ireland that was first applied to the 1986 Census (Haase and Pratschke, 2005, 2008). The original study on the seven case study neighbourhoods was carried out with respect to the situation in 1997–8, and the follow-up study focuses on 2007–9. This chapter focuses on the analysis of data from the 1996, 2002, and 2006 censuses, as these most closely resemble the study period.

The Pobal HP Deprivation Index

The PHDI employs three variables measured by means of ten socioeconomic indicators to assess disadvantage. These are: demographic growth (which is examined using data on population change, age dependency, and residents with third-level educational qualifications and primary education only); social class (assessed with reference to residents in professional and semi-skilled/unskilled classes, residents with primary education only/third-level education and housing quality); and labour market deprivation (assessed using the male and female unemployment rate and levels of lone parenthood). The methodology for the index has been revised on a number of occasions to take account of the distinctive nature of disadvantage in Ireland (for instance, the large rural population in this country) and improve the statistical models underpinning the calculations to facilitate the direct comparison of deprivation scores over time (Haase and Pratschke, 2005, 2008).

The area units on which the index is based consist of electoral divisions (EDs), the smallest spatial units for which census data was available at the time of writing. In the case of Fettercairn the boundaries of the ED in which it is located (Tallaght Fettercairn) perfectly match the boundaries of the neighbourhood, thus the PHDI data provide a spatially exact picture of disadvantage in this case. As Image 2.1 explains, the situation in the other six neighbourhoods is somewhat more complex. The boundaries of South Finglas are not exactly coterminous with the boundaries of the relevant EDs (Finglas South B and C) but this neighbourhood makes up the vast bulk of these EDs. The match between Moyross and the two relevant EDs is also relatively strong, because Moyross encompasses most of the Ballynanty ED and the other (Limerick North Rural) encompasses a predominatly rural area with a small population. However, both Deanrock and Fatima Mansions cover a smaller proportion of the land area of the EDs where they are located. The EDs in which Muirhevnamore and Cranmore are located cover most of the towns of Dundalk and Sligo, so in these cases the PHDI data does not provide a robust picture of disadvantage within these neighbourhoods. Thus the PHDI does not provide a picture of disadvantage that is spatially accurate for all of the seven case study neighbourhoods, but it does provide the best one available at the time of writing. As far as possible the analysis presented below endeavours to take account of the shortcomings in the data on which this index is based.

The national context: unprecedented economic growth and social change

Before looking at the experience of the seven neighbourhoods or, more precisely, the individual electoral divisions in which they are located, we will start with a brief summary of the overall economic performance of the country over the 1996 to 2006 period.

There are many indicators that could be used to describe the economic performance of a country, but the most commonly used one is that of gross national income (GNI) per capita, which is calculated by adding gross domestic product (GDP) to net receipts from abroad of wages, salaries, and property income and dividing the result by the number of inhabitants. In 2006, the Irish GNI per capita figure was over 40 per cent higher than ten years before (when measured in constant

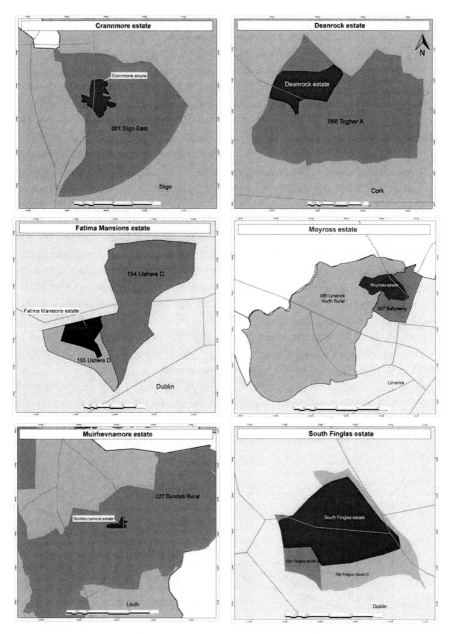

IMAGE 2.1 Map of the electoral divisions in which the case study neighbourhoods are located

2005 prices), which means that the average GNI growth was just over 4 per cent per annum (Central Statistics Office, various years b).

Such growth was not only unprecedented for Ireland, but also exceptional when compared with the experience of other countries. Figure 2.1 shows the growth of GNI per capita based on purchasing power parity for Ireland and a number of comparison countries for the ten-year period under consideration. The graph clearly shows the extraordinary boom that the Irish economy had experienced during our period in question. Whereas Irish GNI per capita amounted to about 75 to 85 per cent of its major European partners in 1996, within the short time of only one decade it climbed to equal Denmark and exceed all other major European countries in 2006.

The 1996–2006 period was distinguished not only by unprecedented economic growth, but equally marked an unparalleled change in the social conditions in Ireland. It is important to understand the magnitude of these changes, as it is otherwise impossible to situate the experience of the seven neighbourhoods under examination in this book within this broader development. To this end, Figure 2.2 outlines changes in the distribution of absolute Pobal HP Deprivation Index scores for Ireland as a whole between 1996 and 2006. The absolute index scores measure the affluence or disadvantage of all 3,429 EDs in the country on a single fixed scale, which, for 1991, has a mean of zero and standard deviation of ten.

This graph reveals a moderate decline in the levels of disadvantage between 1991 and 1996, marked by the slight rightward shift of the distributional curve (see Figure 2.2). This coincides with the onset of the period of economic growth highlighted above, but precedes our period of interest. The main change in the

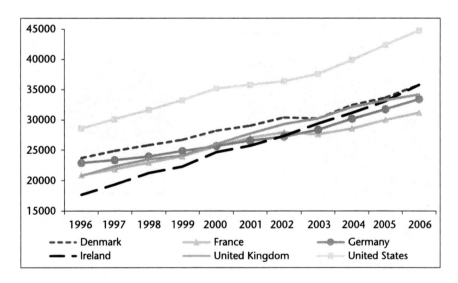

FIGURE 2.1 Irish GNI per capita based on purchasing power parity (PPP), 1996–2006

Source: OECD, various years

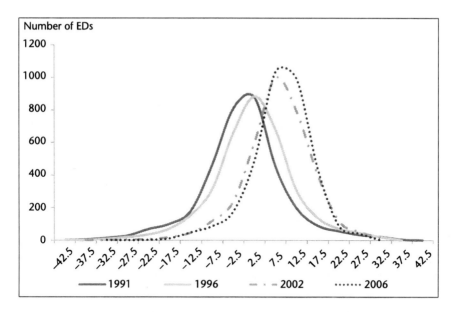

FIGURE 2.2 Distribution of absolute Pobal HP Deprivation Index scores, 1991, 1996, 2002, and 2006

Source: Haase and Pratschke (2008)

PHDI scores occurred between 1996 and 2002, marked by the significant rightward shift in the curve, which points to a sharper decline in disadvantage. This period coincides with the height of the 'Celtic Tiger' boom. During the 2002 to 2006 period, the curve shows only a marginal shift to the right, thus indicating the imminent end of the boom, and a smaller decline in disadvantage.

Thus the entire 1991–2006 period was distinguished by a marked decline in disadvantage, albeit at varying rates during different years, which was driven by the following changes in the variables and indicators that made up the Pobal HP Deprivation Index:

1   population increase of 17 per cent;
2   age dependency rate dropping from 35 per cent to 31 per cent;
3   lone-parent rate rising from 14 per cent to 21 per cent;
4   the proportion of the adult population with primary education only dropping from 30 per cent to 19 per cent and the proportion with third-level education rising from 20 to 31 per cent;
5   higher and lower professional classes rising from 27 per cent to 33 per cent of the total population while the semi- and unskilled manual classes declined from 24 per cent to 19 per cent;
6   male unemployment dropping from 16 to 9 per cent and female unemployment dropping from 12 per cent to 8 per cent;

7 households living in local authority rented (social) housing dropping from 8 per cent to 7 per cent of all households.

Interestingly, and of importance to our research on the seven case study neighbourhoods, micro-spatial analysis at the level of the 3,429 EDs shows that the increase in affluence has reached into more or less every corner of the country. Thus at neighbourhood level, the rising tide had indeed 'lifted all boats' during this period of exceptional growth. This has two important implications: first, almost every neighbourhood in Ireland saw a broadly similar degree of improvement and, second, this also meant that the relative position of local areas remained practically unchanged. With the exception of Dublin's inner city, the most disadvantaged areas of the early 1990s were still the most disadvantaged in 2006 (Haase and Pratschke, 2008). A more detailed analysis of these changes in the seven neighbourhoods is presented later in this chapter. When combining the above indicators into a single deprivation measure and comparing it over successive census waves, a powerful picture emerges that mirrors the economic development depicted in Figure 2.1.

Disadvantage in the seven neighbourhoods

Having discussed disadvantage at the national level, we now proceed to examine the seven case study neighbourhoods in relation to the country as a whole and ask whether their situation has improved or worsened over the past decade. To this end, we utilise PHDI, but focus only on the 1996 to 2006 inter-censal period that most closely reflects the timing of our fieldwork on these neighbourhoods. In addition, the focus here is on relative rather than absolute PHDI scores (absolute PHDI scores in the seven study neighbourhoods, in common with the country at large, also improved in all cases). Relative scores are derived from the absolute scores by deducting the underlying trend as it applies for Ireland as a whole.

Thus, the data presented in Table 2.1 show the relative position of each of the seven neighbourhoods in the index in 1996, 2002, and 2006. The data in the last column of this table indicates that the experience of the seven neighbourhoods (or more precisely of the EDs in which they are located) has been hugely diverse over the past decade. Two neighbourhoods (Fatima Mansions and Fettercairn) have seen a significant improvement in their position, three (Muirhevnamore, Cranmore, and South Finglas) experienced a slight deterioration, and two neighbourhoods (Deanrock and Moyross) a significant worsening of their situation.

By far the most marked decline in relative disadvantage occurred in Fatima Mansions (Ushers C+D EDs), which improved by 9.1 index points. As is examined in Chapters 3 and 4 of this book, the improvement is clearly related to the ambitious regeneration of the neighbourhood – which was originally entirely social rented but was demolished and rebuilt as mixed use and mixed tenure (including private housing and social housing provided by the local authority) between 2004 and 2008 (Norris and Redmond, 2009; Whyte, 2005). In addition, the construction of large numbers of mainly private rented new apartment complexes in the

TABLE 2.1 Relative Pobal HP Deprivation Index scores for the seven case study neighbourhoods and nationwide, 1996, 2002, and 2006

Case study neighbourhood and ED(s) in which it is located	Relative index score 1996	Relative index score 2002	Relative index score 2006	Change in relative index score 1996–2006
Cranmore (Sligo East)	–2.0	–2.7	–6.1	–4.1
Deanrock (Togher A)	–8.8	–16.2	–19.1	–10.3
Fatima Mansions (Ushers C+D)	–24.9	–18.3	–15.8	9.1
Finglas South (Finglas South B+C)	–19.9	–17.0	–25.7	–5.8
Fettercairn (Tallaght–Fettercairn)	–24.6	–10.9	–17.5	7.1
Moyross (Ballynanty)	–21.1	–23.9	–32.3	–11.2
Muirhevnamore (Dundalk Rural)	–6.6	–10.9	–9.3	–2.7
Ireland	*3.0*	*3.3*	*2.1*	*–0.9*

Note: The score for Ireland is not zero because the ED level index scores are calculated on the unweighted index scores, whilst the nationwide figure takes account of the different population weights as they apply to each ED

neighbourhood surrounding the estate during the late 1980s and 1990s, many of which were funded by the tax incentives available as part of the Irish government's urban renewal scheme, is likely to have reduced the disadvantage profile of the wider ED. Research on the residents of these complexes indicates that the vast majority were in employment and had third-level qualifications (Haase, 2009; Norris and Gkartzios, 2011). To the extent that improved PHDI scores in this case were driven by the introduction of private housing into the area, disadvantage among existing residents may not have actually declined but rather may have been *diluted* by the introduction of new, more affluent, residents.

Table 2.1 indicates that the neighbourhood with the second best improvement is Fettercairn – its relative PHDI score rose by 7.1 points between 1996 and 2006. Unlike Fatima Mansions, it is reasonable to assume that this rise in Fettercairn reflects improving fortunes among its existing residents. Its boundaries are fully coterminous with those of the ED on which the PHDI scores are calculated and are not skewed by developments in surrounding neighbourhoods. Moreover, although Fettercairn was subject to some modest regeneration in this period (involving upgrading of dwellings and public spaces – see Chapter 4 for more details), this did not involve any tenure mixing or other measures intended to attract new, higher-income residents. Indeed, the evidence indicates that the population of the neighbourhood stabilised during the period. The proportion of Fettercairn residents who were living at the same address one year prior to the census rose from 88 per cent in 2002 to 94.2 per cent in 2006 (Central Statistics Office, various years a).

The data for both the Dundalk Rural (– 2.7) and Sligo East (– 4.1) EDs, which encompass Muirhevnamore and Cranmore respectively, reveal a slight worsening in the relative PHDI score. The precise import of these index movements for our study neighbourhoods is unclear since, as mentioned above, the data relate to much larger spatial units within which the neighbourhoods are located. Furthermore, both of these EDs experienced significant population change. In Dundalk Rural population grew by 10 per cent between 1996 and 2006, whilst in Sligo East it fell by 10 per cent. In addition, in Dundalk Rural the share of households accommodated in local authority rented housing fell on account of the rapid growth of private housing in the ED as a whole. Since private housing is likely to have attracted slightly more affluent residents, the likelihood is that the fall of 2.7 points in the relative PHDI score for this ED between 1996 and 2006 masks a larger relative worsening of disadvantage in Muirhevnamore. With regard to Cranmore, the underlying population decline, combined with a disproportionate increase in the share of households headed by lone parents and a below-average decline in the share of adults with primary education, points to an increase in relative disadvantage in both this neighbourhood and in the surrounding ED.

The Finglas South neighbourhood encompasses all of the Finglas South B + C Electoral Divisions, which allows a straightforward interpretation of the implications of the relative PHDI scores for this neighbourhood. The scores for Finglas South declined by 5.8 between 1996 and 2006. As is discussed later in this chapter, this worsening of relative disadvantage was driven by a 9 per cent decline in population coupled with a substantial increase in the proportion of the households headed by lone parents (+28.0 per cent) and a below average improvement in educational achievement. Taken together, these developments point to the beginning of a negative cycle of disadvantage in this neighbourhood, characterised by the exodus of relatively advantaged households and their replacement by people with greater social needs.

Table 2.1 also reveals that Deanrock (or more accurately the Togher A Electoral Division) slipped 10.3 scores on the relative PHDI, thus moving one full standard deviation from being slightly below the national average in 1996 to falling into the category of 'disadvantaged neighbourhood' in 2006. As is discussed below, this development is the result of the loss of almost one-quarter of its population, a near doubling in the share of lone parents among all resident households and a failure to share in the nationally occurring improvement in educational standards. As there was little new housing development in this ED during this period (indeed part of the neighbourhood was demolished), this development would appear to be related to increasing disadvantage among existing residents and the entry of new, disadvantaged residents, probably via the allocation of social housing tenancies.

In terms of relative disadvantage Moyross is by far the worst performing amongst the seven neighbourhoods. In 1991, Moyross was one of three very disadvantaged neighbourhoods in the sample, the other two being Fatima Mansions and Fettercairn (see Table 2.1). However, where the other two had both improved by 2006, the score for Moyross declined by 11.2 index points, making it by far the most deprived of the seven neighbourhoods by 2006. Indeed, relative PHDI scores for all areas in Ireland in 2006 reveals that Moyross by then was the most deprived neighbourhood in the country. Rising disadvantage in this case is related to significant population decline (−22.0 per cent between 1996 and 2006), a marked increase in lone parenthood, as a result of which two out of three families with children in this neighbourhood were now headed by a single parent, low educational attainment, and a lack of improvement in education over the previous decade. Moyross also had the highest unemployment rates of the seven neighbourhoods − more than a quarter of all males in Moyross where unemployed in 2006, the year that marked the height of the Celtic Tiger economic boom and a 4 per cent unemployment rate in the country as a whole.

Interpreting changing disadvantage in the seven neighbourhoods

The opening section of this chapter pointed out that the years 1996 to 2006 were a period of unprecedented economic growth and social advance. To explore the experience of the seven neighbourhoods in that context, this section looks at changes in a number of key socioeconomic indicators (some of which are included in PHDI calculations) in the case study neighbourhoods between 1996 and 2006 and compares them with trends in Ireland as a whole.

Demographic change: Ireland's population grew by 16.6 per cent between 1996 and 2006 and by 20.3 per cent between 1991 and 2006. This was the first prolonged and substantial increase in the Irish population since the 1840s, with many of the other social and economic changes at least in part being linked to this underlying growth. The largest increase in population occurred in the commuter belt surrounding Dublin (the Mid-East Region, comprising the counties of Kildare, Meath, and Wicklow). The fastest growing area within that was the western suburbs of Dublin (the operational area of Fingal County Council), which exactly doubled its population over the decade up to 2006. Population growth was strongly urban-led, with many rural areas failing to benefit. However, as existing built-up urban areas have only limited scope for increasing their population, the growth was overwhelmingly concentrated in the peripheral and commuting areas that service the main cities and towns.

Thus, population trends in the seven case study neighbourhoods were heavily influenced by location both in terms of regional population trends and also by the degree to which land use in the neighbourhoods could facilitate ancillary re-zoning and development of greenfield or brownfield sites (see Table 2.2). Because all of the neighbourhoods were constructed prior to the economic boom, they had limited opportunity to facilitate additional population growth.

The main exception to this is Fatima Mansions, sections of which were demolished in the mid-1980s as part of a refurbishment scheme, and further sections of which were vacated in the late 1990s to prepare for a second regeneration project (see Chapter 4). The 8.6 per cent population growth over the past decade thus marks the partial repopulation of the redeveloped neighbourhood. Population

TABLE 2.2 Population change in the seven case study neighbourhoods and nationwide, 1996, 2002, and 2006

Case study neighbourhood and ED(s) in which it is located	Population 1996	Population 2002	Population 2006	Population change 1996–2006 (1991–2006)
Cranmore (Sligo East)	5,961	5,568	5,334	−10.5 (−10.2)
Deanrock (Togher A)	2,680	2,451	2,055	−23.3 (−29.9)
Fatima Mansions (Ushers C+D)	4,373	4,460	4,747	8.6 (5.8)
Fettercairn (Tallaght – Fettercairn)	5,513	6,488	6,600	19.7 (23.7)
Finglas South (Finglas South B+C)	6,516	6,077	5,922	−9.1 (−20.4)
Moyross (Ballynanty)	4,448	4,110	3,468	−22.0 (−25.1)
Muirhevnamore (Dundalk Rural)	14,188	14,715	15,534	9.5 (10.7)
Ireland	*3,626,087*	*3,917,203*	*4,239,848*	*16.6 (20.3)*

growth of one-fifth between 1996 and 2002 in Fettercairn was also driven by a regeneration project as part of which new 'in-fill' social rented housing was constructed (see Chapter 4). In Muirhevnamore, where no new building took place, population growth of nearly 10 per cent was most likely due to an increase in the wider ED rather than in the neighbourhood itself.

In contrast to both the national population trends and the three neighbourhoods mentioned above, four of the case study neighbourhoods experienced considerable population decline during the period under examination. To correctly interpret this development, we have to look at the various factors than can stimulate such decline. Some population decline can naturally occur in any social housing neighbourhood as part of its normal lifecycle. Until recent years in Ireland, newly built housing neighbourhoods, and particularly those with a high proportion of social housing, were designed to cater for families with children. As the children grow older and move out of the parental home, a decline in population density will automatically result. It will occur in particular where the local authority is successful in selling dwellings to tenants, thus facilitating the stabilisation of mixed communities in the area. Thus, population decline in a maturing social housing neighbourhood could be a positive phenomenon.

However, population decline can also be indicative of neighbourhood decline, with dwellings remaining unoccupied or even derelict due to low demand for housing and an area's increasing undesirability. Whether such a situation prevails in any of the four housing neighbourhoods that have registered a population decline cannot be gauged from statistics alone, but needs to be verified by local knowledge. There is a strong suggestion that the population loss in Finglas (9.1 per cent), Moyross (22.0 per cent) and Cranmore (10.5 per cent) were indicative of a downwards movement in demand for housing. Deanrock is quite different in that population decline was driven in large measure by demolition of eight blocks of flats that had contained almost one-third of the dwellings in the estate. These blocks of flats had been identified in our original study as the poorest quality dwellings in all the seven estates from a physical build point of view. Though paradoxically reflecting the strong appeal of Deanrock as a whole, they were in relatively high demand among tenants – and thus were an instance where the social attractions of housing trumped poor physical conditions (see Norris, 1999). In the years up to the end of our fieldwork, other indicators of demand for housing, such as housing waiting lists and house prices for privatised social housing, held up strongly in Deanrock. This issue is discussed further in Chapter 3.

Lone parenthood: Our second demographic consideration is the share of lone parent-headed households in the neighbourhoods. The lone parent rate is important for two reasons: first, studies on poverty and social inclusion in Ireland have consistently shown that lone parents are at considerably greater risk of living in poverty and experiencing social exclusion. Second, the rate of lone parenthood has risen dramatically in Ireland in recent decades – from 13.8 per cent in 1996 to 21.3 per cent in 2006 (see Table 2.3).

However, in this regard, there are marked differences between urban and rural areas, and lone parent rates in the major cities are again up to twice the national average. In Dublin city in 2006, more than one-third of families with dependent

TABLE 2.3   Lone parent rate in the seven case study neighbourhoods and nationwide, 1996, 2002, and 2006

Case study neighbourhood and ED(s) in which it is located	Lone parent % rate 1996	Lone parent % rate 2002	Lone parent % rate 2006	Change in lone parent rate 1996–2006
Cranmore (Sligo East)	23.2	30.8	35.9	12.7
Deanrock (Togher A)	23.8	36.0	42.4	18.6
Fatima Mansions (Ushers C+D)	51.2	56.2	58.4	7.2
Fettercairn (Tallaght – Fettercairn)	36.8	44.5	53.3	16.5
Finglas South (Finglas South B+C)	23.5	34.1	51.6	28.0
Moyross (Ballynanty)	37.8	55.5	63.9	26.1
Muirhevnamore (Dundalk Rural)	18.0	32.2	37.9	19.9
Ireland	*13.8*	*16.7*	*21.3*	*7.5*

children (35.8 per cent) were headed by a single parent. If we look only at the inner city of Dublin, lone parenthood is even more common – every second household with dependent children (50.0 per cent) was headed by a single parent in 2006. After Dublin, Limerick city had the second highest rate of lone parenthood (39.1 per cent) of any local government area in Ireland.

Lone parents are strongly concentrated within the social rented tenure in Ireland. This distribution is principally related to two inter-related factors: (a) their incomes are significantly lower than average and their benefit dependency rates higher so they often face housing affordability problems and consequently are eligible to apply for social housing, and (b) many lone parents apply for social housing and make up a large proportion of those on waiting lists for access to this tenure (38 per cent of households assessed as qualified for social housing in 2005) (Open, 2009). This concentration of lone parents in social housing is evident in most of the seven neighbourhoods examined here. Table 2.3 reveals that while the lone parenthood rate in Ireland increased by 7.5 per cent between 1996 and 2006, in three of the case study neighbourhoods (Cranmore, Deanrock, and Muirhevnamore) this household type increased by more than twice the national average, while in two neighbourhoods (Finglas South and Moyross) lone parenthood increased by more than three times the national average. This development points to increased socio-spatial segregation in Ireland between 1996 and 2006, characterised by the increased concentration of lone parent households in some mainly social rented neighbourhoods.

Educational achievement: in the absence of reliable data on social class or income levels in the Irish census, educational attainment is the best proxy for the overall affluence or deprivation of an area that can be gleaned from this source. The indicator is closely correlated to the underlying social class of the people living in the area.

There has been an unprecedented improvement in the level of education amongst Irish adults in recent decades. In 1991, 36.7 per cent of the adult population had primary education only but this had dropped to half that level (18.9 per cent) in 2006. In some ways this development is to be expected since some reduction in the proportion of adults with primary education only occurs naturally over time as each successive cohort of school-going students tends to attend school for longer than the previous one. Nevertheless the rise in educational standards in Ireland during the period of the economic boom is particularly marked by international standards (OECD, various years).

This development is positive for the individuals concerned and should also bode well for the economy's future competitiveness, but it also creates challenges as unskilled jobs continue to be lost to lower-wage countries, newly developing job opportunities tend to require a higher skills set and puts those without adequate education at an increased risk of unemployment and social exclusion (Smyth and McCoy, 2011). Table 2.4 reveals some worrying trends in this respect. Whilst all of the case study neighbourhoods experienced declines in the numbers of adults with primary education only, these declines exceeded the national average in only

TABLE 2.4 Proportion of adult population with primary education only in the seven case study neighbourhoods and nationwide, 1996, 2002, and 2006

Case study neighbourhood and ED(s) in which it is located	% of low education 1996	% of low education 2002	% of low education 2006	Change in low education 1996–2006
Cranmore (Sligo East)	30.1	24.6	21.9	−8.2
Deanrock (Togher A)	34.2	34.4	32.2	−2.0
Fatima Mansions (Ushers C+D)	50.9	36.0	29.9	−21.0
Fettercairn (Tallaght – Fettercairn)	41.4	27.0	25.8	−15.6
Finglas South (Finglas South B+C)	46.9	39.4	39.8	−7.1
Moyross (Ballynanty)	45.8	40.3	39.6	−6.2
Muirhevnamore (Dundalk Rural)	32.5	28.0	23.8	−8.7
Ireland	*29.5*	*22.2*	*18.9*	*−10.6*

two cases (Fatima Mansions and Fettercairn). Furthermore, in the case of the former neighbourhood this development is probably due to the introduction of new, better-educated residents, rather than to any improvement in the educational attainment of existing residents. The five other neighbourhoods experienced a below-average improvement in their educational profile between 1996 and 2006. This data therefore suggests that the improvement in educational attainment during Ireland's economic boom was spatially uneven and failed to reach into many disadvantaged neighbourhoods. Over the longer term this spatial pattern of educational attainment is likely to predicate similar spatial inequalities in the distribution of employment and unemployment.

Table 2.5 examines the opposite end of the education spectrum – the proportion of the population with third-level education, which has increased dramatically during the period under examination. In 1991, 13 per cent of Irish adults had completed third-level education and this grew to 30.5 per cent by 2006. Not surprisingly, trends in this regard are the inverse of the trends in low educational attainment that were outlined above.

The proportion of residents with third-level education increased in all of the seven case study neighbourhoods, but among these Fatima Mansions is the only neighbourhood where the increase exceeded the national average. As mentioned above, this development may be related to an influx of new, higher educated residents rather than to any improvement in educational attainment among the existing population. All the other case study neighbourhoods performed well below the national average on this indicator between 1996 and 2006, further lending credence to the notion that social housing neighbourhoods did not share fully in the social benefits of the boom.

Employment and unemployment: Unemployment rates in Ireland broadly halved during the period of the Celtic Tiger boom. However, female unemployment rates, which historically have tended to be slightly below male unemployment rates, did

TABLE 2.5   Proportion of adult population with third-level education in the seven case study neighbourhoods and nationwide, 1996, 2002, and 2006

Case study neighbourhood and ED(s) in which it is located	% of third-level education 1996	% of third-level education 2002	% of third-level education 2006	Change in third-level education 1996–2006
Cranmore (Sligo East)	19.1	24.3	25.7	6.6
Deanrock (Togher A)	9.5	10.7	11.6	2.1
Fatima Mansions (Ushers C+D)	10.9	19.8	28.3	17.3
Fettercairn (Tallaght – Fettercairn)	3.8	9.5	10.5	6.8
Finglas South (Finglas South B+C)	3.5	8.5	10.7	7.2
Moyross (Ballynanty)	4.9	6.3	6.0	1.2
Muirhevnamore (Dundalk Rural)	16.3	19.1	23.0	6.7
Ireland	*19.7*	*26.0*	*30.5*	*10.8*

not fall at the same pace due to the increasing levels of female labour force participation. The male unemployment rate fell from 18.4 per cent in 1991 to 8.8 per cent in 2006, whilst the female unemployment rate fell from 14.1 per cent to 8.1 per cent concurrently (Central Statistics Office, various years a). For the past ten years, the reductions in male and female unemployment are 7.6 and 3.9 percentage points respectively.

Unlike the changes in educational attainment outlined above, which were concentrated in the 1991 to 2002 period, the reduction in unemployment was concentrated in the 1996 to 2002 period. During this narrow time span, with the exception of Muirhevnamore (which in any event is not well captured by the ED data), the case study neighbourhoods experienced a decline of around half in unemployment (see Table 2.6). In view of the relatively low educational attainments of residents of these neighbourhoods, this development suggests that at the height of the Celtic Tiger boom even more marginal labour became employable, albeit for a relatively short period in time. However, between 2002 and 2006, Ireland's urban regions already saw a significant downturn in employment rates, with many of the cities and towns already seeing a reversal of their previous good fortune. This reversal is also evident in several of the case study neighbourhoods – Finglas, Fettercairn, Moyross, and Cranmore all experienced an increase in unemployment over the period 2002–6.

Taking all these observations on education and employment trends together, the employment outlook for these neighbourhoods following the sharp contraction of the Irish economy in 2008–9 seems poor and it is likely that unemployment in these neighbourhoods will rise significantly in excess of national increases.

TABLE 2.6 Male and female unemployment in the seven case study neighbourhoods and nationwide, 1996, 2002, and 2006

Case study neighbourhood and ED(s) in which it is located	% of male (and female) unemployment 1996	% of male (and female) unemployment 2002	% of male and (female) unemployment 2006	Change in male (and female) unemployment 1996–2006
Cranmore (Sligo East)	25.3 (14.5)	15.0 (10.5)	15.3 (9.2)	−10.1 (−5.3)
Deanrock (Togher A)	28.0 (20.8)	18.8 (18.9)	16.7 (13.1)	−11.4 (−7.7)
Fatima Mansions (Ushers C+D)	45.1 (35.2)	25.3 (17.3)	19.4 (16.3)	−25.7 (−18.9)
Fettercairn (Tallaght – Fettercairn)	52.1 (39.8)	19.6 (18.3)	22.8 (14.0)	−29.2 (−19.2)
Finglas South (Finglas South B+C)	34.4 (26.8)	15.2 (14.0)	18.6 (14.0)	−15.8 (−12.7)
Moyross (Ballynanty)	40.9 (28.6)	26.1 (14.2)	28.8 (18.7)	−12.1 (−9.8)
Muirhevnamore (Dundalk Rural)	23.0 (15.7)	23.6 (19.1)	16.6 (15.1)	−6.4 (−0.6)
Ireland	*16.4* *(12.0)*	*9.4* *(8.9)*	*8.8* *(8.1)*	*−7.6* *(−3.9)*

Housing tenure: the proportion of Irish households living in social housing provided by local authorities declined from 9.8 per cent in 1991 to 7.5 per cent in 2006. The decline has been most pronounced in the Dublin region, but was also significant in Limerick and Waterford cities and, to a lesser degree, in Ireland's second city of Cork. The disproportionate decline in the four cities is most likely the result of a combination of factors – the overall reduction in the state's involvement in the direct provision of social housing and increasing reliance on indirect supports, the developer-led character of the house-building boom, and the desire by planning officials to reduce the high level of concentrations of social housing (these issues are discussed in more depth in Chapter 4). In 2006, the highest concentrations of local authority rented housing are found in large urban centres – Cork City (15.8 per cent), Waterford City (13.9 per cent), Limerick city (13.2 per cent), and Dublin City (12.5 per cent).

Between 1996 and 2006 all of the seven case study neighbourhoods saw reductions in local authority rented accommodation significantly in excess of national and even regional trends (see Table 2.7). The reduction was most pronounced in Fettercairn, where local authority tenants declined from over 70 per cent of households in 1996 to 56 per cent in 2006, probably as a result of sales of dwellings to tenants. The reduction of 8 percentage points in local authority tenant households in Deanrock during this period may be related to the demolition of the

TABLE 2.7   Social (local authority) and private (for profit) renting households in the seven case study neighbourhoods and nationwide, 1996, 2002, and 2006

Case study neighbourhood and ED(s) in which it is located	% of LA rented (private rented) 1996	% of LA rented (private rented) 2002	% of LA rented (private rented) 2006	Change in LA rented (private rented) 1996–2006
Cranmore (Sligo East)	18.8	15.2	16.2	–2.6
	(11.7)	(15.6)	(17.9)	(6.2)
Deanrock (Togher A)	35.0	31.4	26.9	–8.0
	(3.4)	(5.0)	(5.8)	(2.5)
Fatima Mansions (Ushers C+D)	35.4	29.2	30.8	–4.6
	(18.6)	(23.1)	(25.8)	(7.2)
Fettercairn (Tallaght – Fettercairn)	71.3	55.1	55.5	–15.7
	(2.1)	(3.4)	(7.8)	(5.7)
Finglas South (Finglas South B+C)	26.6	17.8	22.0	–4.6
	(1.9)	(3.1)	(6.1)	(4.2)
Moyross (Ballynanty)	48.3	41.1	44.3	–4.0
	(4.1)	(6.2)	(4.0)	(0.0)
Muirhevnamore (Dundalk Rural)	19.6	16.0	15.3	–4.4
	(8.8)	(10.7)	(15.5)	(6.7)
Ireland	*8.3*	*7.1*	*7.5*	*–0.8*
	(9.9)	*(11.4)*	*(13.8)*	*(3.9)*

blocks of social rented flats in the neighbourhood as well as the attractiveness of the social rented houses in the neighbourhood for tenant purchases.

The contraction in local authority renting households in the other case study neighbourhoods was more modest between 1996 and 2006 – in the region of four percentage points in all cases. This may reflect the challenges residents faced in purchasing their home. Rates of tenant purchase of social housing were low during the Celtic Tiger boom, compared to the historic norm. This was due mainly to the marked rise in house prices during this period, which rendered purchase unaffordable for many social housing tenants even taking into account the discounts of up to 30 per cent of market value that were available to incentivise sales (Norris, Coates, and Kane, 2007).

One feature of the housing boom that accompanied rapid economic growth was a significant increase in dwellings rented from private landlords, thereby reversing a century-long pattern of decline in private renting in Ireland. Table 2.7 reveals that the private rented sector now accommodates a significant share of households in some of the case study neighbourhoods. In the ED in which the redeveloped Fatima Mansions is located, one-quarter of housing units in the area were privately rented in 2006. Muirhevnamore and Cranmore also have significant shares of private rented accommodation (15.5 per cent and 17.9 per cent respectively), although it again has to be remembered that these data relate to a wider geographical area than the neighbourhoods in question. It can safely be assumed that the actual share in the two specific housing neighbourhoods is more likely to be around 5 per cent. Finglas and Fettercairn have both seen some privately rented accommodation coming into the dwelling mix between 1996 and 2006: accounting for less than 1 per cent in 1996, the private rented sector now accounts for about 6 and 8 per cent in these two areas respectively. In both cases this is likely to be related to infill developments of new housing or to the letting to private tenants of former social housing that previously had been privatised through tenant purchase. Deanrock and Moyross have only experienced a very small growth in the privately rented sector, accounting for still less than 5 per cent of households in 2006.

Conclusions

This chapter has examined trends in disadvantage in the seven case study neighbourhoods between 1996 and 2006 using a multi-variate index, the Pobal HP Deprivation Index, which is derived from census small area data. The PHDI is a sophisticated measure of disadvantage, which allows us to compare developments in the seven neighbourhoods with the Irish population-at-large. The chapter first highlighted some challenges associated with applying the PHDI to the case study neighbourhoods since the index relates to spatial units that are not always coterminous with the neighbourhood boundaries.

The results of the analysis reveal rather mixed developments among the case study neighbourhoods. On the one hand, when measured in absolute terms, almost every neighbourhood in Ireland, including the seven case study neighbourhoods, experienced a decline in disadvantage between 1996 and 2006. However, when the same analysis is conducted in relative terms, by benchmarking all of the neighbourhoods in the country against each other, a rather different picture emerges. In relative terms, two neighbourhoods (Fatima Mansions and Fettercairn) saw a significant improvement in their position over this decade, three (Muirhevnamore, Cranmore, and Finglas) experienced a slight deterioration and two neighbourhoods (Deanrock and Moyross) a significant worsening of their situation. The data for Fatima Mansions include the surrounding districts so we cannot be sure that its improving relative deprivation score is entirely due to neighbourhood-level factors, although these are likely to have contributed at least in part. In the case of Fettercairn, however, the data on which the PHDI scores are based capture the neighbourhood very accurately, so in this case it is reasonable to conclude that its improving relative disadvantage scores are related to the improving fortunes of its residents, particularly in relation to educational attainment and employment. The deterioration in Deanrock's relative PHDI score is an exceptional case where population decline may have entailed some improvement in the circumstances of remaining residents since it arose from the demolition of flats that had been the main weak spot in Deanrock in the late 1990s. Moyross, on the other hand, was among the most disadvantaged neighbourhood in the early 1990s, but its position worsened during the decade under review, making it by far the most disadvantaged of the seven neighbourhoods by 2006. Indeed, its relative PHDI score indicates that by then it was the most disadvantaged neighbourhood in the country (see also Chapter 10).

References

Central Statistics Office (various years a) *Census of population of Ireland*, Dublin: Central Statistics Office.
— (various years b) *Measuring Ireland's progress*, Dublin: Stationery Office.
Haase, T. (2009) *Divided city – The changing face of Dublin's inner city*, Dublin: Dublin Inner City Partnership.
Haase, T. and Pratschke, J. (2005) *Deprivation and its spatial articulation in the Republic of Ireland*, Dublin: Area Development Management.
— (2008) *The new measures of deprivation in the Republic of Ireland*, Dublin: Pobal.
Kennedy, K., Giblin, T., and McHugh, D. (1988) *The economic development of Ireland in the Twentieth century*, London: Routledge.
Nolan, B., O'Connell, P., and Whelan, C. (eds) (2000) *Bust to boom? The Irish experience of growth and inequality*, Dublin: Institute of Public Administration.
Norris, M. (1999) The impact of the built environment. In T. Fahey (ed.) *Social housing in Ireland: A study of success, failure and lessons learned* (pp. 101–24), Dublin: Oak Tree Press.
Norris, M. and Gkartzios, M. (2011) 'Twenty years of property-led urban regeneration in Ireland: outputs, impacts, implications', *Public Money and Management*, 31 (4), 257–64.
Norris, M. and Redmond, D. (2009) *Private sector involvement in regenerating social housing estates: A review of recent practice in Dublin*, Dublin: Combat Poverty Agency.
Norris, M., Coates, D., and Kane, F. (2007) 'Breaching the limits of owner occupation? Supporting low-income buyers in the inflated Irish housing market', *European Journal of Housing Policy*, 7 (3), 337–56.
OECD (various years) *Country statistical profiles*, Paris: OECD.
Open (2009) *Making social housing and accommodation provision more one parent friendly*, Dublin: Open.
Smyth, E. and McCoy, S. (2011) 'The dynamics of credentialism: Ireland from bust to boom (and back again)', *Research in Social Stratification and Mobility*, 29 (1), 91–106.
Whyte, J. (2005) *Eight great expectations: A landmark and unique social regeneration plan for Fatima Mansions*, Dublin: Fatima Regeneration Board.

3

LIVEABILITY AND THE LIFEWORLD OF THE SOCIAL HOUSING NEIGHBOURHOOD

Mary P. Corcoran

Introduction

> The nature of an individual's relationships with others in their household, their community and beyond, as well as with institutions and policies, are fundamental influences on quality of life.
>
> *(Fahey, Whelan, and Nolan, 2003, p. 1)*

In this chapter we focus on the subjective perceptions of residents and service providers as they reflect on the 'lifeworld' of the neighbourhoods that constitute their homes or places of work. The analysis presented is based on testimonials gathered from more than 165 residents and service providers through interviews and focus groups across the seven neighbourhoods between 2007 and 2008, and the 203 interviewees who participated in the first phase of the study in 1997–8. The qualitative approach affords the opportunity to explore how residents view neighbourhood change through the lens of social liveability – how well does the neighbourhood accommodate people and their needs, to what extent does it support well-being and the pursuit of individual aspiration and goals? We are interested in the physical and social attractiveness of the neighbourhood, and residents' perceptions of the resources available to them locally. How do they 'read' and rate their local environments? What kinds of educational and economic opportunities have they access to? What kinds of access do they have to recreational facilities, arts, and culture? Are there particular barriers that exist to prevent participation or particular practices locally that militate against participation?

In particular, we are interested in identifying the broad direction of change in residents' and service providers' assessments of liveability over the ten-year time period covered by this study. We explore the extent to which life in the neighbourhood – the lived everyday experiences as seen primarily through the eyes of residents and service providers – has moved along a similar trajectory for all neighbourhoods, or whether there are significant differences within and between them. A key question is whether or not the neighbourhoods and their environs are *perceived* to be improving, remaining more or less static, or deteriorating across time. Perceptions are important because they can shape people's responses and behaviour in ways that are consequential for the individual and the community (see, for instance, Sampson, 2009). One might expect that the seven case study neighbourhoods, in response to wider changes in society, have been moving in a progressively more improved situation. On the other hand, it is also possible that each neighbourhood has a unique local set of circumstances that remain crucial in determining the rate and direction of change. Part of our aim here is to plot the *narrative accounts* of each neighbourhood, and identify where and how their individual liveability trajectories converge or diverge.

The context: liveability in 1997–8

The initial study conducted in 1997–8 pointed to a number of key features of liveability in the seven social housing neighbourhoods under examination.

On the negative side it found that most of the neighbourhoods suffered from either poor housing quality or a weak physical infrastructure, or in some cases a combination of both. However, the relationship between the quality of the built environmental and liveability was generally weak (Norris, 1999). For instance, despite refurbishment, housing quality was poor in Deanrock, a neighbourhood that originally had been 'system built' and was laid out in a monotonous grid

IMAGE 3.1 Fatima Mansions in 2004, prior to its demoltion and reconstruction
Photo by Matt Kavanagh

pattern, yet residents rated it well. In contrast, housing in Finglas South was structurally sound and generally well kept by occupants but some districts of the neighbourhood were characterised by high rates of anti-social behaviour. In Fatima Mansions, both the flats and the general infrastructure and public areas surrounding the dwellings had fallen into an acute spiral of decline by the time of our first round of fieldwork in 1997–8. Many residents at the time were actively seeking to be re-housed elsewhere.

An aspect of the built environment that hampered liveability was the social and spatial segregation of all of the case study neighbourhoods from their surrounding areas, either through physical boundaries (Moyross and Deanrock) or through symbolic boundaries (simmering tensions between Fatima Mansions and the surrounding Rialto neighbourhood). Cranmore in Sligo and Muirhevnamore in Dundalk were tucked away from the main axis of activity in their respective towns. The effect of such patterns of segregation is to divide, isolate, and exclude rather than integrate urban communities. Such polarisation is not unique to Ireland, but has become characteristic of many urban centres where increasingly 'urban space, while it is functionally and economically shared, is socially segregated and culturally differentiated' (Robins, 1993, p. 313).

In addition, the neighbourhoods were internally differentiated and stratified. This was particularly evident in Moyross in 1997–8 but also in Fatima Mansions, Finglas South and Cranmore. As a consequence, the capacity of residents to coalesce around shared interests and represent those interests to wider audiences varied not just *between* neighbourhoods, but also *within* neighbourhoods. In all the neighbourhoods, to a greater or lesser extent, residents spoke of being embattled. From a liveability perspective the neighbourhoods tended to be perceived as unsafe and unsupportive environments by the residents. Quality of life was greatly affected by the problems of drug and alcohol abuse, vandalism, intimidation, and harassment. Our 1997–8 research concluded that 'social order problems are a dominant influence on the quality of life of residents and a crucial element in differentiating between success and failure in [these neighbourhoods]' (O'Higgins, 1999, p. 149). This dovetails with international research, which suggests that social disorder constitutes a fundamental dimension of social inequality at the neighbourhood level and beyond. Residents are thought to read signs of disorder as evidence of a deeper neighbourhood malaise, undermining personal health and trust (Sampson and Raudenbush, 2004; Sampson, 2009).

The palpable alienation of residents in some of the case study neighbourhoods described in 1997–8 was tempered to some extent by a strong sense of social and communal solidarity anchored in everyday social relations and practices. Despite the problems faced, in general residents registered high levels of satisfaction with *their communities*, if not with the physical environment in which the communities were housed or the locality. Even in a neighbourhood as blighted as Fatima Mansions was in 1997–8, a majority (58 per cent) of those surveyed at the time felt that was some sense of a community spirit in the neighbourhood (Corcoran, 1998). These were communities that endured both in the sense of suffering, but also in the more positive sense of continuing to sustain themselves in the face of challenges.

IMAGE 3.2   A settled, well-kept part of Moyross in 2004. Note that horses are commonly
                kept by residents
Photo by Brenda Fitzsimons

There was tension between the negatives of living in an area marked by dereliction
and substance abuse problems, and the positives derived from being enmeshed in
intense familial and neighbourhood networks. The proximity of other family
members acted as a bulwark against social isolation and contributed to liveability
and quality of life. On all the neighbourhoods people derived considerable happiness
from the presence of good neighbours. In some cases, the worse things were in
terms of social order and security, the more important the role of neighbours
became in staving off feelings of despair and alienation. In the absence of a
supportive physical environment, residents generated solidarity based on a strong
sense of identity and sense of place, the significance of which to the concept of
liveability is noted by Lynch (1981). Furthermore, residents of all the neighbourhoods
engaged in acts of resistance to the deterioration of their living environment. Where
community activism brings success, people's sense of themselves as agents, rather
than as subjects that are acted upon, was enhanced.

   In terms of criteria of liveability (demand for and satisfaction with dwelling,
quality of social life and community cohesion, reputation and quality of built
environment) Fatima Mansions was the least liveable neighbourhood and Deanrock
was the most liveable in the eyes of the residents. Despite the work of committed
community activists, social fragmentation was very striking in Fatima Mansions.
Whereas Deanrock, also blighted by poor housing conditions, exhibited a high level
of social solidarity. Moyross was under significant pressure in 1997–8 and closer to
the 'low' end of the liveability continuum. Both neighbourhoods were grappling

with problems of anti-social behaviour and criminality, which impacted on the general liveability of place. South Finglas was a very mixed neighbourhood incorporating both very settled and troubled sub areas. Fettercairn was at a tipping point, mid-way along the continuum. Muirhevnamore and Cranmore were relatively more stable than Fettercairn and therefore closer to the 'high' end of the liveability continuum. Though relatively positively evaluated as liveable by residents they nevertheless were facing challenges (multi-problem families, youth integration, anti-social behaviour) that if left unchecked would intensify their marginalisation.

The changes: liveability in 2007–9

Much has changed since the first round of fieldwork was carried out. Fatima Mansions has undergone a major transformation as part of a comprehensive regeneration conducted between 2004 and 2008, resulting in a total regeneration of both the built and social fabric of the neighbourhood (Norris and Redmond, 2009). The neighbourhood has access to excellent local amenities and is more closely integrated with its surrounding locale (see Image 3.3). As such, it would now be deemed successful in terms of a liveability trajectory. Deanrock has managed to hold its own in the intervening years and the evidence suggests that community engagement remains high and that locals still identify the neighbourhood as a good place to live. Fettercairn, which was in danger of deteriorating, has stabilised and experienced improvement in quality of life in part as a result of access to additional resources and programmes. The neighbourhood has matured, and become more socially integrated than it was in the past. Cranmore, in Sligo (see Image 3.4), and Muirhevnamore, in Dundalk, have benefited from piecemeal refurbishments rather than more comprehensive programmes of regeneration (although one was planned for Cranmore at the time of writing). Nevertheless, they appear to have stabilised over time. Our data makes evident the successes garnered across these five neighbourhoods in terms of generating greater levels of community activism, raising aspirations, reclaiming and improving public spaces and services for residents. All of this contributes to improved liveability. Moyross, which entered a severe spiral of decline at the turn of the twenty-first century, has now been ear-marked for an ambitious multi-year regeneration, although there remains a degree of uncertainty about the precise scale of the programme and the timeframe for delivery (Fitzgerald, 2007; Limerick Regeneration Agencies, 2008). Quality of life in Moyross, however, has deteriorated significantly since the earlier study, with residents and service providers reporting heightened levels of crime, drug use, and anti-social behaviour in the intervening years. Regimes of fear impact very negatively on the quality of life of residents, to a much greater degree now than in the past. The troubled sub areas of Finglas South became less liveable, but despite this large sections remained settled.

Therefore, in summary, the overall picture is a mixed one. The worst neighbourhood in 1997–8, Fatima Mansions, may now make legitimate claims to be the best. Deanrock continues to reap the benefit of a high level of community spirit locally, which enhances its overall liveability. The neighbourhoods that

IMAGE 3.3 Fatima Mansions following its demolition and reconstruction in 2004–8. Photo by Matt Kavanagh

IMAGE 3.4 A section of Cranmore after its refurbishment in 2000–1. Photo provided by Clūid Housing Association.

featured in the middle of the liveability continuum in the earlier study – Cranmore, Muirhevnamore, and Fettercairn – have moved closer to the successful end of this continuum. Both Moyross and Finglas South experienced further decline in liveability in the 1990s, which was acute and widespread in the former and less highly localised in the latter. The complexity of this portrait serves to underline the fact that social rented neighbourhoods are not all the same; local factors such as the history of the neighbourhood, its spatial configuration, tenanting history, transience of population, and the presence or absence of problem families result in different liveability perceptions and experiences.

Below we outline – under the broad rubric of liveability – some of the key themes that emerged from the analysis of data collected from residents and service providers across the seven case study neighbourhoods. In the first instance, we focus on the positives that can be gleaned and which indicate an improvement in liveability across time. There has been a generalised *raising of aspirations* that may bode well for the future trajectories of residents. In this sense, what Veenhoven (2000) describes as 'life-ability' – the inner qualities of a person that can positively impact on life chances – improved across the neighbourhoods between 1997–8 and 2007–9. Second, there is considerable evidence of *sustained engagement* by residents in attempts to improve quality of life in some neighbourhoods, and third, these communities demonstrate *enhanced capacity* to act in their own interests.

On the other hand, respondents' perceptions suggest that liveability remains a key challenge in these neighbourhoods. There is an ongoing problem of stigmatisation and marginalisation of parts of the neighbourhoods and of sub-sections of the community, which continue to threaten their overall liveability. First, there is evidence that internal neighbourhood stratification or a form of *social apartheid* is still present across the neighbourhoods, although this has become more salient in some neighbourhoods and less so in others. Second, a significant proportion of residents are more inclined towards passivity than active engagement, they display a considerable degree of alienation from their neighbours and key service providers, and remain a 'hard-to-reach group'. Finally, there is also evidence of a deeper institutionalisation of an inter-generational *dependency culture*. Service providers across a number of neighbourhoods expressed concern about the internalisation of norms and values that militate against individual capacity building and self-actualisation. These issues are elaborated below.

Drivers of improved liveability

Raised aspirations: There is evidence that raised expectations are a feature of the case study neighbourhoods and this is particularly apparent in relation to attitudes towards educational attainment. In the earlier study, early school leaving was recognised as a chronic problem across the seven neighbourhoods under examination. All of the neighbourhoods in the meantime have benefited from targeted educational interventions either directly or through the ancillary projects available through regeneration programmes (see Chapter 7). People in key roles in the community such as teachers and other service providers readily attest to the raising of aspirations among the people whom they serve. This is illustrated by the following quotations from teachers in the schools serving Deanrock and Fettercairn respectively:

> I can see it here that parents are starting to believe that their child might get to a secondary school that they might never have aspired to. They might get to college–, and I'm not necessarily saying that every child should go to college [third level education].

> . . . I would say the majority of parents now would expect their children at the very least to go to Leaving Cert [school leaving exam] and quite a substantial proportion would also expect that they would go to some third level form of education.

In the same vein, an adult education teacher who worked with Fatima Mansions' residents observed that the regeneration of the neighbourhood had 'collectively raised the spirit of the place'. She added that there had been an uptake in adult education programmes in the neighbourhood in recent years and that one of the outcomes of adults returning to learning was that they were 'adamant that they will keep their children in school'. Service providers in Finglas South also noted the importance of educational role models. When parents take learning seriously there is a potentially positive impact on their children's engagement with the education system. It is difficult to quantify or measure the impact over time of an increasing number of adults returning to education, but service providers report that there has been a tangible benefit within the *family* milieu. In Finglas South programmes that enable people to return to education were praised as providing a pathway to self-fulfilment for people who had historically – and cross-generationally – been excluded or excluded themselves from further education:

> . . . you've got a mother or father going back to education, doing a Leaving Cert [school leaving exam], even at that level, that's helping the children, that's a role model. Finally it's there for them, and we can't quantify it in any way. And just being able to do it, but the few pieces of research that were done . . . certainly people are really happy with the Back to Education [social security benefit scheme]. And they did not do it for the system to return to work, they did it because they hadn't got it, they never had the chance to get it and they wanted to have their Leaving Cert, or their degree or whatever, to say, they had it.

In Deanrock respondents also noted the positive ripple effect of people staying on at school and achieving, thereby acting as an exemplar for others:

> We had people who had never dreamed about it coming down here completing FETAC [vocational] courses. I can think of one mum, and her

starting point would have been 'afraid of her life to come into the place, you know, schools and fellows in suits and whatever' and as we speak she is delivering a sewing, dress-making course to fellow parents, and over a ten-year period this girl is now a tutor with FETAC [formal government] accreditation.

Raised aspirations have the potential not only to improve the life-ability of the individuals concerned but also to have a secondary effect on the aspirations of their children. Education comes to be perceived as an opportunity structure that can enhance life chances and ultimately life outcomes. Nevertheless, it was also noted that there are ongoing high levels of disengagement from schools and that more role models are needed to demonstrate to people the value of education.

Community engagement: There is considerable evidence of sustained engagement by residents in their communities. Arts and cultural initiatives in particular have sought to engage residents in the representation and celebration of aspects of their own cultural realities and lived experiences of place. Borer (2006) points out that the ways that people make sense of the world they live in, once lived in, or hope to build are tied to the places where they *practice* their culture. Identity and sense of place have been noted as key attributes of urban liveability by Lynch (1981). Veenhoven (2000) also notes the crucial dimension of culture in contributing to the liveability of the environment.

Fatima Mansions has been at the forefront of this 'cultural turn' having created as part of its regeneration agenda an arts and culture programme that has become integral to the regeneration process. As one informant observed 'the soul of Fatima is the heritage on the ground'. For instance, learning to appreciate Fatima heritage, to salvage memories, and bring traditions forward into the new Fatima were viewed as crucial to the success of the regeneration programme. Several informants spoke movingly of their participation in cultural events such as 'Bury my Heart in Fatima' and the 'Tower Songs' projects, both organised to provide closure on the neighbour-hood's past, and empower residents to move forward into the future following the regeneration. Such events provided people with an opportunity 'to mourn the life that had been' and gave people the chance to express their emotions on the passing of the old and the arrival of the new. Commenting on the Bury my Heart festival (see Image 3.5), which brought together current and past residents of the complex to bid farewell to the flats, one resident captured the mixed emotions felt by many:

> I can't explain how I felt because I felt really sad, you know, but at the same time looking forward. It was like saying goodbye to the old and hello to the new all at once and seeing all the ex-residents coming back and all, it was very emotional.

Arts and cultural practice offer more than just an opportunity for creative expression, but also a mechanism for expressing and channelling feelings and for building self-esteem. Furthermore, there is a significance attached to community-bonding initiatives expressed through arts and cultural practice that helps to encourage

IMAGE 3.5 The 'Bury my Heart in Fatima' festival which was held to mark the demolition of Fatima Mansions.
Photo by Chris Maguire

pro-social behaviour and give people a pride in place. This theme resonates through a number of the testimonials gathered from people in Deanrock and Fettercairn:

> Like bonfire night was fantastic, that we had an organised fire in the park, who thought you would do that? But we had 2,000 people there all day, do

you know what I mean. And even though there was still bonfires going on, all of the young people stayed until our bonfire was finished. So it was a very small thing, it was only €5–6,000 worth of money but it made a huge difference to the community of [Deanrock]. So small things like that would have a big impact.

We also got involved in urban art so we have a junior aspect to the estate management committee and we have a lot of youngsters involved in that. That is a picture of a mural we did in Kilmartin [neighbourhood adjacent to Fettercairn]. The mural hasn't been touched now, it has been up there for two years.

Environmental projects also have the capacity to encourage social participation locally. One positively evaluated initiative has been undertaken in Fettercairn that focused on improving the aesthetic appeal of the public areas in the neighbourhood:

We try to do clean ups, planting days, that is a picture of a planting day that we did there recently and we try and involve as many people as possible keeping the estate clean. Now we provide brushes and bags and all that kind of thing. I do that, I have a depot for officers where we are able to get supplies for people if they are willing to get involved. So that is quite successful in Fettercairn.

Mechanisms of integration extend to sports and these also may have very positive effects serving as a means of engaging members of the community and offering pro-social models of behaviour particularly for young people. One example of such a successful initiative is the Boxing Club in Muirhevnamore. Local volunteers coach during the week and supervise matches at the weekends. The boxing club has staked out a claim to space in the community centre, and would like to expand their service to provide paid workers who could engage children during the summer holidays. A Community Garda in Fettercairn pointed out that boxing in particular is a disciplined sport that acts as a bulwark against young people engaging in anti-social activity. In Fatima Mansions, a number of young boys interviewed in a focus group praised the summer projects that they had been involved in as having a positive impact, but they singled out their local football team as the most important project that had made a difference to their lives because 'it kept us out of trouble'.

A key point that links all of these kinds of interventions is that they are about people reclaiming their public space for social participation. In the process they help to transform the public realm of the neighbourhoods and their environs. Previously, many neighbourhoods suffered from the problem that the spaces in and around their homes were unsafe, easily colonised by undesirable elements, and ultimately indefensible. Children had to be kept at home, and those that were not kept under tight surveillance tended to roam wild. Public areas became 'no-go' areas, or what Lash (1994) has called 'wild zones'. For Dines and Cattell (with

Gesler and Curtis, 2006) public spaces represent sites of sociability and face-to-face interaction, and at the same time their quality is commonly perceived to be a measure of the quality of urban life. Poor physical surroundings have been identified as a causal factor in violent racist attacks and other types of crime, creating a permissive environment in which offending becomes almost more acceptable (Bauman, 1998).

One of the achievements of social housing regeneration over the last decade, in particular in Fatima Mansions and Fettercairn, is that public space has been reclaimed for the common good. Community centres are, as one informant stated, 'a hive of activity' and these activities spill over into the public space around the neighbourhood through arts and cultural events, parades, sporting activities, landscaping projects, community trips to public amenities, and so on. All of this has had the effect of generating higher levels of what Vertovec (2007) has described as 'civil integration', and encouraging residents to become actively involved in the enhancement and preservation of their community and community resources.

Community capacity: An important way in which residents can exercise efficacy is by finding a voice that can challenge stigmatisation and stereotyping by external audiences. So successful has been the Fatima regeneration project that the neighbourhood is now routinely held up as an exemplar of what neighbourhood regeneration and better social housing policy can achieve (for instance: Kenny, 2007; Treadwell Shine and Norris, 2006). From the start the presence of a cadre of residents and local community workers, willing and committed to the project of regenerating the neighbourhood, was crucial to the changes it experienced. With this cadre in place it worked hard to develop its own leadership, build allies with and links to community power nodes, leverage resources from other community groups, and communicate its efforts to wider publics. In short, residents became more professional and sophisticated in their claims making (Conway, Corcoran, Cahill, 2011). All of this is made clear in the canonical document *Dream / dare/do* produced by Fatima Groups United (FGU – the umbrella body for community groups in the neighbourhood) in 2006, which sets out the lessons it learned via its attempts to bring about positive social and economic change from the early 1990s onwards (Donohue and Dorman, 2006). Early on in this document, FGU emphasises the importance of evidence-based research in underwriting its change efforts and in garnering media attention for them. The report argues that successful regeneration turns on a community's ability to relate in an effective way to internal and external audiences and to exercise strategic control over how it is represented in media spaces:

> When we embarked on this regeneration journey, Fatima was in the news for all the wrong reasons – drugs, crime, joy riding. And despite the fact that many quality services and initiatives were happening, we couldn't get a positive story on Fatima. We knew we needed allies . . . we set out deliberately to portray a very different, more accurate image of Fatima and its residents . . .

we made sure that the regeneration work was 'sold' to the media at key moments and for key reasons.

(Donohue and Dorman, 2006, p. 21)

In the case of Fatima Mansions, underwriting neighbourhood revitalisation through empirical research, building a strong resident organisation, developing residents' communicative competencies, forging alliances with important community power nodes, and the presence of a favourable political opportunity structure made a residents' voice possible. Unusually, the case of Fatima Mansions instances how a rarely heard and sometimes disengaged social group can mobilise and exert power and strength in agenda-setting processes and institutional politics. It is noteworthy that a key factor in Fatima Mansions' success has been the continuity of personnel over the last ten to 15 years. It is impossible to underestimate the impact that 'local champions' can have in terms of motivating the community, being imaginative about possibilities and being able to hold their own at the negotiating table. A set of core advocates for Fatima Mansions were able to make important strategic interventions at key points in the regeneration trajectory and they remain committed to the consolidation of the renewal of the neighbourhood to the present day. That continuity has created optimal conditions for mentoring residents to take on new tasks and crucially to take on responsibility for the re-development. The Limerick urban regeneration initiative, closely modelled on that of Fatima Mansions, is in its infancy and it remains to be seen whether it can make a similar difference to Moyross residents' self-definition and capacity to assert themselves (Limerick Regeneration Agencies, 2008).

Drivers of declining liveability

Social segregation and stigma: Counteracting the advances outlined above there is evidence of continued stigmatisation and marginalisation, themes that resonated very strongly in the original study. These are related processes as groups or individuals that are stigmatised are often marginalised within the case study neighbourhoods, and marginalised groups or individuals who engage in anti-social behaviour provide further 'evidence' of the dysfunctionalism of the neighbourhood to external audiences, thereby reinforcing stigmatisation. It is apparent that stigmatisation continues to operate at the level of the neighbourhood, sub-areas within neighbourhoods, the family, and of the individual. This is frequently linked to negative media portrayals that tend to dominate in national and to a lesser extent local news. While the media representation of Moyross is analysed closely in Chapter 10 of this volume, it is fair to say that all of the neighbourhoods in the study have had to grapple with the stigmatisation that follows from the promulgation of bad news stories. Only one, Fatima Mansions, has managed to generate positive news stories largely arising from its successful regeneration programme (Conway, Corcoran, and Cahill 2011). The situation is less positive for neighbourhoods that have not had the benefit of regeneration programmes and that remain spatially divided and socially deprived. For instance, as the following quotations from service providers working in Moyross and Muirhevnamore reveal, the internal differentiation of the neighbourhood into 'good' and 'bad' places to live remains salient in these neighbourhoods:

> The lower end of Moyross [formerly called Glenagross] was more problematical than the rest of the estate, but this difference is not as marked now. The Respond housing has helped [transfer of ownership to Respond! Housing Association]. However, people living in the lower end feel neglected, and there is a very real sense of 'them and us' vis-à-vis residents in the upper end of the estate.

> I don't think we have ever got to the stage where we would be 100 per cent attractive, that there would be a queue to get in [to Muirhevnamore]. And then there are parts of the estate that people will not live in . . . up the top end of the estate, people don't really want to live there because it is . . .The profile of people is a lot younger, there are younger families, a lot of parents on their own, it is quite a challenge to live up there so there is a bit of a stigma attached to up there and people don't necessarily want a house in that part of the estate.

This comment is reminiscent of what residents told us during the 1997–8 fieldwork when Fatima Mansions and Fettercairn were compared to Beirut. Over the years both of those neighbourhoods have successfully sought to counter that image. In the process they have generated positive local identification with place that has at times diffused into the media.

The 2007–9 fieldwork revealed that nowadays, it is parts of Muirhevnamore that are perceived as 'the Wild West'. This seems to suggest that neighbourhoods may go through a lifecycle where they become destabilised across time leading to a spiral of decline. The latter may provoke an intervention that, if successful as in Fatima Mansions and Fettercairn, puts the neighbourhood back on a stable trajectory again. If conditions change, however, the spiralling of decline may escalate as is the case in Moyross. In this vein a professional based in Moyross told us:

> In the late 1980s and early 1990s the outlook for the estate had been bright, with the refurbishment of Glenagross, and seven different youth clubs active in the area. The houses in Castle Park had been finished to a very high standard. The decline in the area coincided with the loss over a number of years of a group of particularly active and effective individuals, including priests and nuns . . ., the former principal of the primary school and a particular social worker, who after he left was replaced by a stream of different workers – no continuity. Many of these were people who even if they didn't actually live in the community were nevertheless highly accessible to the community. There is now very little community capacity

in Moyross: if four or five key individuals were removed from the area it would collapse.

Regeneration does not necessarily lead to de-stigmatisation (Hastings and Dean, 2003). The redevelopment of Bank's Drive in Cranmore (identified as a black spot in our 1997–8 research) by the housing association Clúid has not fully removed the stigma attached to that part of Cranmore as it is still not seen as a 'good place to live' (O'Toole, 2008). There is great difficulty in attempting to divest a 'bad name', even though in this instance the name of the area was changed following the redevelopment. Furthermore, both the 1998–8 and 2007–9 rounds of fieldwork revealed that, even in relatively well-functioning neighbourhoods, a small troubled sub-area may cause problems for the wider locality. In 1997–8 we found that several neighbourhoods, and in particular Fatima Mansions, felt themselves under siege and this epithet is still employed to describe present day Moyross, evidenced in 'people erecting huge fences, often on top of walls, around their houses, and residents bringing their cars to the community centre to be locked in overnight for security', according to a local community activist.

The regeneration programme in Fatima Mansions transformed both the private and public spaces of the complex and the hope is that the Moyross regeneration can accomplish the same for the residents there. In a small number of districts in Finglas South the situation seems to have worsened over the years. The threat of serious crime has intensified with knock-on effects. Some respondents complained that people are reluctant to leave their homes at night to attend meetings, and are particularly nervous if the meetings are on crime or anti-social behaviour. There is a fear of being seen as 'a rat' and what might happen if you were identified as an informer:

> And you would know from the amount of tit for tat murders that have taken place in the area over the last while, there is certainly a serious problem of gangland activity in certain areas that undermines a lot of the work that's been done. And it probably also undermines in no small way the willingness of people to maintain their contact with residents associations or to be community representatives or to put themselves out there in the community because they can end up being targeted and they're afraid. And there's no way of saying that they're not afraid.

Furthermore, there is a sense that the difficulties of the neighbourhood are often hidden to outsiders particularly during the day time. People 'don't see' what is going on there. But, as the following quotations from residents of Finglas South reveal, at night the area becomes severely compromised and people again feel besieged in their own homes:

> It wouldn't be that here, but there'd be houses, a road where people are just … certain roads where people … they're just no go areas in the night time,

people just won't go near them and people don't leave their houses, and that's constantly going on,

And we did establish what is called the Finglas Safety Forum which is a joint forum between ourselves, the local Gardaí and local residents' associations. We set it up about three years ago, it died a death and we've reinstated it this year again. It is working very slowly but there is a real level of nervousness around people feeling that they might be intimidated, targeted or otherwise if they work too closely with us and the guards basically. You would hear people saying I'll say hello to you at the meeting but if you pass me in the street, don't pretend to know me.

This problem of intimidation and the wall of silence that it induces is also present in Moyross, where according to one informant:

There are too many young unmarried mothers/single parents who are very vulnerable to threats and anti-social behaviour. The culture of threatening people is now very pervasive in the area: residents are constantly been told that they will be burned out if they fall foul of certain families or individuals.

Attempts can be made to address this through mobilising the community but it is challenging work that requires a sustained effort over a long period of time with no guarantee that the culture of intimidation can be countered. In fact, the evidence suggests that it is extremely difficult to tackle a situation where power has been abrogated by a small number of tightly knit families who exercise and maintain control in their localities through a regime of fear (Hourigan, 2011).

Alienated minorities: Engaging 'hard-to-reach' groups is a thorny problem that continues to impact on the liveability of these neighbourhoods. A common complaint of service providers across the seven neighbourhoods is the persistence of anti-social behaviour perpetrated by youth whom the service providers see as part of a wider matrix of dysfunctional families in the neighbourhood. Paradoxically, Ireland consistently ranks highly on international indices of quality of life because of the relative stability of the Irish family (Fahey *et al.*, 2003). Yet in places like Moyross in Limerick, it is precisely such tightly knit family groupings' control over local fiefdoms that contributes to widespread social pathology (Hourigan, 2011). A professional working in Muirhevnamore observes:

I suppose again it can be the youths in the estates, it can be either youths causing damage, youth, noise or stuff like that, that would be kind of it, youth and children, you know, coming from dysfunctional houses, maybe the parents would be away and won't take responsibility for the children and stuff like that. Now you can get the adults I suppose, parties, noise, music.

A concern raised by interviewees relates to the 'ripple effect' caused by anti-social behaviour. It renders public spaces unsafe for the community in general and, therefore, results in communal and public spaces becoming 'no-go' areas. The ongoing challenge for these communities is how to foster a culture of civil integration (Vertovec, 2007) where youth respect public space and publicly provided services. It is noteworthy that in Fatima Mansions considerable resources were put into counteracting anti-social behaviour at the earliest opportunity during the regeneration cycle in order to prevent the destabilisation of the process. In particular, the Fatima Mansion's Regeneration Board sought to work with families rather than individuals to address behavioural problems (Whyte, 2005). Multi-problem or what one service provider called 'chaotic' families are seen as particularly troubling because of their basic lack of skills to socialise their children adequately, and to pass on the kinds of norms and values that can contribute to fomenting resilient communities. Service providers on the ground note the negative effects of poor parenting skills and the absence of role models. On each neighbourhood, there are troubled children growing up without access to some of the basic resources that are crucial to personal and intellectual development, or what Veenhoven (2000) calls 'life-ability'. Given the lack of behavioural guidelines and constraints, anti-social behaviour takes root and becomes normalised over time, as the following quotations from service providers working in Muirhevnamore, Moyross, and Deanrock respectively illustrate:

> The parents are sitting drinking in the house, their kids see this every day, the parents doing drugs and all that, it is natural to them, it comes natural. I mean some of our kids would say, it is only hash, they are only smoking hash. . . . they are oblivious, it is natural to them, it is just natural, the same as the graffiti on the walls and the general clean up, they don't care. They take a wrapper off a lolly and throw it on the ground. There is no educating and saying, your environment, there is none of that education. It is just monkey see, monkey does.

> We'll say of 720 families, at most you have a core of maybe ten bad ones, dysfunctional families . . . And who then have their little acolytes who are kind of hangers on. But there are, at most, ten, and I would even put it at less than ten . . . The reason those families are dysfunctional is that no work is actually being done with the families . . . They just don't know how to parent themselves because the chances are they came from a dysfunctional family. You learn how to parent from your own parents. If you haven't been parented properly yourself you are not going to parent your own children properly.

> There is still kind of a semi-chaotic lifestyle within the Deanrock estate. The Guards would say when they are passing by, there will still be lights on at 4:00 and 5:00 in the morning but there would be no life there before 4 o'clock in the afternoon in some pockets of the estate.

As was the case in 1997–8, the service providers interviewed during our 2007–9 fieldwork recognised that the concentration of a critical mass of dysfunctional families can reverberate outward into the community, creating further challenges for those charged with providing services and those trying to maintain the social fabric. The inability of multi-problem families to raise children adequately, to participate in their communities, and to resolve conflicts amicably makes them prime targets for exploitation by unscrupulous drug dealers. Thus, one informant explains how the social configuration within Moyross facilitates an exploitative and oppressive social structure:

> [You have a] pyramidal structure with broad base of individuals and families that have little skills to engage socially. This is the group that have been most exploited by the criminal element to whom they are highly vulnerable e.g., through owing money – easily compromised and forced into criminal activity.

Given the continued problems experienced in the neighbourhoods, and the troubling presence of a critical mass of multi-problem families in particular, it is not surprising that service providers and residents report evidence of pathologies at an individual level. In Finglas South this is manifested in local concerns about increasing violence, incivility and drug use in the area. It is noteworthy that the latter were not seen as a major concern in 1997/1998, but are now:

> I was just saying it's gotten really unsafe, and it's not the unsafe that there was years ago, but it's the guns and the drugs and the knife crime, the riots on St. Patrick's Day. We haven't had riots in Finglas in years, and there were the riots on Halloween up in the South there where things got out of control. Although people might think we've had them for years, we haven't.

> The other thing about this community is that it's very normalised to take drugs, and that's the scary part with the young people growing up and I think cocaine really normalises it. There's some families, some pockets where it's just normalised anyway.

Ironically, the community spirit has declined even as the physical landscape of the neighbourhood has changed for the better. According to key informants, there has been an exacerbation of the division between the better-off and the worst-off over the years. On the other hand, Fatima Mansions has undergone a renaissance while managing to keep the challenge of anti-social behaviour and drug use in check (yet those problems are by no means solved).

Disengagement and institutionalised capacity deficit: Despite all the community initiatives undertaken over the years a problem persists in terms of significant numbers of people remaining on the fringes or outside the community ambit. The problem of how to integrate marginalised young men, for instance, remains salient. And the descriptions of some of the problems that these disengaged teenagers generate is reminiscent of the problems caused by the so-called 'filthy fifty' gang of young men in Finglas South that we encountered during our 1997–8 fieldwork. As one service provider in Muirhevnamore observed:

> Now the boxing club and the football club in the community centre and all have made a difference because they are taking kids off the street and they are reducing all that sort of anti-social. But then there are older guys there who don't engage with football or boxing, they are in their late teens, early twenties and they just want to mess, drink, drugs, act the ejit [idiot]. There is a big problem going on at the minute actually, anti-social problem at the minute.

One problem is that there are few positive male role models for many young people in these neighbourhoods. Many children in multi-problem families are inducted into crime and anti-social behaviour at a young age and miss out on having a positive male role model in their lives. If they only infrequently attend school they do not develop positive relations there with teachers. People working with young people recognise the importance of interventions and the need for male leaders in the community:

> Yes volunteering is totally female dominated at this stage, you know, which isn't a good thing for young people, we are particularly trying to engage young men or sort of 15, 16, 17. And we see in areas where there are males involved that they have higher success rate in that age group.

Gardaí working in Fettercairn have put significant efforts into developing relations with young people at risk of progressing along a criminal path who have been referred to them through the Garda Youth Diversion Projects (GYDPs):

> So during the period of nearly 15 years say of Gardaí diversion projects, every young person who we saw has been potentially at risk and had already committed crime would have been on our programme and we would have worked with them on a daily basis. ... It is just a matter of, first of all, identifying them, go to the parents. The parents are of course delighted to see them getting involved in the projects ... suddenly I think for the first time in their lives they were given some attention, that is really what it was. They were given the opportunity of working on computers, going fishing – which is a simple thing.

Youth service providers in Finglas South identified transience as a particular problem, their young male clients require high levels of intervention in the management of even basic tasks:

> I suppose one of the issues for the young men is that there wasn't really an option for them to move out of home, you know, that most of the social

housing is for women and their kids and they might live with them for a while but that might not always work out or whatever . . . That's why a lot of them would end up staying on the couches of people, or a lot of them would just move home or stay with an older sibling. But most of the males we deal with would be all living at home. A lot of them, even into their twenties would still be living at home, driving their parents up the wall. A lot of the work that the task street workers do would be to physically get the young people out of bed and take them to their court appearances and wait and see what the result would be and then phone their mother with what the result has been and then in probation.

Such problems are not confined to younger men and are also identified among older cohorts in the local population. There is a pattern of people who have not become embedded in social ties either through marriage or having children or being able to sustain a relationship across time, becoming increasingly socially isolated and disengaged within the neighbourhoods. In this vein an interviewee from Finglas South told us:

I also believe that . . . what I said about suicide earlier on, some of those suicides have been people in the forties, men in their forties, and there's a need there for something to happen around that age group. And again, some of the men that we know are either separated or never got married, and they're in a family home and the mother might have died off, the father, and gone, in their own family home and they have nothing to do but drink.

In Finglas South, the capacity of the community to organise itself is seen as being at a low level. The area has no community centre as such (St Helena's Resource Centre is a state provided project) and never had an independent community organisation of the type that there are in other parts of Dublin. In contrast to other areas, where community development projects and family resource centres have played key roles in providing and mobilising for services locally, the Finglas South Community Development is not regarded as a success and a number of interviewees were critical about its work: 'They should be taking the lead role in pulling residents' associations together, in trying to maybe amalgamate resident's associations representing a broad area from a resident's point of view, and it's simply not happening, it's just not happening'.

Even in a neighbourhood such as Fatima Mansions, where there has been active engagement of residents in a highly successful regeneration project, a kind of learned helplessness can be discerned in the attitudes of some of the residents. Many residents remain unaware of activities in the neighbourhood. For instance, some service providers noted that they had to go door to door to try to engage residents in programmes delivered on site. Some may lack a sense of agency as one resident wryly recalls: 'I remember one day there was someone knocked at me door and she said, people are throwing stones at my door. And I said to her 'Go out and tell them to stop!'. An expectation develops that someone else will solve the problem, and it becomes naturalised in the community to pass the buck of responsibility to someone else. Learned helplessness is a problem that is identified by service providers across all of the neighbourhoods and points toward the institutionalisation of a capacity deficit:

> The point is that people got things – e.g. fully-kitted out house – too easily over the recent years. This simply fed a dependency culture, and when people get stuff for nothing they tend to have no respect for it.

Several service providers addressed the issue of getting people to think about and act in their own interests rather than waiting for someone else to do it for them. Furthermore, some service providers noted that while the actual number of people living in precarious circumstances may have declined, the problems of those who are still precarious have intensified. One way this is manifested is in the continuity of a cycle of deprivation across generations, and frequently those at the coalface are at a loss as to how this might be addressed. In this vein the principal of a school serving one of the estates told us:

> We would say that the 17 and 18 year olds, children that came through our school, are now producing as single parents the next generation coming to us. And we're saying to ourselves, sometimes you get disheartened ... do we break the cycle? How do we break the cycle? And you think you are breaking it and then you see the next generation coming through and you wonder what impact you're making. Now this may be on a bad day, it's not being negative, being realistic. You just wonder sometimes. We have them coming now, into junior infants as four year olds. Their mums are still seventeen-, sixteen-, and eighteen-year-old single girls and the dads are the boys who came through our school. Small amount, it is true to say, but it hasn't gone away.

Conclusions

Atkinson and Kintrea (2004) have observed that life chances are in part locally determined and that the emergence of the 'area effects' thesis has invigorated long-standing debates about how place and society are linked. Veenhoven (2000) argues that life chances are the outcome of the interaction between liveability of the environment and the life-ability of the person. More recently, the *Commission on the Measurement of Economic Performance and Social Progress* has argued for an interpretation of quality of life that captures both the quality of people's health, education, everyday activities and participation *and* the social and natural environment in which they live (Stiglitz, Sen, and Fitoussi, 2009). The Commission also notes that measuring these features requires both objective and subjective data. Accordingly, the purpose of this chapter was to provide a subjective interpretation of liveability in social rented neighbourhoods across time.

Residents and service providers in the seven case study neighbourhoods with whom we have consulted at two intervals, ten years apart, provide ample testimony to support the claim that place matters in the determination of quality of life. Educational interventions, regeneration initiatives, and environmental enhancement projects across the seven neighbourhoods have had a positive impact. They have reduced physical isolation, boosted community morale, and raised people's aspirations. The physical locales of several of the neighbourhoods and the public areas around them have been aestheticised through a range of cultural and environmental initiatives. Internal stratification remains salient, however, and each neighbourhood must still contend with troublesome youth and multi-problem families. The neighbourhoods continue to suffer stigmatisation arising from how they are externally perceived by the media and society, and it takes considerable commitment and resources to counter a negative image. In terms of norms and expectations, there has been a growth in social participation. In addition, non-traditional pathways into education through programmes such as community employment schemes are deemed to have been locally successful. Nevertheless, there remains a dearth of positive role models of success in education and employment for young people, and this is likely to worsen given the present conditions in the economy.

The positives in terms of the general re-enfranchisement of many residents is countered by the presence of a capacity deficit among a persistent minority that reproduces marginalisation cross-generationally, and which limits the horizons and aspirations of many children growing up on these neighbourhoods. Residents of social housing neighbourhoods and of low-income districts more broadly continue to be hampered by their relatively restricted social and geographical networks. They have little or no access to opportunity structures beyond the confines of their own neighbourhoods and their own communities. We conclude that definite advances have been made in the neighbourhoods over the ten years under examination. However, while at an individual level it is possible to point to small successes in such areas as promoting pro-social behaviour, encouraging children to stay in school longer, developing school-based multi-cultural programmes etc., at a collective level, serious social exclusion problems remain. The process of improving the liveability of the neighbourhoods and the life-ability of their residents continues if further social fragmentation is to be avoided.

References

Atkinson, R. and Kintrea, K. (2004) Opportunities and despair it's all in there: Practitioners' experiences and explanations of area effects and life chances. *Sociology*, 38(3), 437–55.

Bauman, Z. (1998) *Work, consumerism and the new poor*. Buckingham: Open University Press.

Borer, M. (2006) The location of culture: The urban culturalist perspective. *City and Community*, 5(2), 173–97.

Conway, B., Corcoran, M., and Cahill, L. (2011) The 'miracle' of Fatima: media framing and the regeneration of a Dublin housing estate. *Journalism: Theory, Practice and Criticism*, 13(6), 551–71.

Corcoran, M. (1998) *Making Fatima a better place to live*. Dublin: Fatima Groups United.

Dines, N. and Cattel, V., with Gesler, W. and Curtis, S. (2006) *Public spaces, social relations and well-being in East London*. Bristol: Policy Press.

Donohue, J. and Dorman, P. (2006) *Dream/dare/do. A regeneration learning manual*. Dublin: Fatima Groups United.

Fahey, T., Whelan, C., and Nolan, B. (2003) *Monitoring quality of life in Europe*. Dublin: European Foundation for the Improvement of Living and Working Conditions.

Fitzgerald, J. (2007) *Addressing issues of social exclusion in Moyross and other disadvantaged areas of Limerick city*. Limerick: Limerick City Council.

Hastings, A. and Dean, J. (2003) Challenging images: tackling stigma through estate regeneration. *Policy and Politics*, 31(2), 171–84.

Hourigan, N. (ed.) (2011) *Understanding Limerick: Social exclusion and change*. Cork: Cork University Press.

Kenny, B. (2007) Making golden age of regeneration a reality, *Irish Times*, 28 November.

Lash, S. (1994) Reflexivity and its doubles: Structure, aesthetics and community. In U. Beck, A. Giddens, S. Lash (eds) *Reflexive modernisation* (pp. 110–73). Cambridge: Polity Press.

Limerick Regeneration Agencies (2008) *Limerick regeneration programme: A vision for Moyross, Southill, Ballinacurra Weston and St Mary's Park*. Limerick: Limerick Regeneration Agency.

Lynch, K. (1981) *A theory of good city form*. Boston, MA: MIT Press.

Norris, M. (1999) The impact of the built environment. In T. Fahey (ed.) *Social housing in Ireland: A study of success, failure and lessons learned* (pp. 101–24). Dublin: Oak Tree Press.

Norris, M. and Redmond, D. (2009) *Private sector involvement in regenerating social housing estates: A review of recent practice in Dublin*. Dublin: Combat Poverty Agency.

O'Higgins, K. (1999) Social order problems. In T. Fahey (ed.) *Social housing in Ireland: A study of success, failure and lessons learned* (pp. 149–72). Dublin: Oak Tree Press.

O'Toole, J. (2008) *Cranmore, 1998–2008*, unpublished report commissioned for the present study.

Robins, K. (1993) Prisoners of the city: Whatever could a postmodern city be? In E. Carter and J. Donald (eds) *Space and place: Theories of identity and location* (pp. 236–75). London: Lawrence and Wishart.

Sampson, R. (2009) Disparity and diversity in the contemporary city: social (dis)order revisited. *British Journal of Sociology*, 60(1), 1–31.

Sampson, R. and Raudenbush, S. (2004) Seeing disorder: Neighborhood stigma and the social construction of broken windows. *Social Psychology Quarterly*, 67(4), 319–42.

Stiglitz, J., Sen, A., and Fitoussi, J.-P. (2009) *Report of the commission on the measurement of economic performance and social progress*. Paris: CMEPSP.

Treadwell Shine, K. and Norris, M. (2006) *Housing policy discussion series: Regenerating local authority estates – review of policy and practice*. Dublin: Centre for Housing Research.

Veenhoven, R. (2000) The four qualities of life: ordering concepts and measures of the good life. *Journal of Happiness Studies*, 1(1), 1–39.

Vertovec, S. (2007) *New complexities of cohesion in Britain: Super-diversity, transnationalism and civil-integration*. Oxford: ESRC Centre on Migration, Policy and Society.

Whyte, J. (2005) *Eight great expectations: A landmark and unique social regeneration plan for Fatima Mansions*. Dublin: Fatima Regeneration Board.

4

REFORMING SOCIAL HOUSING MANAGEMENT

Michelle Norris and Cathal O'Connell

Introduction

The neighbourhoods that are the focus of this study were all built originally by local authorities for letting to social housing tenants. It was already the case when we studied these neighbourhoods in 1997–8 that a significant minority (and in some cases a majority) of the dwellings here had been privatised through sales to tenants (known as the tenant purchase scheme in Ireland) (see Table 1.1 in Chapter 1). Also, the growth of area-based initiatives has meant that the range of local agencies that are relevant to life within the neighbourhoods has extended well beyond the mainstream local government sector in recent years. Yet, these neighbourhoods continue to draw much of their identity and character from their origins in the social housing system and from the continuing relationship that many residents have with local authorities as landlords. Even former tenants who have bought out their homes often still think of themselves and their neighbours as having a link with local authority housing departments. This link would be absent in housing neighbourhoods originating in the private sector. It is therefore relevant to locate the present study in the context of developments in social housing policy.

Like many other elements of the welfare state, the social housing sector has contracted in many Western European countries in the past two decades as cuts in state capital funding have reduced new housing output (Stephens, Burns, and MacKay, 2002). In some cases, such as the UK, Germany, and the Netherlands, this trend has been augmented by various privatisation and externalisation measures, such as: increased reliance on private sector funding, sales of dwellings to tenants, and transfer of ownership of the housing stock and/or of responsibility for providing some key housing management services to alternative providers (Gibb, 2002; Whitehead, 2003). As a result of these developments, low-income and often multiply disadvantaged households are now more heavily concentrated in social housing than was traditionally the case (Scanlon and Whitehead, 2007). Concerns about the implications of this and about the physical quality of neighbourhoods more generally have inspired a greater emphasis on the regeneration of social housing neighbourhoods (Kintrea, 2007). The regulatory environment has also changed, though in different ways in different countries. In many countries, the withdrawal of government financial support has increased the management autonomy of social landlords (Gruis and Nieboer, 2007). However, in the UK, central government has subjected social housing providers to much greater levels of scrutiny, to greater monitoring, evaluation, and regulation, and has used both financial incentives and legal enforcement to shape their behaviour (Cowan and McDermont, 2006).

This chapter examines developments in social housing management reform in Ireland during the last decade, using evidence from the seven neighbourhoods, and compares these to the wider European context. At the time of our original study of the seven neighbourhoods in 1997–8, the bulk of the social rented dwellings in these neighbourhoods and in the Irish social housing sector more broadly were owned and managed by local authorities. We found that their housing management arrangements focused on property management, rather than a tenant welfare focus, and they operated within a hierarchical, rigidly demarcated, rule-driven, desk-bound culture and delivered services in a highly centralised fashion from headquarters (O'Connell, 1999). Although relatively benign and paternalistic in its treatment of tenants, this organisational culture fostered minimal interaction with them and provided no opportunities for cooperation or consultation on housing management. Our 1997–8 fieldwork revealed, at best, indifference towards local authority housing departments among tenants, and, at worst, outright hostility. Despite this we did uncover many examples of able and committed local authority housing managers who were engaged in innovative practice and partnership working with residents and community groups, but this was generally driven by individuals, rather than systems or policies, and therefore was patchy and often not sustained if these individuals moved on from their posts (O'Connell and Fahey, 1999; Guerin, 1999).

In the decade since then, developments in Irish social housing policy and management arrangements have in some ways echoed wider European trends, but the sector has retained some distinctive features. In relation to the latter, uniquely in Western Europe, in 2007–9 the Irish government continued to fund 100 per cent of the capital cost of social house building and this funding had increased significantly since 1997–8, with the result that output doubled during this decade, albeit from a low base (see Figure 1.1 in Chapter 1). In addition, unlike the vast majority of EU members, social housing rents in Ireland are linked to the income of tenants and bear no relationship to the costs of managing and maintaining dwellings (Scanlon and Whitehead, 2007). Some of the social housing reforms that parallel wide European trends were already emerging in 1997–8 – many were flagged in the mid-1990s in policy statements from the housing ministry (Department of the Environment), but in recent years they have been realised in practice (Department of the Environment, 1991; 1996). For instance, in the early 1990s the government announced that housing associations would play a greater role in Irish social housing provision, reflecting the norm in most other Western European countries (Department of the Environment, 1991). Increased funding and the fact that, unlike local authorities, housing association dwellings cannot be bought by tenants has enabled this sector to expand since then. In 1997, housing associations provided 15 per cent of social housing in Ireland (approximately 15,000 dwellings), and this rose to 18.6 per cent (25,442 dwellings) by 2006 (Department of the Environment, Community and Local Government, various years; Mullins, Rhodes, and Williamson, 2003). Housing ministry policy statements issued in the early 1990s also emphasised the need to more effectively regenerate social housing neighbourhoods and suggested that management standards in the local authority housing sector needed improvement and from this time a series of measures to achieve this were put in place (see Norris and O'Connell, 2002). While on foot of recommendations made in the 1996 policy statement on local government reform – *Better Local Government: A Programme for Change* – management arrangements in the sector were reformed in an effort to encourage more strategic and evidence-based management (Department of Environment, 1996).

The function of this chapter is to document the key changes in housing management in the seven neighbourhoods between our first visit there in 1997–8 and our second in 2007–9, to examine the extent to which these reforms were driven by the policy changes outlined above and to explore their impact on tenants. The discussion is organised into four sections that reflect the most significant housing management reforms we have identified. These are:

1   the changing role of the social housing officer (reconceptualisation);
2   the emergence of more sophisticated strategies to address the physical and social decline of neighbourhoods (regeneration);
3   the entry of the new actors into the social housing sector (externalisation);
4   and reforms to the management of the social housing service (managerialisation).

Reconceptualisation

One of the most dramatic changes evident in the seven neighbourhoods during the decade under examination is a transformation in the relationship between local authorities and tenants. With some exceptions, the 1997–8 research revealed that tenants had very negative views of both their general interactions with local authorities and of the quality of housing management services provided. Tenants reported significant difficulties in making contact with local authority staff and complained that their views were not dealt with satisfactorily when they did. A resident of Deanrock reported in 1997–8 'you are constantly fobbed off and not listened to' by the local authority housing department and a Fettercairn resident suggested that 'hassling them' is the only way to access housing management services. At this time tenants in all seven neighbourhoods also complained about the inefficiency of the housing maintenance service, of procedures for allocating tenancies, and, in particular, about arrangements for dealing with anti-social behaviour in neighbourhoods. In contrast, the 2007–9 research revealed that in most (but not all) cases tenants' perceptions of local authorities improved radically. Ten years earlier complaints about the housing management service were central to tenants' concerns, but in 2007–9 they were rarely mentioned and the focus of their concerns had shifted to the failings of other service providers in areas such as health, social care, and local development.

This occurrence is related principally to the reconceptualisation of the social housing management function. As mentioned above, in 1997–8 this was defined as primarily a property focused, bureaucratic task and was delivered in a centralised, paternalistic manner. In most neighbourhoods rent collectors, who still visited most dwellings on a weekly basis, provided the only regular contact between tenants and their landlord. In 1997–8 only one of the seven neighbourhoods (Moyross) was serviced by dedicated, estate-based, housing management staff and only one of the six local authorities under examination (Dublin City Council) had begun to decentralise its housing management services from head office. By 2007–9, a transformation in interactions between tenants and housing managers was evident, characterised by: greater visibility of housing managers on the ground in social housing neighbourhoods and the development of stronger relationships with tenants, which in turn led to a more responsive service that has contributed to a strong focus on addressing the problem of anti-social behaviour. As is discussed in Chapter 9, the latter is now redefined as a core housing management responsibility, rather than entirely outside the landlord's remit, as was the case in 1997–8 (Guerin, 1999). These changes were operationalised by the appointment of local estate officers, responsible for the management of individual neighbourhoods or groups of neighbourhoods in all of the local authorities under examination, and the appointment of officials with specific responsibility for combating anti-social behaviour in most of these. As a result, spending nationally on estate management grew from 12.9 to 33.8 per cent of total expenditure on local authority housing management between 1997 and 2001 (Indecon, 2005).

These developments are the result of both local and national drivers. National policy statements on housing and local government reform emphasised the need to provide a more responsive service to tenants and identified the establishment of local housing management structures as a key means of achieving this (Department of the Environment, 1991, 1996; O'Connell, 1998). Practical guidelines on how to implement these reforms were provided by the reports of the Housing Management Group (1996, 1998) and the Centre for Housing Research, and a central government grant aid was provided by Housing Management Initiative Grants Scheme. The 1997 Housing (Miscellaneous Provisions) Act also gave local authorities additional powers to evict tenants engaged in anti-social behaviour and for the first time offered a legal definition of such activity, thereby delimiting their responsibilities in this regard (Kenna, 2006).

Interviews with Dublin City Council staff also highlighted the influence of local concerns regarding the standard of housing management in the 1990s, from both elected councillors (Dublin Corporation, 1993), council managers (Keegan, 1995; Kenny, 1998), and tenants' representatives (Ballymun Task Force, 1988; Fatima Groups United, 2000). Efforts to address these initially centred on the Ballymun estate in Dublin's northern suburbs. Here a series of measures intended to address the serious management problems in the neighbourhood were piloted, including: a local housing management structure and estate office and action to evict squatters and anti-social tenants (Power, 1997). These arrangements were ultimately extended to cover the city as a whole, a development that was facilitated by significant restructuring of staffing arrangements at the time. The traditional system of door-to-door rent collection was phased out and many of the former rent collectors were redeployed into new estate-based housing management roles. Dublin City Council was the pathfinder in this regard, but all of the other local authorities under examination have subsequently followed suit with locally modified variations of the same. In Cork and Limerick the impetus for this came from service reviews commissioned from external organisations (Guerin, O'Connell, and Norris, 1998; Norris, 2000). In South Dublin County Council it came from the establishment of this new local authority, as part of a reorganisation of local government in Dublin in 1993, which necessitated the establishment of new housing management arrangements.

The 2007–9 research indicates that this reconceptualisation of the housing management function has positive material impacts on neighbourhoods and the localisation of housing management has been particularly beneficial. Both tenants and housing managers agreed that the latter had improved relations between them. For instance, a Cork City Council manger claimed that the estate officer structure

> gives you the opportunity to get to know people better. They can put a face to you and build a relationship. They see you as a point of contact and feel they are heard. It's not just an organisation – it's the person.

While a resident of Deanrock reported:

> We also had a tenant liaison officer . . . who was very helpful to us, pushing things that we wanted, asking the City Hall [local authority headquarters], saying 'they really need this, ye need to do this, they need ye to do that' [sic].

There was also widespread agreement that localisation improved housing manage-ment standards and, thereby, the reputation of neighbourhoods. For instance, a Deanrock resident claimed:

> City Hall [Cork City Council] often come around, you mightn't even see them on the street yourself, but you hear of someone saying it. I think City Hall today are more assertive. . . . they cleared up a whole house, provided furniture, put windows in, changed the doors, the flooring, put in heating. City Hall now I believe are going around now making sure they are not

going to have dirty houses any more cos it's their property, which is a good thing [sic].

Similarly, a Fettercairn resident told us:

We don't want it to go back to where it was before the Nineties when there was absolutely nothing in the community. South Dublin County Council took over [from the local authority formerly responsible for this area] after that and we did see big changes. We had, sort of the landlord was on the doorstep then rather than somebody in [the city centre] who never got to see anybody. [Under the previous local authority] . . . huge rent arrears mounted up on houses and then houses became run down. . . . it created a bad standard.

Regeneration

The second significant development in the social housing sector during the decade under examination is the emergence of more sophisticated regeneration strategies to overcome the physical and social decline of some social rented neighbourhoods. In 1997–8, a number of the seven neighbourhoods had been regenerated but interventions were heavily focused on physical improvements – mainly refurbishment. Fatima Mansions and Deanrock were both subject to extensive refurbishment prior to our first visit in 1997–8, which involved improving the physical structure of dwellings and open areas in both cases and the demolition of one block of flats in the former (Norris, 1999). This emphasis reflected the dominant approach to social housing regeneration at the time (Norris, 2001).

By 2007–9 the emphasis of regeneration programmes had shifted significantly in two ways. First, although a strong emphasis on built environment solutions persisted, the focus of these actions changed from refurbishment of existing dwellings to their demolition and, in most cases, replacement with new dwellings. For example, the Fatima Mansions complex was demolished in 2005 and rebuilt between 2006 and 2008 (see Images 3.1, 3.3), a large section of Cranmore was de-tenanted in 2006, demolished in 2009, and rebuilt by a housing association in 2000–1 (see Image 3.4), the flats in Deanrock were demolished in 2006 and work is currently underway to demolish significant sections of Moyross as part of a wider programme to regenerate the entire social housing stock in Limerick city. Second, regeneration strategies were broadened to include social, community, and housing management interventions. The origins of this development can be traced to efforts to consult tenants about the design of regeneration schemes and the estate management reforms highlighted earlier in this discussion. Efforts to promote community development and address social problems as part of regeneration schemes are more recent and are linked to the growth of area-based social inclusion initiatives examined in Chapters 5 and 6. Most recently, regeneration projects have also attempted to diversify the tenure structure of social housing neighbourhoods usually by introducing private owners (but in some cases by introducing other types of social landlords). The logic of this intervention is that owner-occupiers tend to have higher incomes than social housing tenants, so providing dwellings for the former will help to break up the concentrations of disadvantaged households and associated stigma often associated with large social rented estates (Musterd and Andersson, 2005; Norris, 2006).

The evidence from the case study neighbourhoods indicates that inclusion of community development, social inclusion, and housing management interventions as part of regeneration projects has generally had a positive impact. This finding reflects international experience in this field, which indicates that multi-faceted interventions are necessary for effective regeneration (Kintrea, 2007). However, in contrast to the norm elsewhere in Europe, social and community interventions in Ireland are provided by agencies external to local authorities or other social landlords. This created significant coordination problems on some of the seven neighbourhoods, and necessitated the establishment of quite elaborate coordination structures in Cranmore and to a lesser extent Fatima Mansions (see Chapter 7). If local authorities had more direct control over the funding and delivery of community and social services, less elaborate and less costly coordination arrangements would have been required in these cases.

The available evidence indicates that tenure diversification can be a useful regeneration strategy particularly in the case of very large social housing neighbourhoods that are associated with large concentrations of disadvantage (Musterd and Andersson, 2005). However, in Ireland, neighbourhoods in this category are very few in number. Among the seven neighbourhoods under examination here, only Moyross and South Finglas could be considered large (> 1,000 dwellings) and both already include a large number of non-social renting households as a result of sales of dwellings to tenants. In smaller social rented neighbourhoods located in mixed tenure areas, such as Fatima Mansions, the arguments for tenure diversification are less convincing. In this case the number of social rented dwellings was reduced from 320 to 150 due to the demolition and rebuilding of the neighbourhood in 2006 – 70 dwellings for sale at below market value to low-income households (called 'affordable housing' in Ireland) and 396 private apartments for sale on the open market were also provided as part of this project, the net reduction in social housing provision was very substantial, and this took place at a time of high demand for these tenancies. Although interviewees argued convincingly that the introduction of private housing helped mitigate the acutely stigmatised public image of the neighbourhood, the Fatima Mansions case highlights the limitations of tenure diversification as an income diversification strategy. In this case most of the private apartments have been acquired by investors rather than owner-occupiers and several proved difficult to sell after house prices began to decline rapidly in late 2007. Kintrea and Muir's (2009) research on Ballymun in north Dublin found that the vast majority of the private housing built as part of its regeneration programme was also sold to investors. In many cases these dwellings were let to claimants of rent supplement (an income-related housing allowance paid to private renting households in Ireland), who must be benefit dependent in order to qualify for this support.

In addition, the inclusion of private rented or indeed owner-occupied dwellings in social rented neighbourhoods may also raise housing management challenges because their occupants have no legal relationship with the social landlords. This created problems in Moyross and South Finglas, as Limerick and Dublin City Councils evicted tenants engaged in anti-social behaviour but were powerless to address similar activities by homeowners (see Chapter 9).

Between 1997–8 and 2007–9 the built environment aspects of regeneration projects in the seven neighbourhoods also grew more sophisticated and generally more successful in recent years. For instance, as part of the demolition and rebuilding of Fatima Mansions efforts were made to improve the 'permeability' of the neighbourhood to the wider district by building a new pedestrianised street and community and sports centre to encourage non-residents to visit. This significantly improved the public image of the neighbourhood. In Deanrock and Fettercairn, the strategic provision of new 'infill' housing closed off alleyways and increased the opportunities for passive surveillance by residents of open areas that had previously been sites for anti-social behaviour. In contrast to the norm in 1997–8, the physical aspects of recent regeneration programmes in the case study neighbourhoods were guided by detailed masterplans in 2007–9. On the other hand, the overreliance on built-environment-related interventions evident during our first visit to the seven neighbourhoods remained apparent during our second visit. Three of the seven neighbourhoods (Moyross, Fatima Mansions, and Cranmore) were extensively refurbished between 1997 and 2006; two (Fatima Mansions and Deanrock) were refurbished the preceding decade and two (Cranmore and Moyross) are due to be refurbished in the near future. Moreover, by 2007–9, radical built environment interventions such as demolition were used more often than was the case a decade before. This was sometimes appropriate and successful (as in the case of the flats in Deanrock and Fatima Mansions, which were poorly constructed and their design facilitated anti-social behaviour), but not always. In Cranmore, a significant number of structurally sound and well-designed dwellings were demolished in 2009 to no obvious benefit. In Muirhevnamore interviewees expressed concern that if plans for the demolition of large sections of the neighbourhood are implemented, this will have a very negative impact on community cohesion.

Externalisation

The third significant development in the social housing sector during the last decade is that certain functions that were previously the direct responsibility of local author-ities, such as the provision of social housing and regeneration of neighbourhoods, were externalised to quasi-governmental, non-profit, and private-sector organisa-tions. This process began in the early 1980s with greater reliance on private rented housing subsidised by rent supplement to accommodate low-income households and the introduction of public subsidies for housing associations (Norris, Healy, and Coates, 2008). The 1990s saw the establishment of quasi-governmental agencies, responsible to central government, such as the Dublin Docklands Development Authority and Temple Bar Properties, charged with implementing schemes to regenerate inner city areas that would have previously been the sole responsibility of local authorities, and since 2000 the private sector has become more involved in the regeneration of local authority neighbourhoods via Public-Private Partnership (PPP) arrangements (Montgomery, 1995; Moore, 2008; Redmond and Russell, 2008). These developments were in part a pragmatic response to funding constraints by both central and local government, but they also reflected the growing scepticism at central government level regarding the capacity of local authorities, which inspired the establishment of area-based initiatives outside of the local government structure that are examined in Chapters 6 and 7 of this volume.

Many of these developments impacted on the seven neighbourhoods under examination here. For instance, sections of Cranmore and Moyross were transferred into the ownership of housing associations as part of regeneration schemes. PPP arrangements were employed to regenerate Fatima Mansions and were proposed for Deanrock but had not been implemented at the time of writing. A regeneration agency, under the direction of the housing ministry rather than Limerick City Council, was established in 2007 to regenerate the city's social housing stock. Many of the seven neighbourhoods now include rent supplement households (living in dwellings sold under the tenant purchase scheme), as do the neighbourhoods surrounding them. Coates and Norris' (2006) research highlights particularly high concentrations of rent supplement claimants in areas around Fatima Mansions and Fettercairn.

However, by the time of our 2007–9 visit, it was clear that some aspects of this externalisation process had been reclaimed by the local authorities as part of their growing strategic management remit and, for various reasons, the limits of other aspects of this agenda had been reached.

Rent supplement is an example of the former development. Due to concerns about the escalating costs of this benefit, in 2004 the government decided that local authorities would take over responsibility for all long-term rent supplement claimants. Under the Rental Accommodation Scheme (RAS) they will lease accommodation from private landlords, which will be sublet to households that have been claiming rent supplement for 18 months or more (Department of the Environment, Heritage and Local Government, undated). Currently rent supplement claimants negotiate a lease directly with private landlords, but it is envisaged that local authorities will be able to secure better value for money than individual claimants (Coates and Silke, 2011).

The use of PPPs for social housing regeneration, which has to date been done only in Fatima Mansions, is an example of a locally, rather than central-government, driven externalisation, as a senior Dublin City Council official interviewed for this study acknowledged that the impetus for its establishment came from this organisation. In addition to the opportunity for raising private sector funding, he pointed out that this model enabled the provision of community and leisure facilities that would not have been eligible for central government regeneration funding because this covers only the refurbishment of buildings and public spaces in neighbourhoods (Treadwell Shine and Norris, 2006). He also suggested that PPPs are particularly useful for procuring complex schemes such as Fatima Mansions, which incorporates a mix of housing tenures and land uses, because they employ a single contract. Whereas, in order to achieve the same outcome using the traditional direct procurement model, he claimed 'we might have had maybe five phases, maybe five developers, a stop/start approach' and would have had less control over its design and implementation.

For residents and community sector representatives from Fatima Mansions, the provision of €6.5 million towards the cost of a social regeneration plan to be implemented by a dedicated Regeneration Board was a key benefit of the PPP scheme (Whyte, 2005). This 'community dividend' was earmarked for social and community projects for which mainstream, public funding is not available. Thus it has enabled the implementation of a more holistic regeneration project, tailored to address the particular needs of Fatima Mansions residents, than would have otherwise been possible considering the rigidity of the terms of the public funding available to this sector (Treadwell Shine and Norris, 2006).

Although the PPP regeneration scheme delivered very significant benefits in Fatima Mansions, developments since its completion have cast doubts on the transferability of this model to other contexts and some critics have raised concerns about the desirability of this (e.g. Bissett, 2009; Hearne, 2011; Redmond and Russell, 2008). Criticisms of the use of these PPPs for social housing regeneration have focused on the loss of public land and, in some cases, social rented units necessitated by the use of parts of target neighbourhoods for private development. Although the evidence collected during our second visit to Fatima Mansions indicates that, in this case, this loss was outweighed by a reduction in the stigmatised reputation and concentrations of disadvantaged households, these countervailing factors are not relevant to all regeneration projects. The Fatima Mansions scheme was also negotiated in the context of an unprecedented housing market boom. However, in 2008 negotiations with the preferred private sector bidder for similar schemes to regenerate social housing neighbourhoods in Dublin collapsed, against the background of a sharp decline in house and land prices (see Bissett, 2009; Hearne, 2011).

Externalisation of social housing provision to housing associations has continued unabated during the decade under examination, principally via the construction of new housing association dwellings because, in contrast to the UK, stock transfers have been employed very rarely in Ireland (Pawson and Mullins, 2010). The local authority officials we interviewed in 2007–9 expressed mixed views about this. Some criticised housing associations for 'cherry picking' tenants and complained that the inclusion of housing association dwellings in some of the seven neighbour-hoods created logistical difficulties in relation to neighbourhood management and regeneration. Others welcomed competition from these organisations and suggested that it would lead to improved service and choice for tenants. One senior local authority manager expressed the hope that they would take over as the main providers of social housing in Ireland, as this would enable local authorities to concentrate on strategic planning and would also increase the independence of the social housing sector from central government. However, he raised concerns about the structure of the housing association sector. It is dominated by a handful of very large providers that own approximately half of the stock and which he suggested 'are as large and bureaucratic as any local authority' and a multitude of very small providers, with no paid staff, many of which he argued are not interested in developing new housing schemes (see also Mullins *et al.*, 2003). Therefore, he suggested that the structure of the sector required more hands-on management by the housing ministry.

Managerialisation

The 1997–8 research was conducted during a time of unprecedented levels of criticism by central government of the local authority's strategic management of the social housing service. Concerns in this regard were flagged initially in the housing ministry's 1991 housing policy statement and spelled out in more detail two years later, in a memorandum to local authorities (Department of the Environment, 1991). This memorandum set out a devastating catalogue of weaknesses, which the ministry considered were then common in strategic management practice in housing departments, such as:

1   too much focus on day-to-day operations and insufficient long- and medium-term planning;
2   inadequate management information, and insufficient monitoring of the information that is available;
3   management activity is uncoordinated and pays too little attention to the combined impact of activities on neighbourhoods; and
4   the focus is solely on reducing expenditure rather than on getting better value for money.

The framework for the reform of the management of the local authority housing service was outlined initially in the 1996 policy statement *Better Local Government* (Department of the Environment, 1996). Since then, this framework has been further developed in other policy statements and underpinned by legislation. Its most significant elements are:

1   The establishment of Strategic Policy Committees (SPCs) responsible for making policy in each of the authorities' functional areas, including housing. Unlike the committees they replaced, SPCs have a corporatist structure. In addition to councillors, they include representatives of business and the non-profit sectors.
2   The introduction of additional local housing policy-making responsibilities such as the formulation of housing strategies (from 2001) and social and affordable housing action plans (from 2004).

3   The appointment of senior managers in each of the local authority functional
     areas called Directors of Service responsible for supporting this policy-making
     function, and the redesign of many junior posts.
4   The introduction of performance monitoring requirements in 2000 (extended
     in 2003 and 2008) to enable evidence-based central and local government
     policy making.

The local government reform programme has been the subject of a number of
reviews by central government and independent commentators, which have
proffered broadly positive conclusions regarding its implementation and impact
(e.g. Boyle, Humphries, and O'Donnell, 2003; Callanan, 2005). However, most of
this analysis is macro-level in focus and takes little account of the impact of these
reforms on specific services such as housing. Furthermore, it is based mainly on
consultation with the (largely uncritical) key stakeholders involved in this process
and assessment of the outputs generated (for instance: services provided) rather than
the outcomes achieved (in terms of their impact on service quality). Our 2007–9
fieldwork in the seven case study neighbourhoods did not examine these reforms
in sufficient depth to enable definitive assessment of their impact on housing
services. However, it does provide some insights into this issue, which indicate that
various measures have been implemented successfully, but their impact has been
more uneven than the aforementioned assessments imply.

Compliance with the managerialisation reform agenda is high among the local
authorities under examination. All of these organisations produced housing
strategies (a legal obligation) and action plans (not a legal obligation when the
research was conducted, but this has recently changed) and many have produced
policies addressing numerous other housing issues, in addition they have established
housing SPCs, reformed staffing structures and adhered to the performance
mentoring regime. In a minority of authorities, notably Dublin City Council, the
Housing SPC worked particularly well and initiated several new policies, reformed
others and increased policy debate by initiating an annual conference, amongst
other reforms. In several authorities (Dublin and Cork City Councils, South
Dublin County Council) the Directors of Housing Services played a key role in
improving local policy making and housing management standards.

Among the managerialist reforms under examination, the performance
monitoring arrangements have had the least positive impact on housing management
standards. The meaningfulness of the indicators used, the weakness of arrangements
for addressing poor performance and the lack of information technology supports
necessary to collate the management information required are the principal reasons
for this. Details of these indicators are set out in Table 4.1, which reveals that these
suffer from the same problem as the aforementioned assessments of the local
government reform programme – they measure output rather than outcomes
(see also Local Government Audit Service, 2000). Notably, in this regard the housing
service indicators are weaker than those applied to other local government services
(many of which do measure service outcomes). In addition to the fact that the

performance monitoring regime was devised in consultation with local authority managers, the reasons for this relate to shortcomings in IT supports. Unlike most other local government services the various housing IT systems do not cover the entire spectrum of housing functions and different authorities use different packages. This has mitigated against the establishment of comprehensive performance management arrangements, and according to several of the local authority managers interviewed in 2007–9 rendered compliance with the performance monitoring regime very onerous.

Table 4.1 also highlights marked variations in housing management performance as indicated by these measures, both between authorities and over time, which raises the question: what can central government do to address these variations? The answer until recently has been very little, because in contrast to the UK, central government in Ireland has no regulatory powers over social housing management standards in either local authorities or housing associations. Circulars and memoranda from the housing ministry to local authorities are purely advisory, in legal terms (Kenna, 2006). This situation has recently been changed by the Housing (Miscellaneous Provisions) Act 2009, which affords the housing minister the authority to issue directives or instructions to local authorities regarding their housing functions.

There is also evidence that the poor performance monitoring and management information-generating capacity undermined efforts to improve strategic management and policy making. For instance, Focus Ireland, Simon Communities of Ireland, Society of St Vincent de Paul and Threshold's (2002) review of the first round of housing strategies produced by local authorities in 2001 raises questions of the accuracy of the data on which their estimates of housing need, costs, and supply are based. More recently a report by the Comptroller and Auditor General (2007, p. 11) into the regeneration of the Ballymun social housing neighbourhood in north Dublin complained its evaluation of this project and good management practice more generally was hampered by 'the lack of baseline statistics and inadequate and variable information feedback on programmes'.

The mixed impact of housing SPCs also undermined efforts to promote better strategic management and policy making and various, sometimes contradictory, reasons for this were proposed by the local authority officials interviewed during our 2007–9 visit to the seven neighbourhoods. One senior manager blamed the capacity of councillors for their underperformance. Due to Ireland's strongly clientelist political culture, she argued that they were primarily interested in ensuring access to services for their voters and had very little interest in policy making, so most new policies are initiated by staff. The same interviewee mentioned difficulties in getting the private and non-profit sectors to engage with the SPC process. This view was contradicted by an official at a larger authority, who argued that in an effort to maximise control, housing managers have sometimes 'bamboozled' the SPC members with unnecessary technical details and data, thereby minimising the opportunity for the latter to initiate policy reform. He suggested that 'Where SPCs have been properly supported, they have been effective'.

TABLE 4.1 Results of local authority housing service performance monitoring, 2004, 2006

Service indicator	Cork City Council		Dublin City Council		Limerick City Council		Louth County Council		Sligo County Council		South Dublin County Council		National; median (34 local authorities)	
	2004	2006	2004	2006	2004	2006	2004	2006	2004	2006	2004	2006	2004	2006
Total number of dwellings in local authority stock	7,801	7,891	26,915	26,990	3,223	3,201	2,899	2,967	1,701	1,815	7,688	8,034	1,901.5	2,026.5
Overall % of dwellings that are let	97.7	94.6	92.6	91	93	90.9	98	97	96.1	94	99.5	99.1	97.4	96.5
Overall % of dwellings that are empty	4.6	5.4	7.4	9	7	9.1	2	3	3.8	6	0.5	0.9	2.8	3.5
Empty dwellings subject to major refurbishment schemes (%)	55.1	53.8	17.7	11.0	88	21.5	14	50.0	29.2	14.0	34.7	1.4	21.8	16.2
Empty dwellings unavailable for letting (%)	79	79.3	69.9	75.9	80	90.0	100	95.0	80.4	83.0	93.7	70.0	73.1	68.8
Empty dwellings available for letting (%)	21	20.8	30.0	24.1	20	10.0	0	5.0	90.6	17.0	6.3	30.0	26.9	31.2
Average time taken to re-let dwellings available for letting (weeks)	4.0	6.0	4.0	6.0	1.0	1.0	1.5	0.7	3.5	1.4	1.0	0.3	4.0	3.8
Repairs completed as a % of valid repair requests received	93.0	86.7	88.0	91.6	74.0	83.0	72.8	84.0	95.6	53.0	96.5	97.5	85.0	87.8
Average time to inform applicants of local authority housing (days)	32.0	27.0	40.0	55.0	56.0	56.0	8.0	9.0	13.7	7.3	21.0	29.0	28.0	29.5
Housing rent collected at year end as % of amount due	92.8	93.0	85.0	85.9	94.57	87.0	88.8	88.8	84.0	90.0	78.0	83.0	89.0	89.0

Source: Local Government Management Services Board (2004, 2006)

The same interviewee also highlighted marked inter-local authority differences in the impact of the Directors of Housing Services. In some cases they have improved strategic management and policy making, but in others 'people are still doing the same administrative jobs they always did, but now at a higher grade'. There was widespread support for this view among the local authority staff we interviewed in 2007–9 but less consensus around the reasons why this is the case. Some blamed promotions systems in local authorities, which afford too much weight to qualifications and interview performance, too little to candidates' achievements in their current jobs. Other interviewees working at smaller local authorities in the regions suggested that the tendency for managers to move between authorities in order to secure promotion undermined management capacity, because it promotes a conservative management style and means that they are often not *in situ* for long enough to gain the in-depth knowledge of the service necessary to drive extensive service reform. Notably this practice was identified as a barrier to improving housing management standards in our 1997–8 research and our 2007–9 interviewees suggest that it is a particular problem in Limerick City Council, which was among the strongest housing departments in the former year.

The other key contribution to poor management standards we identified in 1997–8 – the staffing of housing departments by non-specialist, generally untrained housing managers – had dissipated by 2007–9, at least in the larger local authorities we examined. Many of the Dublin and Cork City Council and South Dublin County Council staff we met during our 2007–9 visit had spent substantial portions of their career in housing and undergone significant specialist training, which in our view has contributed to the strong strategic management performance of these authorities. In smaller local authorities the modest size of the housing service reduced the possibility of pursuing a specialist career in housing, and more broadly in Ireland, the small social housing stock and its dispersal among a large number of small public and non-profit sector landlords has, to date, largely stifled the development of housing management as a profession and of associated training and education provision.

Conclusions

This chapter has examined the impact of ten years of reforms to arrangements for social housing provision and management on the seven case study neighbourhoods. Among the four most significant developments in this regard, the reconceptualisation of the housing management function has had by far the most positive impact on the views of tenants and, our research indicates, this was the main driver of the marked improvement in their relationships with local authorities between 1997–8 and 2007–9 and of the associated improvement in the liveability of several neighbourhoods. Some significant improvements in regeneration practice are also evident, particularly in the case of Fatima Mansions, but this analysis has also highlighted a continuing over-reliance on radical built environment interventions such as demolition. Some aspects of the externalisation of social housing provision, such as the growth of the housing association sector, have also been positive, however, the future of other aspects of the externalisation agenda, such as the externalised model of regeneration procurement using PPPs, is uncertain. Whereas the impact of the various reforms to the management of the social housing service, such as the advent of strategic policy making and performance monitoring, has been uneven in some cases and uniformly low in others, and has had a negligible impact in terms of improving the liveability of social rented neighbourhoods.

The introduction to this chapter mentioned that recent decades have seen marked reductions in government subsidisation of social housing in most Western European countries, but in some cases (such as the Netherlands) this has been accompanied by increased management autonomy for social landlords, whereas in others (most notably the UK) social landlords have been subject to increasingly interventionist supervision by central government. Ireland is distinctive in the international context, therefore, because public spending on social housing increased significantly in the 1990s and early 2000s (albeit not to levels that matched investment during the first half of the twentieth century). In terms of reforms to the governance of social housing, the Irish case has more in common with the UK than with the Dutch end of this spectrum. Several of the reforms described in this chapter mirror those introduced in the UK as part of the Blairist project of modernising the welfare state (Walker, Reid, and Mullins, 2006). In the UK social housing sector the modernisation agenda was characterised by: increased managerialisation and central government control; attempts to apply private sector incentives by, for instance, affording clients a greater say in management decisions; the promotion of partnership and multi-agency working, and the transfer of responsibility for services traditionally provided directly by government to the non-profit and (for-profit) private sector (Pawson, 2006; Walker, 2001). However, the reforms to Irish social housing examined here are relatively conservative compared to the UK and also to other aspects of the Irish welfare state, most notably the health service (Taylor, 2005). For instance, stock transfers from the local authority to the housing association sector in Ireland have been minimal to date, the results of performance management have not been linked to public funding availability and minimal use was made of private finance during the period under examination in this chapter.

The reasons for this are both ideological and practical. Social housing in Ireland was not subject to the sustained ideological attacks common elsewhere in Western Europe in recent decades and, in the context of a rising population and plentiful tax revenue during the Celtic Tiger economic boom, the government's key priority for the sector was to increase output, which is difficult to do in tandem with structural reform.

The unravelling of the practical part of this equation, in the emergence of the fiscal crisis in 2007–8, indicates that more radical reform is likely in the future and the public spending and legislative developments since then signal the likely trajectory of this process. In relation to the latter the Housing (Miscellaneous Provisions) Act 2009 enables the housing minister to intervene in local authorities' housing management decisions, by, for instance, specifying the factors they must take into account when determining rent levels and to issue directives forcing errant authorities to comply. In addition, the Residential Tenancies (Amendment) (No. 2) Act 2012 extended the powers of the Residential Tenancies Board to include the regulation of housing association tenants as well as private renting tenants and thereby for the first time regulated secure occupancy rights of housing association tenants. Read in tandem with the aforementioned performance monitoring arrangements these legislative developments indicate that Ireland is moving towards the more regulated social housing provision arrangements that have been adopted in the UK, rather than towards increased landlord autonomy. Notably, the 2009 Act also legally underpins the Rental Accommodation Scheme, which it defines as equivalent to social housing in legal terms and enables local authorities to lease dwellings for letting as social housing, as well as building or buying them. Furthermore, between 2008 and 2010, the capital budget for constructing/purchasing social housing units was cut from €980 million to €367 million and the vast majority of new social housing units delivered since these cuts have been financed using leasing (Department of Public Expenditure and Reform, 2011). These indicate that, irrespective of whether local authorities or housing associations are responsible for managing social housing in Ireland in future, this country is moving towards a model of social housing provision similar to that currently employed in Germany and Belgium, whereby private landlords play a central role in its supply (Scanlon and Whitehead, 2007).

References

Ballymun Task Force (1988) *Programme of renewal for Ballymun: An integrated housing policy.* Dublin: Ballymun Task Force.

Bissett, J. (2009) *Regeneration: public good or private profit?* Dublin: Tasc.

Boyle, R., Humphries, P., and O'Donnell, O. (2003) *Changing local government: A review of the Local Government Modernisation Programme.* Dublin: Institute of Public Administration.

Callanan, M. (2005) Institutionalizing participation and governance? New participative structures in local government in Ireland. *Public Administration*, 83(4), 909–29.

Coates, D. and Norris, M. (2006) *Supplementary welfare allowance, rent supplement: implications for the rental accommodation scheme.* Dublin: Centre for Housing Research.

Coates, D. and Silke, D. (2011) *Comparative financial appraisal of long term costs of social housing delivery mechanisms.* Dublin: Housing Agency.

Comptroller and Auditor General (2007) *Special report No 61: Ballymun regeneration.* Dublin: Stationery Office.

Cowan, D. and McDermont, M. (2006) *Regulating social housing: Governing decline.* London: Routledge.

Department of Public Expenditure and Reform (2011) *Comprehensive review of expenditure, thematic evaluation series: Social housing supports.* Dublin: DPER.

Department of the Environment (1991) *A plan for social housing.* Dublin: Department of the Environment.

— (1996) *Better local government: A programme for change.* Dublin: Stationery Office.

Department of the Environment, Community and Local Government (various years) *Annual housing statistics bulletin.* Dublin: Department of the Environment, Heritage and Local Government.

Department of the Environment, Heritage and Local Government (undated) *Rental Accommodation Scheme (RAS): General overview of scheme.* Dublin: Department of the Environment, Heritage and Local Government.

Dublin Corporation (1993) *Lord Mayor's commission on housing.* Dublin: Dublin Corporation.

Fatima Groups United (2000) *11 acres: 10 steps.* Dublin: Fatima Groups United.

Focus Ireland, Simon Communities of Ireland, Society of St Vincent de Paul and Threshold (2002) *Housing access for all? An analysis of housing strategies and homeless action plans.* Dublin: Focus Ireland.

Gibb, K. (2002) Trends and change in social housing finance and provision within the European Union. *Housing Studies*, 17(2), 325–36.

Guerin, D. (1999) Relationships with Local Authorities. In T. Fahey (ed.) *Social housing in Ireland: A study of success, failure and lessons learned* (pp. 224–38). Dublin: Oak Tree Press.

Guerin, D., O'Connell, C., and Norris, M. (1998) *An estate management strategy for Cork.* Cork: unpublished report for Cork City Council.

Gruis, V. and Nieboer, N. (2007) Government regulation and market orientation in the management of social housing assets: Limitations and opportunities for European and Australian landlords. *European Journal of Housing Policy*, 7(1), 45–62.

Hearne, R. (2011) *Public private partnerships in Ireland: Failed experiment or the way forward?* Manchester: Manchester University Press.

Housing Management Group (1996) *First report.* Dublin: Department of the Environment.

— (1998) *Second report.* Dublin: Department of the Environment.

Indecon (2005) *Review of local government financing: Report commissioned by the Minister for the Environment, Heritage and Local Government.* Dublin: Indecon International Economic Consultants.

Keegan, O. (1995) *A review of Dublin Corporation's rent scheme, rent payment methods and arrears and account management procedures.* Dublin: Dublin Corporation.

Kenna, P. (2006) *Housing law and policy in Ireland.* Dublin: Clarus Press.

Kenny, B. (1998) *Report on estate management.* Dublin: Dublin Corporation.

Kintrea, K. (2007) Policies and programmes for disadvantaged neighbourhoods: Recent English experience. *Housing Studies*, 22(2), 261–82.

Kintrea, K. and Muir, J. (2009) Integrating Ballymun? Flawed progress in Ireland's largest estate regeneration scheme. *Town Planning Review*, 80(1), 83–108.

Local Government Audit Service (2000) *Review of performance indicators.* Dublin: Department of the Environment and Local Government.

Local Government Management Services Board (2004, 2006) *Service indicators in local authorities.* Dublin: Local Government Management Services Board.

Montgomery, J. (1995) The story of Temple Bar: Creating Dublin's cultural quarter. *Planning Practice and Research*, 10(2), 135–72.

Moore, N. (2008) *Dublin Docklands reinvented: the post industrial regeneration of a European city quarter.* Dublin: Four Courts Press.

Mullins, D., Rhodes, M.L., and Williamson, A. (2003) *Non-profit housing organisations in Ireland, North and South.* Belfast: Northern Ireland Housing Executive.

Musterd, S. and Andersson, R. (2005) Housing mix, social mix and social opportunities. *Urban Affairs Review*, 40(6), 761–90.

Norris, M. (1999) The impact of the build environment. In T. Fahey (ed.) *Social housing in Ireland: A study of success, failure and lessons learned* (pp. 106–44). Dublin: Oak Tree Press.

— (2000) *Managing in partnership: Developing estate management in Limerick city.* Limerick: PAUL Partnership.

— (2001) Regenerating run-down public housing estates: A review of the operation of the Remedial Works Scheme. *Administration*, 49(1), 25–45.

— (2006) Developing, designing and managing mixed tenure housing estates. *European Planning Studies*, 14(2), 199–218.

Norris, M. and O'Connell, C. (2002) Local authority housing management reform in the Republic of Ireland: Progress to date – impediments to further progress. *European Journal of Housing Policy*, 2(3), 245–64.

Norris, M., Healy, J., and Coates, D. (2008) Drivers of rising housing allowance claimant numbers: evidence from the Irish private rented sector. *Housing Studies*, 23(1), 89–109.

O'Connell, C. (1998) Tenant involvement in local authority housing: A new panacea for policy failure? *Administration*, 46(2), 25–46.

— (1999) Local authorities as landlords. In T. Fahey (ed.) *Social housing in Ireland: A study of success, failure and lessons learned* (pp. 57–78). Dublin: Oak Tree Press.

O'Connell, C. and Fahey, T. (1999) Local authority housing in Ireland. In T. Fahey (ed.) *Social housing in Ireland: A study of success, failure and lessons learned* (pp. 35–56). Dublin: Oak Tree Press.

Pawson, H. (2006) Restructuring England's social housing sector since 1989: Undermining or underpinning the fundamentals of public housing? *Housing Studies*, 21(5), 767–83.

Pawson, H. and Mullins, D. (2010) *After council housing, Britain's new social landlords*. London: Palgrave.

Power, A. (1997) *Estates on the edge: the social consequences of mass housing in Northern Europe*. London: Macmillan.

Redmond, D. and Russell, P. (2008) Social housing regeneration and the creation of sustainable communities in Dublin. *Local Economy*, 23(3), 168–79.

Scanlon, K. and Whitehead, C. (2007) Social housing in Europe. In K. Scanlon and C. Whitehead (eds) *Social Housing in Europe* (pp. 8–34). London: London School of Economics.

Stephens, M., Burns, N., and MacKay, L. (2002) *British social rented housing in a European context*. Bristol: Policy Press.

Taylor, G. (2005) *Negotiated governance and public policy in Ireland*. Manchester: Manchester University Press.

Treadwell Shine, S. and Norris, M. (2006) *Housing policy discussion series: Regenerating local authority estates – review of policy and practice*. Dublin: Centre for Housing Research.

Walker, R. (2001) How to abolish public housing: Implications and lessons from public management reform. *Housing Studies*, 16(5), 675–96.

Walker, R., Reid, B., and Mullins, D. (2006) *Managing Social Housing: Modernisation, Reinvention and Management Reform*. London: Routledge.

Whitehead, C. (2003) Financing social housing in Europe. *Housing Finance International*, Summer, 3–8.

Whyte, J. (2005) *Eight great expectations: A landmark and unique social regeneration plan for Fatima Mansions*. Dublin: Fatima Regeneration Board.

5

WHY TARGET DISADVANTAGED NEIGHBOURHOODS?

Rationale for area-based interventions

Eileen Humphreys and Des McCafferty

Introduction

A key policy trend in Ireland and other European countries has been the development of area-based interventions to respond to problems of spatial deprivation at local level. These approaches entail the application of resources, both public and private, to specific geographical areas, as opposed to particular sectors of society. As such, they represent a significantly different model of state intervention from that developed in liberal democratic societies throughout the twentieth century. This is especially the case in those countries that traditionally have had strongly centralised systems of government, such as Ireland and the UK, where area-based interventions have introduced a significant 'new localism' to public policy and administration. The purpose of this chapter is to outline and critically review the rationale for area-based interventions in Ireland, with reference to the wider international experience with this policy approach. This requires an understanding of the contextual issues that led to the introduction of the area-based approach and shaped its evolution over time. This is provided in the opening section, which looks at the development of area-based interventions internationally. The background to, and some key trends in, the development of these initiatives in Ireland is outlined briefly in the next section, and this is followed by a detailed account of the rationale underpinning the area-based approach. The final section summarises some recent assessments of area-based anti-poverty interventions internationally, as well as the key elements of the case for these measures in Ireland.

Re-emergence of the area-based approach

The development of area-based interventions in Ireland has been shaped by external influences, particularly EU structural policies. It has also been influenced strongly by area-based policies in the UK, where there is a longer history of this approach and where systems of governance and public policy development are similar to Ireland. In turn, the implementation of area-based interventions in the UK has borrowed from the US experience, which, like that in the UK but unlike Ireland, has been strongly urban based. In the US, public policy interventions targeted on areas with a concentration of problems were driven by problems of racial tensions and ghetto poverty in the cities, which particularly affected the black population (Wilson 1987, 1991). Similarly, the first UK intervention – the Urban Programme – was developed in England in the late 1960s in response to the growing evidence of urban decay in inner cities, and fears of social unrest and ethnic tensions (Parkinson, 1996).

Internationally then, area-based interventions to counteract poverty and deprivation emerged in crisis situations. The aims of these programmes were generally based on one or more of the following: (i) addressing economically inefficient imbalances in the spatial distribution of economic growth and development that resulted from market failure; (ii) promoting social justice by augmenting or complementing redistributive and structural policies to combat inequality in access to resources; (iii) tackling policy failures, including those resulting from poor responsiveness of centrally designed policies to changed macroeconomic conditions and to variations in needs at local area level, as well as the unintended reinforcing and spatially concentrating effects of certain policies (e.g., welfare, planning, and housing policies) on the problems of inequality and dependence. The changing focus of area-based programmes in relation to the changing weight accorded to economic efficiency versus social equity goals is outlined in the next sub-section, while the link between policy failures and area-based initiatives is explored in the following sub-section.

Local responses to globalisation, restructuring, and uneven development: By the late 1970s, policy responses in advanced Western states generally emphasised structural economic change and its social consequences as the root causes of the spatial concentration of problems in cities. Economic restructuring from manufacturing to service activities associated with globalisation and the transition to a post-industrial society, and the resulting loss of employment opportunities for both skilled and unskilled production workers, led to the increased polarisation of the labour market into high- and low-wage sectors (Wilson, 1991; Sassen, 2000). This polarisation was translated into pronounced spatial disparities by the operation of housing markets and housing systems, resulting in the spatial concentration of poverty in certain localities. Such areas appeared both in inner cities and in the large-scale post-Second World War housing estates located on the outskirts of cities (Andersen and van Kempen, 2003; Skifter Andersen, 2002). While these problems were most acute in industrial regions – particularly those with specialised dependence on declining industries such as coal mining, steel, textiles, and shipbuilding – spatially concentrated deprivation at a small area level affected even successful cities and regions.

In the UK, the response of the Labour government to the intensifying local concentration of poverty in the 1970s involved organisational changes, including new partnerships between central government departments and local and community interests. While there were elements of policy continuity under Conservative governments in the 1980s and 1990s, there were also differences. Greater centralisation of urban regeneration, less engagement with local government, promotion of private sector-led partnerships and entrepreneurialism were key policy shifts. In a marked divergence from the neo-corporatist models evolving elsewhere in the European Community (EC), trade unions were excluded from partnerships. Fiscal initiatives in favour of property development, targeting resources on capital rather than revenue projects, and direct economic rather than social objectives were key features of (area-based) urban policy at this stage (Parkinson, 1996). These features are exemplified by initiatives such as the inner city task forces (led by officials from central government departments), enterprise zones and urban development corporations targeted in 'tightly defined geographic areas' (Rhodes, Tyler, and Brennan, 2005, p. 1920).

By the late 1980s, a new emphasis was emerging in local development policy throughout Europe. This entailed a much greater focus on endogenous or 'bottom-up' policies of development (Cappelin, 1992), and on the potential contribution of deprived areas and disadvantaged groups to the wider economic development of the city and region. Under neo-liberal administrations in several states, there was also a strong emphasis on reducing the costs of welfare payments. This arose from demographic trends towards ageing population structures, and emerging labour market skills shortages (producing a coincidence of unfilled vacancies and high unemployment in some areas). An additional factor in some cases was the erosion of the fiscal base of cities, due to processes of suburbanisation and counter-urbanisation. Already, in analysing types of strategies to deal with problems of deprived local areas, a distinction could be made between 'inward'- and 'outward'-looking strategies (Hall, 1997; Cameron and Davoudi, 1998) – the former focusing on specific problems within deprived areas, the latter on wider structural factors and neighbourhood–city–region connectivity. The new emphasis on the economic contribution of deprived areas was accompanied in the early 1990s by the introduction of competitive bidding by local areas for regeneration funds (e.g., City Challenge from 1991 and the Single Regeneration Budget from 1994 in the UK). The thinking was that area-based programmes should not only focus on the most deprived areas (the needs-based criterion) but that they should target areas that could show potential to improve, and the capacity to manage the process (Tunstall and Lupton, 2003).

The election of the 'New' Labour government in 1997 in a context of economic growth but increasing problems of social dislocation led to a renewed and stronger focus on the social aspects of regeneration, and the prioritisation of social inclusion. This resulted in wider application of the area-based approach, and the broadening of the sectoral policy areas applying it. Examples at this time were Education Action Zones, Health Action Zones, Employment Action Zones, and programmes like Sure Start in early childhood education. By the late 1990s, the problems of deprived areas were also being increasingly articulated in terms of deficits in social resources and with an emphasis on the social relational aspects of disadvantage. These concerns were reflected in policy objectives to promote community development and social cohesion, and to augment social capital, defined as the norms and networks that promote civic behaviour in territorial communities, including neighbourhoods, and facilitate access to economic and social mobility opportunities via socially heterogeneous networks (Putnam, Leonardi, and Naretti, 1993; Putnam, 2000). From the late 1990s and into the current decade, while 'the emphasis has shifted back to need ... competition, innovation and improvement potential remain features of some programmes' (Tunstall and Lupton, 2003, p. 2).

Policy delivery at the present time is characterised by a stronger emphasis on localisation through local partnership structures, local strategies, and the empowerment of communities and disadvantaged groups in the process of change. It also emphasises local involvement in the management of funds (Rhodes et al., 2005) and meeting the needs of neighbourhoods within a more comprehensive framework for local government – in England, for instance, the Local Area Agreement (Joseph Rowntree Foundation, 2007). These approaches were reflected in later rounds of the Single Regeneration Budget (five and six), and at the neighbourhood level in programmes such as New Deal for Communities (1998 onwards) and the Neighbourhood Renewal Fund (2000). Contractual agreements that set out the framework for the implementation of action and are linked to measurable goals/targets have been a feature of recent urban regeneration programmes in the UK, France, the Netherlands (Andersen and van Kempen, 2003), and other advanced countries. Local authorities, typically working with other local stakeholders including social and civil society organisations, are the key players. Examples here include, in France, the *Contract de Ville*, agreed between the state and the local authorities, which were replaced in 2007 by *Contracts Urbains de Cohésion Sociale (CUCS)*; in the Netherlands, the *Large Cities Policy (I, II and III)* operating up to 2009, with a revised framework developed from 2010 onwards that includes a strengthened neighbourhood approach based on more than 40 districts (the 40+ Community Action Plans). Similarly, in Sweden, the first development agreements between central government and municipalities were introduced in 1999 in the framework of national Metropolitan Policy. These agreements placed a strong emphasis on reducing social, ethnic and other forms of discriminatory segregation into small-scale residential areas and promoting social integration. More recently (from 2008), municipal regulations have strengthened the framework for coordination of urban development at local level (European Urban Knowledge Network, 2010).

A further trend in several advanced European countries is institutional innovation at local level, centred on local authorities and how they operate to engage and work with other stakeholders in decision making. This is identified as an 'implicit' and 'indirect' characteristic in the implementation of national urban policies – i.e. aiming at providing others with capacity and improved conditions for tackling urban challenges (d'Albergo, 2010). Examples here include greater decentralisation of power to local level and multi-level relationships (UK, France, Spain), reforms of local government (UK, Spain), and reforms of structures and processes of public action (UK, France). With the recent change of government in the UK, the Big Society initiative and the renewed emphasis on local growth focus on a transfer of power from central government to local communities and community empowerment via planning reforms. It involves a strengthening of local government, removal of the regional layer of institutions (Regional Development Agencies) and a much stronger emphasis on citizen and community involvement in local decision making, using innovatory methods of participation (e.g. use of participatory budgeting schemes). It also places a renewed focus on voluntary activity and the role of charitable organisations in delivery of public services, as part of the public service reform agenda.

Addressing policy failures and policy reform: While globalisation as a factor in uneven development is generally emphasised in the literature – with reference to the US (Wilson, 1987, 1991; Jargowsky, 1997), the UK (Parkinson, 1998; Hamnett, 1994), and advanced countries of Europe (Allen, 1998; Musterd and Ostendorf, 1998) – this is contested. Skifter Andersen (2002), for instance, argues that segregation in general and deprivation in specific places 'are not fully explained by globalisation and social exclusion . . . There is plenty of evidence that segregation and deprivation continue in situations where the national or local economy is booming and social inequality is decreasing'. He goes on to argue that the causes of place-based deprivation are linked to local and regional conditions, and complicated dynamics that pull certain areas 'into a vicious downward cycle of decline from which they seldom escape unaided' (Skifter Andersen, 2002, p. 768).

As well as local and regional factors, national policies in areas such as planning, housing, and welfare have had a major bearing on socio-spatial inequality. The role of planning and housing in reinforcing tendencies towards concentrated poverty at local area level is linked initially to clearances of inner cities and the construction of large mono-tenure social housing estates on the outskirts of cities in the post-Second World War period in many European states. More recently, housing policies are being used to address problems of concentrated poverty in several advanced states. Instruments include housing mobility programmes out of urban ghettos in the US (de Souza Briggs, 1998; de Souza Briggs and Keys, 2009); promotion of physical renewal based on mixed tenures in the UK (Camina and Wood, 2009); a combination of rent reductions (intended to encourage higher income tenants to move to low-income neighbourhoods), and physical improvements combined with social initiatives and organisational change in Denmark (Skifter Andersen, 2002) and regulation to prevent segregation of ethnic or other vulnerable social groups into specific neighbourhoods in Sweden (European Urban Knowledge Network, 2010).

UK governments have pursued mixed-tenure housing policies since the 1980s but, in recent years, there is a much stronger emphasis on this approach (Department of the Environment, Transport and the Regions, 2000). The principle of tenure mix has now been incorporated into planning policy that requires 'sustainable, inclusive mixed communities in all areas, both urban and rural . . .' to be created via 'a variety of housing particularly in terms of tenure and price' (DCLG, 2006, pp. 6–9 cited in

Camina and Wood, 2009). Tenure mix is seen as an instrument to break up spatial concentrations of poverty at small area level, producing socially mixed areas, with different forms of social interaction and cohesion, and overcoming place-based stigma. The case for mixed tenure draws on notions of social capital, particularly the benefits for poor people of access to more socially heterogeneous networks. Potential benefits include the spread of mainstream norms and values linked to the presence of more affluent residents (drawing on Wilson's 1987 thesis), and the opening up of job opportunities (Camina and Wood, 2009; Atkinson, 2005). Mixed tenure policies are an alternative to reducing the exposure of poor individuals and families to poor neighbourhoods via exit from them, which is difficult and rare for the most vulnerable.

Welfare policy and the objective of reducing the fiscal burden of welfare transfers have also influenced the development of area-based interventions. The reform of welfare by promoting a shift from passive to active labour market programmes (ALMPs) has been a key aspect of policy change in advanced states since the 1980s. This reform is often labelled as a welfare-to-work approach. Some of these reforms involve using the tax system to improve the incentive for people on welfare, wherever they live – i.e. people-based approaches – to engage in training and work (e.g., Family Income Tax Credits in the UK). With the recent change of government in the UK (2010), there is increasing emphasis on the conditionality of welfare support on readiness to work, to enter training, etc. In addition, other aspects of ALMPs are linked to provision of services or new forms of economic or self-help activities (e.g., social economy programmes) in disadvantaged communities, and are implemented through an area-based approach.

Evolution of area-based interventions in Ireland

While Ireland was a late industrialising country, and in the 1970s and 1980s lagged considerably behind the EU average in terms of its economic development, it too was affected by the wider processes of economic adjustment emanating from globalisation. The absence of large mono-industrial areas comparable with those of the more developed European countries, and the smaller population and dispersed settlement patterns, meant that the problems of poverty and deprivation were smaller in scale and qualitatively different in Ireland. Nevertheless, economic restructuring was experienced in a number of forms following EU accession in 1973. These included a major loss of jobs in manufacturing as domestic firms were fully exposed to international competition, and the consolidation in agriculture towards larger and more efficient holdings resulting from the Common Agricultural Policy. The differential impact of these trends on localities depended on the composition of the local economic base, local infrastructure, human capital, and locational factors (e.g., remoteness from new job opportunities, and from services including education).

Difficulties of adjustment at local level were reflected in the emergence in the 1980s of unemployment 'blackspots' and of high levels of long-term unemployment, which particularly affected unskilled manual workers. Long-term unemployment proved to be particularly intractable through the 1980s and into the 1990s. The first integrated area-based interventions in urban (and some rural) environments, the Area-based Response to Long-term Unemployment, was specifically addressed to this issue. This was supported initially under a Global Grant for Local Socio-economic Development (1990–91) co-financed by the European Commission, and later by the Operational Programme for Local Urban and Rural Development in the Irish Community Support Framework (1994–99).

In rural areas, development problems were reflected in high levels of unemployment in some cases, but more typically in under-employment and low rates of labour market participation linked to a lack of local economic opportunities, and imbalanced demographic structures associated with the exodus of young people and females. The first area programme for Integrated Rural Development (1988–90) established by the Department of Agriculture in 12 pilot areas, with a particular focus on community and local enterprise (Walsh, Craig, and McCafferty, 1998), was developed to respond to these problems.

In addition to these urban and rural programmes, area-based interventions in Ireland have also been strongly developed along the border with Northern Ireland. Reflecting the difficulties faced by all international border regions, areas along the Irish border suffer from a range of disadvantages. In addition to remoteness, these include distortions of trade arising from different currency and fiscal regimes, and typically poorer and incomplete infrastructures resulting from different planning and public service systems. In the Ireland/Northern Ireland case, these problems were exacerbated by the spill-over into the border region of the inter-community conflict, associated violence, and public disorder in Northern Ireland over some 30 years. This negatively affected economic development, acting as a disincentive to inward investment and tourism; it weakened labour market integration, disrupted the trading environment, and undermined community cohesion. The Community Initiative INTERREG for the Northern Ireland/Ireland Border Region (from 1989), which had a strong infrastructural and economic development focus, and later the PEACE Programme (from 1994–95) which addressed inter-community conflict, were early interventions applying the area-based approach in this special context.

Economic conditions changed rapidly in the course of the 1990s from those under which area-based interventions first emerged. The most significant aspect of this was the reduction in unemployment levels and in particular in long-term unemployment. Nevertheless, significant differentials in unemployment levels have persisted at the local level, and Ireland now displays in some of its cities and larger towns the patterns of cumulative disadvantage characteristic of the most industrialised states. Economic and labour market interventions (job search, training for the unemployed, addressing low educational qualifications, small-scale enterprise development) have therefore remained a central focus of area-based interventions into the current period. However, and mirroring the trend in the UK, these initiatives have expanded considerably in scope to take on a wider range of issues, including family breakdown, lone parenthood, child behavioural problems, drug abuse, crime and anti-social behaviour, and the health problems among disadvantaged sub-groups in the population. This has resulted in a proliferation of area-based programmes that now include youth diversion projects, family, parenting and child-care services, drugs taskforces, initiatives to tackle educational disadvantage amongst children, and to promote access to further and third-level education for residents of disadvantaged areas (see Chapter 6 for a detailed account of current initiatives). Increasingly, these interventions are characterised by an attempt to address causal processes of deprivation based on greater understanding of the risk and protective factors associated with certain behaviours such as educational drop-out, juvenile crime, and teenage pregnancy. There is also more emphasis on partnership and multi-agency working, integrated action, local service coordination, and leveraging investment into disadvantaged areas (e.g., in the RAPID Programme – Revitalising Areas by Planning Investment and Development).

In parallel with this extension of the sectoral/functional scope of the area-based approach, there has been a significant extension of the local partnership structures used from the outset to implement this approach. Under the 'cohesion' process rolled out by the government from 2004–05, local partnerships and community groups have been established nationwide, in areas that are not designated as disadvantaged as well as those that are. Up to the end of 2009, the Local Development and Social Inclusion Programme (LDSIP) supported 37 Integrated Development Companies, 17 Urban Partnerships and two Employment Pacts, as well as 180 projects in the Community Development Programme. The RAPID Programme was extended from Strand I (the most deprived areas of cities) to also cover provincial towns in Strand II, and now operates in 45 areas throughout the country. Local development structures have recently been restructured. This involves a consolidation of two local and community development programmes that have been in place since the early 1990s, namely (i) the Local Development and Social Inclusion Programme; and (ii) the Community Development Programme and the agreement of a new Local and Community Development Programme, in operation from January 2010. New integrated partnership structures are now in place comprising 52 local development companies and other local development groups. The former LEADER Groups (36), operating in rural areas, have been absorbed into this new arrangement in that they too are reconstituted as integrated local development companies.

Rationale for area-based interventions

The literature identifies several different reasons for area-based anti-poverty interventions. These are reviewed below, with particular reference to the implementation of these initiatives in Ireland. While there are close links between the various reasons, and justification for a particular area-based programme may be based on a combination of considerations, Walsh (1999) notes that different programmes in Ireland tend to be associated mainly with one or another rationale.

Effectiveness, efficiency, and completeness in reaching the poor: An important rationale for area-based interventions is that, if poverty is concentrated spatially, then confining interventions to the worst affected areas as a form of targeting offers 'efficiency' and 'completeness in reaching poor individuals' (Tunstall and Lupton, 2003). The targeting case for an area-based approach became stronger in Ireland in the 1980s, due to changes in the geography of poverty including the emergence of unemployment 'blackspots' as well as spatial concentration of vulnerable groups such as drug addicts and lone parents (Walsh, 1999). However, for this justification of an area-based approach to hold, both the *rate* and the *incidence* of poverty in the targeted areas must be high. In other words, most of the population in these areas must be poor, and most of the poor must live in the areas in question. The lower the rate of poverty in the designated areas, then the greater the number of unintended beneficiaries that will be included (inefficiency in targeting); on the other hand the lower the incidence of poverty then the fewer poor people who will be included (incompleteness). This problem with area-based targeting has been recognised for a long time, with Townsend (1979, p. 560) pointing out that, in Britain, 'however we care to define economically or socially deprived areas, unless we include over half the areas in the country, there will be more poor persons or poor children living outside of them than in them'.

It has been argued that the geography of poverty in Ireland, and specifically the low incidence of the poor in relatively high risk areas, is such that spatial targeting produces inefficiency and incompleteness (Watson, Whelan, Williams, and Blackwell, 2005). The targeting rationale is also undermined somewhat by the relatively dispersed settlement pattern. Whatever the logic for using efficient targeting as a rationale for area-based interventions in urban areas, where housing systems tend to concentrate poorer households spatially, it is less appropriate to the rural context. In disadvantaged rural areas, poverty tends to be widely dispersed and characterised by problems of under-employment (rather than concentrated unemployment), social isolation in a context of population decline and demographic imbalance, poor infrastructure, and poor accessibility to services. Hence Shucksmith (2000), for instance, argues that the area-based approach to social exclusion in rural areas is based on an urban model and is inappropriate in the rural environment.

Even if the underlying geographical conditions for effective spatial targeting of the poor are present, successful implementation of the area-based approach requires that areas of concentrated poverty be identified accurately, based on objective indicators of deprivation. This presents significant methodological challenges and, in the Irish context, practical difficulties linked to mismatches between the boundaries of statistical/administrative units and 'natural' localities or communities characterised by deprivation. Objective measurement is usually based on proxy or surrogate indicators of deprivation derived from census data at a small area level, which are statistically combined to produce composite indices of relative dis-advantage. Two such indicators have been widely used in Ireland: Pobal HP Deprivation Index developed by Haase and Pratschke (2008) (see Chapter 2); and the SAHRU deprivation index (Kelly and Teljeur, 2007). While the two measures are highly correlated nationally, nevertheless there are instances where they give varying indications of local conditions. In general, the smaller the spatial units for which data are available, and the more sophisticated the index, the better the spatial targeting, i.e., the greater the efficiency and completeness in reaching intended beneficiaries. Recent work to assess the effectiveness of the Index of Multiple Deprivation 2000, used in the UK to target the poor, found this to be 'a more complete way of targeting the poor than has been claimed by opponents of area-based targeting in the past'. Nevertheless, while more efficient in reaching some sub-groups (particularly children) than others, spatial targeting based on the index remains relatively inefficient (Tunstall and Lupton, 2003).

The extension of the area-based approach in Ireland to a situation now whereby area-based initiatives effectively cover the whole of the country, suggests that targeting is no longer a primary objective of this approach. Therefore, other justifications for the approach must come into play.

Positive discrimination and rationing: Closely linked to the targeting rationale for area-based interventions is the argument that these measures can be used as a way of rationing scarce resources, making funds available to certain areas and excluding others. According to Walsh (1999) this was an important consideration in the initial development of area-based initiatives in Ireland in the 1980s, when (as is the case again now) there were severe constraints on public expenditure. Rationing, or positive discrimination, may be primarily motivated either by a desire to close the gap in living standards and opportunities between poorer and wealthier areas (i.e., redistribution considerations), or, alternatively, to maximise the return on investment (an efficiency argument). Depending on the relative weight given to these two considerations, designation of areas will be based on needs, or on criteria such as the area's potential and/or capacity to deliver a programme, and to absorb the funding available for specific purposes. As outlined earlier, the latter approach has become more important in recent years. Potential and capacity are typically assessed on the basis of competitive bidding, and the production of strategies and action plans (Tunstall and Lupton, 2003). While the combination of a needs-based criterion (long-term unemployment rates) and organisational capacity at local level was used in the selection of the first 12 local area-based partnerships, competitive bidding has not been a strong feature of area-based initiatives in Ireland. This is reflected in the nationwide extension of the geographic coverage of area-based initiatives.

Positive discrimination based on needs, aimed at promoting the convergence of poorer areas with the mainstream, is in line with EU territorial development policy, with spatial targeting as one of the five principles underlying the 1989 reform of the Structural Funds. The thinking was that European funding, combined and in harmony with national programmes, could have a real impact on economic convergence and social cohesion across the regions of Europe, by achieving the scale of funding required to make an impact. Similar thinking underlies the matching funding requirement of several area-based programmes that are designed to 'leverage' additional funding into the most deprived areas. This is the approach used in the RAPID programme and also the major regeneration programmes introduced in recent years in both Dublin and Limerick. The combination of direct and indirect or leveraged funding under certain programmes adds to the difficulty of evaluating area-based initiatives.

One further justification for confining interventions to the most deprived areas is political visibility, in that it provides evidence that government and policy makers are taking action to address the problems of these areas. Visibility, however, can also have negative effects by adding to the stigma of areas: 'the area deprivation policies of recent years ... actually reinforce inequality and dependence. This can arise by labelling areas, and through their loss of status scare off potential development' (Townsend, 1979, p. 560).

Neighbourhood effects: A third rationale for area-based interventions relates to the widely researched phenomenon of neighbourhood or area effects. These refer to the cumulative and qualitatively different effects for people, infrastructure, and organisations arising from negative externalities associated with the concentration of poverty at neighbourhood level (Tunstall and Lupton, 2003; Watson, *et al.*, 2005). In simple terms, area effects refer to the idea that it is worse to be poor in a poor area than in a mixed area, and that living in a poor area compounds the disadvantage arising from one's own poverty (Atkinson and Kintrea, 2001). Problems linked to area effects include lower incomes, higher rates of physical and mental ill-health, deficiencies in child development, behavioural problems in children, and alienation from mainstream society. In addition, as Kleinman (1999) points out, negative externalities arising from concentrated deprivation (e.g., more crime) can also impact on the wider society. While it is appropriate to respond to people-based poverty through a range of redistributive policies such as social welfare payments, and free or subsidised medical care, education, childcare, and housing, these measures may not be enough, in the presence of area effects, to change the trajectory of places characterised by concentrated poverty. Neighbourhood effects, therefore, justify additional interventions at the area level to support individuals and families, organisations (businesses, public institutions, voluntary bodies), and infrastructure (Tunstall and Lupton, 2003; Watson et al., 2005).

Conceptually, neighbourhood effects can be divided into those that derive from characteristics of the population in poor neighbourhoods, and those that flow from characteristics of the place itself. Most academic attention has been devoted to people-derived effects, explanation of which draws on notions of social capital and social relational aspects of community, including relationships with the mainstream (Putnam *et al.*, 1993; Putnam, 2000; Barnes *et al.*, 2005). Among the mechanisms and factors that underpin people-derived neighbourhood effects are restricted social networks that result in a lack of the 'bridging' social capital that is important, for example, in accessing knowledge about job opportunities as well as in competing for them (Ellen and Turner, 1997). Other aspects of social interaction, including the socialisation of children by adults, and peer influences, may lead to the emergence of an 'underclass' in circumstances of concentrated poverty (Wilson, 1987, 1991; Murray, 1996). The conventional understanding of this relationship is that the social and economic isolation of the poor in areas of concentrated and multiple deprivation leads to the development in these areas of a set of social values, norms and behaviours that are qualitatively different from the mainstream. These include a low value on education and employment, and the expectation of welfare support, as well as high rates of teenage sexual activity, non-marital births, and social pathologies such as delinquency, drug addiction, and crime (Greene, 1991). Such norms and behaviours in turn exacerbate social exclusion, and push the areas affected into a vicious cycle of decline (Wilson, 1987), giving rise to the concept of a 'culture of poverty'.

Place-derived area effects, or what might be referred to more accurately as indirect people-derived effects, arise in a number of inter-related ways. These include deficiencies in both public and private services, poor quality of environment, peripheral or isolated location (exacerbated by poor public transportation), and place stigmatisation. Public services such as schools, primary medical care, and policing may fail to meet the needs of residents in deprived areas, due partly to the greater demands placed on them, and partly to the services being of a lower quality because of difficulties in attracting and retaining professional staff (Duffy, 2000). Low levels of disposable income result in the under-provision of private services, including retail facilities, but service providers can also be deterred by negative place images. In general, stigmatisation is one of the most significant problems faced by poor places and can lead to under-investment in jobs as well as services, to discrimination in employment (particularly when labour markets are 'tight'), denial of access to credit, mortgage finance, and insurance on the basis of address (so-called 'redlining'), and lack of inward mobility of people with choice (and higher levels of education and income).

The measurement of neighbourhood effects is methodologically challenging (Dietz, 2002; Tunstall and Lupton, 2003) and research on the extent of these effects is inconclusive. Several researchers argue that such effects are relatively small in Europe compared with the US, and therefore insufficient to justify a specifically area-based approach to urban deprivation (Musterd and Ostendorf, 1998; Skifter Andersen, 2002). A wide-ranging review by Ellen and Turner (1997) found that area effects are generally much smaller than the effects of family characteristics, and that they diminish when unobserved family characteristics are controlled for. In a recent study of neighbourhood effects on individuals' income, Galster, Andersson, Musterd and Kauppinen (2008) reach a similar conclusion, but nevertheless find that statistically and substantively significant effects persist. However, even if the weight of evidence points to significant area effects, this still leaves open the question of whether such effects are best countered through area- or people-based interventions (Pringle, 1999).

Haase and McKeown (2003) argue that the study of neighbourhood effects is a relatively neglected area of research in Ireland, and furthermore that the main area-based intervention (the Local Development and Social Inclusion Programme) has 'not provided a satisfactory definition of cumulative disadvantage nor specified the remedies needed in order to reverse the decline of deprived areas be they urban or rural' (p. 4). While there is now a plethora of both area-based and target-group-based initiatives (e.g., for lone parents, youth offenders, pre-school, and school-going children) in areas of concentrated disadvantage, conceptually they show little evidence of working to address problems of neighbourhood effects. Moreover, area effects are quite different in disadvantaged rural areas. For example, rural populations are more likely to hold values and attitudes conforming to the mainstream, and rural areas may have better institutional infrastructures (e.g., schools, churches). However, area effects may be present in the lack of certain services or poor accessibility to them.

Innovation through piloting and mainstreaming successful approaches: The fourth rationale for area-based interventions relates to the promotion of innovative approaches in the design and delivery of interventions through the use of pilot projects. Hence, as well as level of need, the potential to develop good models that could be mainstreamed in policy and practice is often a criterion for funding. Area-based initiatives based on local partnership – now the Integrated Local Development Companies – were conceived initially as experimental initiatives. The importance of innovation as an objective of area-based initiatives was strongly influenced by the availability of EC/EU funding for local development from the late 1980s. All community initiatives included a requirement for innovation in policy and/or practice as a criterion for funding. This requirement formed part of the area-based initiatives (LEADER and successive programmes from 1991, and URBAN) as well as people-oriented initiatives implemented through area-based approaches. The latter programmes include POVERTY III, NOW (targeting women), and HORIZON (focused on disadvantaged groups including the disabled), all of which began in the 1980s, special initiatives such as the Territorial Employment Pacts launched in 1996, and, EQUAL (2000–06), addressed 'discrimination and inequality in the labour market through new and innovative policies and practice'. As well as experimentation through the implementation of new initiatives on the ground, the transnational networking component of most of these programmes has provided a further source of innovation through the exchange of information and experience with other localities across the EU.

The emphasis on policy innovation arose in part from the realisation by central government, specifically the Department of Taoiseach (an Irish prime minister), that centrally designed economic and welfare programmes were not sufficiently adaptable to resolve the intractable problem of long-term unemployment in local communities (Haase and McKeown, 2003). By allowing local communities to experiment with employment creation and anti-poverty actions, the central administration could learn from their experience and adapt mainstream programmes accordingly. The Local Employment Service (LES) and the Money Advice and Budgeting Service (MABS) are examples of schemes piloted by local partnerships that were subsequently mainstreamed. However, while Sabel (1996) in his review of the local partnerships was particularly laudatory of their innovative capacity, other studies have questioned the extent of learning from innovation by area-based initiatives (Haase and McKeown, 2003). Moreover, Walsh *et al.* (1998) suggest that the scope for innovation has in fact been restricted through the 'straightjacket application' of the local area-based approach resulting from over-centralised control.

Coordination, integration, and responsiveness to local conditions: The fifth rationale for area-based initiatives is that this approach can bring additional benefits in terms of improved efficiency and effectiveness of anti-poverty policies. These benefits arise from integration and coordination across public service areas, thereby maximising synergies among programmes, as well as from improved responsiveness to local conditions.

The issue of policy coordination and integration is not unique to Ireland but rather one that has highlighted the need for local responses in 'almost all advanced countries' (Sabel, 1996, p. 11). Stand-alone policies in discrete functional areas, such as education, health, housing, or labour market up-skilling, do not respond to the multi-dimensional nature of poverty. There is now a growing realisation of the need to break down the 'silo mentality' in policy making and delivery, and there are mechanisms at national level in Ireland to coordinate and drive the government's social inclusion agenda (e.g., the National Anti-Poverty Strategy and its successor programme the National Anti-Poverty and Social Inclusion Strategy 2007–16). Nevertheless, policy coordination remains weak. Hence problems arising from localised processes of interaction between the labour market, the education and training system, housing, and the environment are more likely to be addressed effectively through an area-based approach (National Economic and Social Council, 1990). Examples include the integration of enterprise support with training, and the integration of training, personal development, and job search with support for childcare and parenting.

Features identifiable as 'the local approach', such as coordinated service delivery and funding, and multi-agency working, were central to the first area-based initiatives for disadvantaged areas in Ireland. These include the Poverty III Programme and the area-based response to long-term unemployment. In the context of the Operational Programme for Local Urban and Rural Development (1994–99), it was argued that 'by integrating development across a range of measures and actions, the benefits will be reinforced and the results much greater than the individual efforts' (Area Development Management, 1995, p. 25). However, achieving local integration remains difficult because of the lack of decision-making autonomy at local level in the key service-providing organisations, as well as the fact that different organisations work to different administrative geographies (Walsh, 1999).

The locally driven approach is also based on the argument that 'no centralised or systematic organisation of development action can take full account of the diversity of local situations' (Commission of the European Communities, 1989). Some areas of mainstream policy that have a strong influence on poverty alleviation, such as health, education, and welfare, are highly centralised in terms of programme design and decision making on funding. The local approach provides a better match to needs, more customised responses allowing for more flexibility, and a more immediate response to new issues as they arise in the local environment. In the UK, for example, the role of local area-based initiatives in 'bending' mainstream programmes has been established from the earliest initiatives. However, the potential to do this requires a high degree of local autonomy at the point of delivery. The evidence is that this is not present in Ireland but rather the scope for action is constrained by prescriptive policy design at central government level (Haase and McKeown, 2003; Walsh et al., 1998).

Community empowerment and the development of local capacity: The need to respond more flexibly to differentiated local needs represents a laudable but nevertheless somewhat passive or reactive rationale for area-based initiatives. A more ambitious remit for these programmes is the mobilisation of local potential through community development, and the empowerment, through inclusion in decision-making structures and processes, of groups affected by poverty. In general, this rationale is closely related to the development of the endogenous approach to local development throughout Europe in the 1980s. From the inception of local area-based initiatives, central government (the Department of the Taoiseach) identified as an important role for local partnership companies the promotion of participative democracy (Sabel, 1996) to complement representative democracy as exercised through the electoral system. In more recent times, government emphasis on community development, both in Ireland and other European countries, has shifted somewhat towards concerns with volunteering and active citizenship, but area-based initiatives continue to be identified as a key means to secure these objectives.

Community development has been strong traditionally in Ireland, and holistic models of development, especially in rural environments, pre-date policy initiatives in favour of area-based development (Walsh et al., 1998). The Community Development Programme and local partnership companies support the development of community organisational structures, capacity building (through information, training, advice, etc.), and service delivery in disadvantaged areas and for disadvantaged target groups. In addition, they have encouraged and facilitated networking and the scaling up of community and voluntary organisations (e.g., the community fora at city and county level). Such interventions are seen to have benefits in terms of creating a vibrant civil society, as well as improving the capacity of communities themselves to engage in anti-poverty initiatives. However, the process and outcomes have been open to criticism. The main criticisms are that there is too much emphasis on consensus in the social partnership model, and not enough recognition of conflicting views; too much emphasis on the role of the voluntary and community sector in service delivery on behalf of state agencies, and not enough on advocacy; strong development of structures in disadvantaged areas that are professionalised but often not strongly embedded in existing social networks and forms of organisation in the local community.

More recently, the potential contribution of area-based initiatives to promoting citizen participation in decision making and improved governance has been emphasised. The recent nationwide extension of partnership companies and community development groups under the 'cohesion' process is largely motivated by such considerations, which were also central to the establishment of City and

County Development Boards and associated developments in local government (e.g., Strategic Policy Committees). These are the structures and processes through which local authorities engage with communities. Other partnership-based structures such as Social Inclusion Measures (SIM) Groups also operate under the City and County Development Board structure. However, these are not considered to be particularly successful in promoting participation and governance, and there is considerable fragmentation of effort. Rather than being fully integrated, local partnership companies tend to be seen as the 'watchdogs' for social inclusion on these structures.

Conclusions

Much of the recent literature is inconclusive about the effectiveness of area-based interventions in narrowing the gap between deprived areas and the mainstream (Andersen, 2002; Rhodes et al., 2005). It is also inconclusive on the relative effectiveness of place-based interventions vis-à-vis person-based policies in areas such as education, employment, and welfare (Griggs, Whitworth, Walker, McLennan, and Noble, 2008). While positive outcomes of area-based interventions have been identified (e.g., Parkinson, 1996; Rhodes et al., 2005; Griggs et al., 2008), the impact in terms of turning around places of concentrated poverty has been limited. For instance, after more than 30 years of area-based interventions in the UK, 'there has been no dramatic change in the relative ranking of the most deprived areas in England on the Indices of Multiple Deprivation' (SEU, 2001, cited in Rhodes et al., 2005).

Reasons for the inconclusive state of research on area-based approaches have been identified in the literature. Among these are insufficient development of evaluation theory and methods (Rhodes et al., 2005; O'Reilly, 2007; Tyler and Brennan, 2007) with arguments pointing to weaknesses in research design, as well as a basic lack of information about the impact of interventions on the key outcomes that they are designed to affect (Rhodes et al., 2005; O'Reilly, 2007). Part of the problem here is the difficulty of disentangling policy effects from other causal factors, and data limitations such as mismatches in boundaries of local area interventions and statistical units (Rhodes et al., 2005). A further issue is that expenditures on area-based initiatives, while they are significant and have increased over the years, are relatively small compared both with mainstream interventions and with the scale of the problems they are intended to address (Rhodes et al., 2005; Parkinson, 1996).

While there has been no comprehensive and in-depth evaluation of the area-based approach in Ireland, experience here with area-based anti-poverty initiatives seems to conform generally to wider European trends. However, some of the features of the Irish implementation of area-based programmes, particularly weaknesses linked to the strongly centralised system of public administration, are not in the spirit of the local approach, and raise questions about the precise rationale for area-based initiatives. The wide geographic application of such measures means that the rationale of efficiency and completeness in reaching the poor does not apply, and likewise the justification of using an area-based approach to ration funds to certain areas based on needs or other criteria (such as potential or capacity) is greatly diluted. Conceptually, or in terms of how area-based initiatives are framed, area or neighbourhood effects are not clearly articulated in the rationale for such interventions. Moreover, there has been relatively little research on assessment of the extent of various types of concentration effects (people-derived as well as place-derived) at local area level. In recent years, the contribution to policy innovation has also been relatively weak. Evaluation to establish what works, and to identify the distinctive contribution of area-based interventions to improvements, has been particularly weak. Localisation based on a central role for local government has been absent, a significant point of contrast compared with the UK and wider EU experience of implementing area-based approaches, and a feature that hardly seems likely to allow the full benefits of this approach to be realised.

References

Allen, J. (1998) Europe of the neighbourhoods. In A. Madanipour, G. Cars, and J. Allen (eds) *Social exclusion in European cities* (pp. 25–52). London: Jessica Kingsley.

Andersen, H.S. (2002) Excluded places: the interaction between segregation, urban decay and deprived neighbourhoods. *Housing, Theory & Society*, 19(3), 153–69.

Andersen, H.T. and van Kempen, R. (2003) New trends in urban policies in Europe: Evidence from the Netherlands and Denmark. *Cities*, 20(2), 77–86.

Area Development Management (1995) *Integrated local development handbook*. Dublin: Area Development Management Ltd.

Atkinson, R. (2005) *Neighbourhoods and the impacts of social mix: Crime, tenure diversification and assisted mobility*. London: Housing and Community Research Unit, ESRC Centre for Neighbourhood Research CNR Research Paper No. 29.

Atkinson, R. and Kintrea, K. (2001) Disentangling area effects: Evidence from deprived and non-deprived neighbourhoods. *Urban Studies*, 38(12), 2277–98.

Barnes, J., Belsky, J., Broomfield, K., Dave, S., Frost, M., Melhuish, E., and The National Evaluation of Sure Start Research Team *et al.* (2005) Disadvantaged but different: Variation among deprived communities in relation to child and family well-being. *Journal of Child Psychology and Psychiatry*, 46(9), 952–62.

Cameron, S. and Davoudi, S. (1998) Combating social exclusion. In A. Madanipour, C. Cars, and J. Allen (eds) *Social exclusion in European cities* (pp. 235–52). London: Jessica Kingsley.

Camina, M. and Wood, M. (2009) Parallel lives: Towards a greater understanding of what mixed communities can offer. *Urban Studies*, 46(2), 459–80.

Cappelin, R. (1992) Theories of local endogenous development and international cooperation. In M. Tykklainen (ed.) *Development issues and strategies in the new Europe* (pp. pp. 1–19). Aldershot: Avebury.

Commission of the European Communities (1989) *Guide to the reform of the Community's Structural Funds*. Luxembourg: Office for Official Publications of the European Communities.

d'Albergo, E. (2010) Urban issues in nation-state agendas: a comparison in Western Europe. *Urban Research & Practice*, 3(2), 138–58.

De Souza Briggs, X. (1998) Brown kids in white suburbs: housing mobility and the many faces of social capital. *Housing Policy Debate*, 9(1), 177–221.

De Souza Briggs, X. and Keys, B. (2009) Has exposure to poor neighbourhoods changed in America? Race, risk and housing locations in two decades. *Urban Studies*, 46(2), 429–58.

Department of the Environment, Transport and the Regions (2000) *Regeneration that lasts: A guide to good practice on social housing estates*. London: DETR.

Dietz, R.D. (2002) The estimation of neighborhood effects in the social sciences: An interdisciplinary approach. *Social Science Research*, 31(4), 539–75.

Duffy, B. (2000) *Satisfaction and expectations: attitudes to public services in deprived areas*. London: Centre for Analysis of Social Exclusion (CASE), London School of Economics.

Ellen, I.G. and Turner, M.A. (1997) Does neighbourhood matter? Assessing recent evidence. *Housing Policy Debate*, 8(4), 833–66.

European Urban Knowledge Network (EUKN) (2010) *Urban development in Europe: A survey of national approaches to urban policy in 15 EU Member States*. The Hague: European Urban Knowledge Network, www.eukn.org/E_library/Urban_Policy/New_EUKN_publication_Urban_Development_in_Europe (accessed 8 February 2011).

Galster, G., Andersson, R., Musterd, S., and Kauppinen, T.M. (2008) Does neighborhood income mix affect earnings of adults? New evidence from Sweden. *Journal of Urban Economics*, 63(3), 858–70.

Greene, R. (1991) Poverty concentration measures and the urban underclass. *Economic Geography*, 67(3), 240–52.

Griggs, J., Whitworth, A., Walker, R., McLennan, D., and Noble, M. (2008) *Person- or place-based policies to tackle disadvantage? Not knowing what works*. York: Joseph Rowntree Foundation.

Haase, T. and McKeown, K. (2003) *Developing disadvantaged areas through area-based initiatives*. Dublin: Area Development Management Ltd.

Haase, T. and Pratschke, J. (2008) *New measures of deprivation for the Republic of Ireland*. Dublin: Pobal.

Hall, P. (1997) Regeneration policies for peripheral housing estates: inward and outward-looking approaches. *Urban Studies*, 31(5–6), 401–24.

Hamnett, C. (1994) Social polarisation in global cities. *Urban Studies*, 31(3), 401–24.

Jargowsky, P.A. (1997) *Poverty and place: ghettos, barriers and the American city*. New York: Russell Sage Foundation.

Joseph Rowntree Foundation (2007) *Changing neighbourhoods: The impact of 'light touch' support in 20 communities*. York: Joseph Rowntree Foundation.

Kelly, A. and Teljeur, C. (2007) *The national deprivation index for health and health services research*. Dublin: SAHRU (Small Area Health Research Unit).

Kleinman, M. (1999) There goes the neighbourhood. *New Economy*, 6(4), 188.

Murray, C. (1996) The emerging British underclass. In R. Lister (ed.) *Charles Murray and the underclass: the developing debate* (pp. 23–56). London: Institute for Economic Affairs.

Musterd, S. and Ostendorf, W. (1998) *Urban segregation and the welfare state*. London: Routledge.

National Economic and Social Council (1990) *Strategy for the nineties: Economic stability and structural change, Report No. 89*. Dublin: NESC.

O'Reilly, D. (2007) Comment on Rhodes *et al.* (2005): Some further thoughts on assessing the effects of area-based initiatives on local outcomes. *Urban Studies*, 44(5–6), 1145–53.

Parkinson, M. (1996) Twenty-five years of urban policy in Britain – Partnership, entrepreneurialism or competition? *Public Money and Management*, July–September, 7–14.

— (1998) *Combating social exclusion: Lessons from area-based programmes in Europe*. Bristol: The Policy Press.

Pringle, D.G. (1999) Something old, something new: Lessons to be learnt from previous strategies of positive territorial discrimination. In D. Pringle, J. Walsh, and M. Hennessy (eds) *Poor people, poor places. A geography of poverty and deprivation in Ireland* (pp. 263–78). Dublin: Oak Tree Press.

Putnam, R.D. (2000) *Bowling alone: The collapse and revival of American community*. New York: Touchstone, Simon & Schuster.

Putnam, R., Leonardi, D., and Naretti, R. (1993) *Making democracy work: Civic traditions in modern Italy*. Princeton, NJ: Princeton University Press.

Rhodes, J., Tyler, P., and Brennan, A. (2005) Assessing the effect of area based initiatives on local area outcomes: Some thoughts based on the national evaluation of the Single Regeneration Budget in England. *Urban Studies*, 42(11), 1919–46.

Sabel, C. (1996) *Ireland – Local partnerships and social innovation*. Paris: OECD.

Sassen, S. (2000) *Cities in a world economy,* second edition. Thousand Oaks, CA: Pine Forge Press.

Shucksmith, M. (2000) *Exclusive countryside? Social inclusion and regeneration in rural Britain*. York: Joseph Rowntree Foundation.

Skifter Andersen, H. (2002) Can deprived housing areas be revitalised? Efforts against segregation and neighbourhood decay in Denmark and Europe. *Urban Studies*, 39(4), 767–90.

Townsend, P. (1979) *Poverty in the United Kingdom*. London: Penguin.

Tunstall, R. and Lupton, R. (2003) *Is targeting deprived areas an effective means to reach poor people? An assessment of one rationale for area-based funding programmes*. London: Centre for Analysis of Social Exclusion (CASE), London School of Economics.

Tyler, P. and Brennan, A. (2007) 'Comment on Rhodes *et al.* (2005) – Some further thoughts on assessing the effects of area-based initiatives on local outcomes': A reply. *Urban Studies*, 44(5–6), 1155–59.

Walsh, J. (1999) The role of area-based programmes in tackling poverty. In D. G. Pringle, J. Walsh, and M. Hennessy (eds) *Poor people, poor place: A geography of poverty and deprivation in Ireland* (pp. 279–312). Dublin: Oak Tree Press.

Walsh, J., Craig, S., and McCafferty, D. (1998) *Local partnerships for social inclusion?* Dublin: Oak Tree Press.

Watson, D., Whelan, C. T., Williams, J., and Blackwell, S. (2005) *Mapping poverty: National regional and county patterns*. Dublin: Institute of Public Administration and the Combat Poverty Agency.

Wilson, W.J. (1987) *The truly disadvantaged: The inner city, the underclass and public policy*. Chicago: University Chicago Press.

— (1991) Studying inner-city social dislocations: The challenge of public agenda research. 1990 Presidential Address. *American Sociological Review*, 56(2), 1–14.

6

A NATIONAL-LEVEL VIEW OF AREA-BASED INTERVENTIONS

Michelle Norris

Introduction

Assessing the generosity of the Irish welfare state, particularly in recent years, and comparing its design to welfare systems internationally raises significant challenges (Cousins, 1997). Most comparative studies of welfare states categorise Ireland with other English-speaking countries in the 'residual' or 'Anglo-Saxon' welfare model (e.g. Esping Andersen, 1990; Kautto, 2002). This is because spending on cash transfers, such as social security payments, is low by Western European standards, and remained so during the Celtic Tiger boom, and the social security system is highly targeted by means testing (O'Connor, 2003). However, spending on public services in Ireland exceeds the norm among most of the Anglo-Saxon countries and the methods used for their delivery are more typical of higher spending 'corporatist' welfare states such as Belgium and Germany (National Economic and Social Council, 2005). Due to lack of resources, which necessitated reliance on voluntary effort, coupled with the central role of the Catholic Church as a service provider, the private and particularly the non-profit sector has traditionally played a central role in mainstream social service delivery in Ireland, especially in the fields of education and health. Between the late 1980s and mid-2000s the reliance on non-statutory providers of social services was reinforced by the growing influence of corporatist arrangements for wage determination and economic and social policy making, colloquially termed 'social partnership', which have afforded representatives of the business, trade unions, and non-profit sectors a role in policy making (Taylor, 2005).

Unlike corporatist welfare states, public services and systems of government more broadly in Ireland are also distinguished by their highly centralised nature and the modest role local government plays in policy making and service delivery – a tendency that has intensified as the twentieth century progressed (Callanan, 2003).

Paradoxically, this is paralleled by a long and rich tradition of voluntary local economic and community development and social service provision, particularly in rural areas and disadvantaged urban communities. According to Lee (2003, p. 49) this was historically an 'essentially conservative' movement, focused mainly on self-help, with strong links to the Catholic Church and other powerful institutions. However, from the 1980s this began to change, as the sector radicalised and professionalised. Thus its focus shifted from self-help to social justice and the community development approach, which emphasises the empowerment of poor communities, building capacity, and lobbying for policy reform, became increasingly central to its activities. During the 1980s these 'second generation' community development organisations attracted scant funding from government, and their activities relied mainly on volunteers and participants in various active labour market programmes that provide work experience for the long-term unemployed (Donnelly-Cox and Faffro, 1999). This situation has changed since the early 1990s, as the Irish government and the European Union provided increased funding for area-based interventions (ABIs), additional to mainstream services (Area Development Management, 2000). Much of this investment was channelled through the non-profit sector, which, as a result, became a significant service provider in poor neighbourhoods and also heavily reliant on funding from government (Geoghegan and Powell, 2006).

The area-based interventions have been subject to extensive research and political scrutiny in Ireland and attracted significant international interest (most notably Sabel, 1996). However, this literature has focused mainly on evaluating the effectiveness of individual schemes (see Motherway, 2006 for a review), measuring the influence of disadvantaged communities in their design and implementation (Muir and Rhodes, 2008), and unpicking the politics of their relationship with government (Powell and Geoghegan, 2004). To date, however, no global analysis of the collective scale, significance, and impact of ABIs has been produced. This chapter aims to address this omission and also to relate the development of these measures to that of the broader Irish welfare state.

The analysis of these issues presented here is organised into four further sections. The next section outlines the expansion in the number and scale of ABIs since the early 1990s. The middle section reflects on public investment in these, and suggests that in this regard they constitute a substantial redirection of resources towards disadvantaged neighbourhoods and add spatial targeting of the Irish welfare state onto existing arrangements for targeting according to income and personal characteristics. The closing part of the chapter assesses the impact of the area-based interventions with reference to the three most prominent themes in the literature on good practice in this field: targeting, programme design, and governance. Although these measures have yielded many positive benefits, this analysis suggests that their impact has been less than would be expected considering their scale and the associated public investment. The reasons for this are discussed in the conclusions.

Defining area-based interventions

No standard definition of the concept of area-based interventions is available because there is no tradition in anti-poverty policy in Ireland and internationally of treating these measures as a type of policy instrument that shares common objectives or methods. This lack of a standardised view of these interventions is itself significant, as it reflects the *ad hoc*, piecemeal manner in which they have grown up over the past two decades and the absence of a strategic approach to their role.

For the purposes of the analysis presented in this book, ABIs were taken to consist of publicly funded programmes that were intended (according to their *stated* aims) to combat spatial concentrations of disadvantage and were targeted on neighbourhoods because they were identified as disadvantaged. Programmes of this type can seek to combat disadvantage either directly by targeting services or benefits on the poor who live in poor neighbourhoods or indirectly by encouraging better-off residents or businesses to move into those neighbourhoods, thus improving their socioeconomic profile. Since most mainstream social services are not area-targeted in this way, area-based interventions, for the most part, can be thought of as 'add-ons' to the mainstream system. In addition, however, there is also a category of ABIs that seek to 'bend' the delivery of mainstream services so that they give special attention to poor areas (as identified above). The latter overlap with the mainstream system and do not have quite the same 'add-on' character as the majority of the area-based programmes that emerged in recent decades. Nevertheless, they are counted here as coming within the scope of area-based programmes.

The loose definition just set out did not yield a precise means of drawing boundaries that would clearly mark off a set of programmes as 'area based', largely because programmes varied in the emphasis they placed on spatial targeting. Some defined it as fundamental and clearly specified the areas they aimed to reach. Other programmes did not accord a central role to spatial targeting but merely indicated with varying degrees of emphasis that some priority in allocation of resources would be accorded to deprived areas. In addition, even though some programmes gave a strong role to spatial targeting in their design, when it came to implementation, the targeting criteria were in some cases relaxed so much that delivery of the programmes actually became quite diffuse and embraced large areas of the country. The present study drew a distinction between programmes that, nominally, were strongly targeted in spatial terms and those that were weakly targeted. It must be acknowledged that in some cases this distinction has limited significance in practice since nominal attention to spatial targeting in some programmes turned out to have limited real significance at the implementation stage.

Number and character of area-based interventions

Based on the approach just outlined, Table 6.1 presents a list of the national ABIs that were in operation between 1996 and 2006, classifies them as 'strong' or 'weak' in spatial targeting terms, and identifies the key implementation strategies they employed and the agencies responsible for their implementation.

TABLE 6.1 Remit, implementation, and spatial targeting of area-based interventions, 1990–2006

Intervention	Dates	Remit/objectives	Implementation strategies	Implementation agencies	Spatial targeting
CLÁR (Ceantair Laga Árd-Riachtanais)	2001–ongoing in 2006/7	Concentrate public expenditure on the most disadvantaged rural areas	Planning, grant aid	Local government, voluntary sector	Strong
Community Development Programme	1990–ongoing in 2006/7	Develop a network of community development resource centres	Grant aid	Voluntary sector	Weak
Community Employment and Jobs Initiative	1994–ongoing in 2006/7	Employment experience and training for the long-term unemployed	Grant aid, social security benefits	Public sector, voluntary sector	Weak
Community Services Programme (called the Social Economy Programme until 2006)	2000–ongoing in 2006/7	Support social enterprises to deliver local services and employment opportunities for the disadvantaged	Grant aid	Voluntary sector	Weak
Delivering Equality of Opportunity in Schools (DEIS) – 8 separate measures until 2005	1984–ongoing in 2006/7	Overcome educational disadvantage by additional investment in schools with a disadvantaged student body	Planning, grant aid	Schools	Strong
Dormant Accounts Fund	2001–ongoing in 2006/7	Disburse of unclaimed funds from credit and insurance institutions to alleviate poverty	Grant aid	Local government, voluntary sector	Strong
EOCP (Equal Opportunities Childcare Programme)	2000–2006/7	Provide childcare to enable parents to return to education or employment	Planning, grant aid	Private sector, voluntary sector	Weak
Family and Community Services Resource Centre Programme	1994–ongoing in 2006/6	Combat disadvantage and improve the function of the family unit	Grant aid	Voluntary sector	Weak
Local Government Social Inclusion Units	2001–ongoing in 2006/7	Enable local government to tackle social exclusion	Service provision, grant aid	Local government	Weak

(*Continued*)

TABLE 6.1 (Continued)

Intervention	Dates	Remit/objectives	Implementation strategies	Implementation agencies	Spatial targeting
Local Drugs Task Forces	1997–ongoing in 2006/7	Facilitate community-based response to drug problems	Planning, grant aid	Voluntary sector	Strong
Local Employment Service (LES)	1995–ongoing in 2006/7	Promote employment reintegration of the long-term unemployed	Service provision, grant aid	LES directly, voluntary sector	Strong
National Childcare Investment Programme (NCIP)	2006–ongoing in 2006/7	Improve the supply and quality of early childhood care and education; support disadvantaged families	Planning, grant aid	Private and voluntary sector	Weak
Partnerships and employment pacts	1991–ongoing in 2006/7	Support local economic, employment, and community development projects	Planning, service provision, grant aid	Partnerships directly, voluntary sector	Strong
Programme of Grants for Locally Based Community and Voluntary Organisations	2004–ongoing in 2006/7	Grants to community groups for equipment, education, training, and research	Grant aid	Voluntary sector	Weak
RAPID (Revitalising Areas by Planning, Investment and Development)	2001–ongoing in 2006/7	Concentrate public expenditure on the most disadvantaged urban areas	Planning, grant aid	Local government, voluntary sector	Strong
Remedial Works Scheme	1985–ongoing in 2006/7	Grants for refurbishing run-down social housing estates	Grant aid	Local government	Weak
Rural Renewal Scheme	1998–2006	Promote the development of commercial and residential buildings	Fiscal relief	Private sector	Strong
Special Projects to Assist Disadvantaged Youth	1988–ongoing in 2006/7	Support out-of-school projects for young people	Grant aid	Voluntary sector	Weak
Springboard	1998–ongoing in 2006/7	Provide intensive support for children at risk	Grant aid	Voluntary sector	Weak

Town Renewal Scheme	1998–2006	Promote the development of commercial and residential buildings	Fiscal relief	Private sector	Strong
Urban Project	1996–2006	Improve living standards in disadvantaged neighbourhoods	Service provision and grant aid	Local government, voluntary sector	Strong
Urban Renewal Scheme	1986–2006	Promote the development of commercial and residential buildings	Fiscal relief	Private sector	Strong
Youth Diversion Scheme	2001–ongoing in 2006/7	Divert young people from crime through community programmes	Service provision and grant aid	Police and voluntary sector	Weak
Young Peoples' Facilities and Services Fund	1998–ongoing in 2006/7	Promote the development of commercial and residential buildings	Grant aid	Local government, voluntary sector	Strong

This table highlights a growing proliferation of separate ABIs in the last two decades. In 1990, only five programmes of this type were in operation, but this had expanded to 11 by 1996 and to 24 by 2006. This is due to the establishment of new area-based interventions and the striking longevity of most existing programmes. Despite the fact that most were established for a limited time only, this period was often repeatedly extended and only five ABIs in existence in the 1990s (the EU-funded Urban Project, the Equal Opportunities Childcare Programme, and the Urban, Town and Village, and Rural Renewal Schemes) were discontinued by 2006.

This table indicates that half of the area-based schemes under examination are weakly spatially targeted and most provide grant aid to fund the provision of services by other agencies rather than provide the services directly themselves or take responsibility for strategic planning of other services. In addition, general or multi-purpose rather than single-purpose agencies dominate.

Among the grant-giving agencies listed here, the Community Development Programme (CDP) is the most significant general purpose measure, in terms of number of projects funded. It funds community development resource centres in disadvantaged neighbourhoods that have a community development remit. It is the latest in a series of funding schemes for interventions of this type, which were initiated in the early 1980s, and is currently the principal source of revenue for community development activity in Ireland (Geoghegan and Powell, 2006; Ó'Cinnéide and Walsh, 1990).

Table 6.1 also identifies a large number of single-purpose area-based grant schemes established to fund interventions relating to: family support (Springboard, Family Resource Centres), childcare (Equal Opportunities Childcare Programme, National Childcare Investment Programme), and youth work (Young People's Facilities and Services Fund, Special Projects to Assist Disadvantaged Youth).

The Partnerships are an example of a strategic planning and funding agency working in this field. As their name implies, these are non-statutory agencies, managed by representatives of government, business, and the third sector, which are tasked with devising a multi-dimensional plan to address spatial concentrations of disadvantage, focused on the following: (1) combat long-term unemployment; (2) assist the development of local economic and employment projects, particularly by promoting social economy projects and entrepreneurs within low-income communities; and (3) support more traditional community development projects, particularly for vulnerable groups (Teague, 2006). This remit is implemented principally by providing grant aid to relevant local community-based organisations and also by support for these organizations from Partnership staff. Twelve Partnerships targeting urban neighbourhoods were established initially in 1991, but in 1994 this was expanded to 20 urban Partnerships and 18 Partnerships targeting rural areas (generally known as Leader Partnerships because they also administer the EU-funded Leader Rural Development Programme). Also at this time a further 33 community groups were established to carry out similar work in small towns outside the large concentrations of disadvantage targeted by the Partnerships (Walsh, Craig, and McCafferty, 1998).

Efforts to provide additional funding for mainstream education services in poor neighbourhoods commenced in the 1980s. Over the next decade eight separate programmes to provide pre-school services and grant aid and additional teachers to schools serving a disadvantaged student body were placed. Following a review, from 2005 these were integrated into a single support programme for qualifying schools called Delivering Equality of Opportunity in Schools (DEIS) (Department of Education and Science, 2005).

During the second half of the 1990s a lively debate took place both about the proliferation of area-based interventions and the need for their coordination (National Economic and Social Forum, 1999) and on their lack of representative democratic underpinnings and their relationship with local government (Department of the Environment, 1996). As a result of this debate and a wider programme of local government reform, the links between local authorities and the Partnerships were strengthened and the former were afforded additional responsibilities in relation to planning for local development (via City and County Development Boards). From 2001 some local authorities responsible for areas of high disadvantage were awarded central government grant aid for the establishment of Social Inclusion Units (see Table 6.1).

Also as part of this debate in 1997 an Integrated Services Project (ISP) was established in four pilot areas, tasked with planning for service integration at local level. This function was subsequently incorporated into the mandate of two new area-based measures established in 2001 – RAPID and CLÁR. These are both examples of the relatively small number of strongly spatially targeted area-based interventions established in Ireland during the decade examination, the former targeted disadvantaged urban electoral divisions, the latter targeted the equivalent neighbourhoods in rural areas. In addition to local development planning, these programmes invest a relatively small amount of dedicated funding to improve the physical, social, and community infrastructure of the target areas, but most of their objectives in this regard are achieved indirectly – by ensuring that these areas are prioritised in decisions regarding the allocation of mainstream government funding (Fitzpatrick Associates, 2006).

Unlike most analyses of area-based measures in Ireland, Table 6.1 also includes some active labour market programmes (ALMPs) and the main funding stream for social housing regeneration within this category. The only two ALMPS that provide work placements and training for the long-term unemployed (Jobs Initiative and the Community Employment schemes, commonly known as JI and CE respectively) are included on the grounds that poor neighbourhoods are prioritised in decisions regarding the allocation of resources under these schemes and that they provide a key source of staff for community development and community-based service providers in these neighbourhoods (Geoghegan and Powell, 2006).

The Remedial Works Scheme, which funds the regeneration of social housing estates, is included because this tenure is very strongly correlated with poverty in Ireland (Watson, Whelan, Williams, and Blackwell, 2005). Consequently, this type of investment is an effective mechanism for targeting spatial concentrations of disadvantage.

All of the aforementioned area-based interventions aim to address spatial concentrations of poverty by providing additional direct public investment targeting the poor households resident in these areas. However, the urban, town, and rural renewal schemes operate differently. They provide tax relief to owner-occupiers and private landlords who purchase new or refurbished residential or business premises in designated, declining, urban, and rural areas. Therefore, unlike most other area-based interventions they provide indirect investment (tax revenue forgone) rather than direct grant aid and these reliefs are unlikely to be taken up by disadvantaged households (who may not be eligible to pay tax and may have difficulty securing a mortgage to purchase a qualifying property) (Goodbody Economic Consultants, 2005). Thus, rather than directly improving the circumstances of poor households, these measures address concentrations of poverty by encouraging more high-income residents to live in poor neighbourhoods.

Expenditure on area-based interventions

In seeking to quantify national expenditure on the area-based interventions identified in Table 6.1, it proved possible to deal only with expenditure from central government. A range of sub-national bodies, such as local government (city and county councils), local education agencies (Vocational Education Committees – VECs), and health authorities (sub-national, administrative units of the Health Services Executive – HSE), also contributed significant funding to special area-based services for disadvantaged areas, sometimes through the co-funding of activities also supported by central government and sometimes through separate projects. The range and number of funding heads and forms of support provided by these sub-national bodies were so great and so often tied up with other services and funding programmes that it was not possible to disentangle them in any comprehensive way. Therefore they are not included in the national picture in this section, though they are included as part of the neighbourhood-level analysis of expenditure presented in Chapter 7. The implication of the lack of central-level data on sub-national programmes is that, short of replicating our analysis of the individual neighbourhoods in every disadvantaged neighbourhood in the country, there is no way of arriving at a comprehensive national summing up of the amount of public funding devoted to area-targeted anti-poverty measures in Ireland at present.

What is presented in Table 6.2 is a next-best alternative – an estimate of central government expenditure on area-based interventions in 2006 – but the exclusion of spending by sub-national public agencies is likely to represent a significant undercount of the total spending on ABIs in Ireland. To ensure consistency, these data were assembled from the smallest possible number of published, official sources – in all except four cases (the urban, rural, and town renewal schemes and community employment/jobs initiative programmes being the exceptions) from the finance ministry's *Revised estimates for public services* and the *Annual report* of Pobal, which administers the funding of many ABIs (Government of Ireland, 1998,

2008; Pobal, 2007). Data on the community employment and jobs initiatives programmes were also adjusted to exclude expenditure that would have been incurred by the state had these schemes not existed; 65.9 per cent of the expenditure on these active labour market programmes is accounted for by replacement of the welfare benefits that participants were previously in receipt of, the balance is accounted for by the 10 per cent additional stipend that participants receive plus training costs and overheads. Only the 34.1 per cent of CE and JI expenditure that makes up this add-on element is counted here as part of spending on area-based initiatives. Dormant Accounts Fund expenditure is all channelled through the other programmes listed, therefore to avoid double counting this fund is excluded from the ABI expenditure estimates presented in Table 6.2.

TABLE 6.2   Central government expenditure on area-based interventions, 1996, 2006

	Expenditure in €m (2006 prices)		Type
	1996	*2006*	
Strong spatial targeting			
CLÁR (Ceantair Laga Árd-Riachtanais)		23.0	Capital
DEIS (Delivering Equality of Opportunity in Schools)	11.4	50.8	Current
Local Drugs Task Forces		16.0	Current
Local Employment Service (LES)	6.2	23.2	Current
Partnerships and employment pacts	18.9	47.6	Current
RAPID (Revitalising Areas by Planning, Investment and Development)		4.1	Capital
Rural Renewal Scheme[1]		90.6	Capital
Town Renewal Scheme[1]		24.5	Capital
Urban Renewal Scheme[1]	402.3	256.2	Capital
Urban Project	12.8		Mixed
Young Peoples' Facilities and Services Fund[2]		40.0	Mixed
Sub-total	*451.6*	*576.1*	
Weak spatial targeting			
Community employment and jobs initiative[2]	158.1	124.0	Current
Community Development Programme	8.0	20.2	Current
Community Services Programme		37.1	Current
Equal Opportunities Childcare Programme[3]		40.0	Mixed
Family and Community Services Resource Centre Programme	0.3	30.5	Current
Local authority social inclusion units		1.0	Current
Programme of Grants for Locally Based Community and Voluntary Organisations		3.0	Mixed
National Childcare Investment Programme[3]		3.8	Mixed

(*Continued*)

TABLE 6.2   *(Continued)*

	Expenditure in €m (2006 prices)		Type
	1996	2006	
Remedial Works Scheme	21.0	120.7	Capital
Special Projects to Assist Disadvantaged Youth		3.3	Current
Springboard		2.6[4]	Current
Youth Diversion Programme	2.2	6.7	Current
Sub-total	*189.6*	*392.7*	
Total (strongly + weakly spatially targeted)	*641.2*	*968.8*	
Total as % of total public expenditure on social security	10.6	7.1	
Total as % of GDP	0.8	0.5	

Source: Government of Ireland (1998, 2008), Pobal (2007), Goodbody Economic Consultants (2005), ministries' annual reports, and information provided by ministries

Notes: Expenditure data includes only central government spending and excludes spending by local government and sub-national government agencies.
[1] These schemes did not involve direct government expenditure, but rather tax reliefs and associated tax revenue foregone. As data for tax revenue foregone in 2006 are not available, the estimate here is based on annual average tax revenue foregone between 1999 and 2004.
[2] Total expenditure has been reduced by 65.9% to take account of the value of social security benefits covered by the wages of participants, because this expenditure would have been incurred in the absence of these schemes.
[3] These schemes funded both private (for profit) and community/voluntary (non-profit) childcare facilities. The data here relate only to community/voluntary facilities, as these are more likely to have been targeted on disadvantaged areas.
[4] Refers to expenditure in 2007.

These data indicate that (in constant 2006 prices) these programmes accounted for €641.2 million of central government spending in 1996 and €968.8 million in 2006, an increase of over 50 per cent over the period. However, the increase occurred at a time of rapid growth in both public expenditure as a whole and the wider economy and represented a small *decrease* relative to those benchmarks. The figure for 2006 was equivalent to 7.18 per cent of social security spending and 0.55 per cent of GDP, which represented a decline of about one-third in these ratios compared to 1996. The urban, rural and village, and town renewal schemes, as outlined earlier, are indirect anti-poverty measures in that they do not directly target the poorer segments of the population in poor neighbourhoods but seek rather to incentivise business investment and better-off residential settlement to move into such neighbourhoods. They accounted for 29 per cent of area-based expenditure in 2006. If we excluded these measures and focused on those that were intended to benefit the poor directly, total area-based expenditure falls to €688 million in 2006 and €239 million in 1996. Of this total for 2006, some €393 million was accounted for by programmes that utilised relatively weak spatial targeting criteria and so would be expected to show only limited concentration in deprived areas, while the balance (excluding the tax expenditure programmes represented by Urban Renewal and Village and Town Renewal) amounted to €295 million.

As the target populations for these spending programmes detailed in Table 6.2 varied greatly from programme to programme and in most cases are not precisely quantified, it is not possible to express the expenditure in terms of spending per person or per household of target population. However, an illustrative indication of what the expenditure might entail can be provided by estimating what the expenditure per household would be if it were wholly directed at the most disadvantaged households. If, for illustrative purposes, we excluded the tax expenditure programmes listed in Table 6.2 and focused on the €688 million accounted for by the other programmes in the table, and if we were to assume that this expenditure were concentrated on the 10 per cent of households in the country that were most disadvantaged (approximately 147,000 households), we would arrive at an estimated average spend per household in that category for the year of €4,680, or €90 per week, a not insignificant amount. If we were to limit our attention to the share of that spending accounted for by programmes with strict spatial targeting criteria (i.e. those most likely to be concentrated in the kinds of disadvantaged areas represented by the neighbourhoods in our study), the spend per household in 2006 would fall to €2,009, or €39 per week.

Due to the proliferation of area-based interventions described in the preceding section, investment in 2006 was channelled through many more separate programmes than was the case in 1996. The proportion of this investment derived from EU funding schemes also declined as Ireland's economic status improved. Between 1991 and 1994, 60 per cent of funding for the Partnerships came from the EU, but by 2007 this had fallen to zero (Department of Finance, 1994, 2007). The Equal Opportunities Childcare Programme (EOCP) was co-funded by EU Structural Funds, but its successor the National Childcare Investment Programme (NICP) was not (Pobal, 2007). Table 6.2 highlights a redistribution of area-based investment in favour of weakly spatially targeted measures during the period under examination. Spending on these grew by 207 per cent between 1996 and 2006, whereas spending on strongly spatially targeted measures rose by 27.1 per cent (albeit from a much higher base). In addition, state agencies, particularly local government and education, played a much stronger role in the implementation of ABIs by 2006, whereas in 1996 most of this investment was channelled through the third sector. By the latter year a larger proportion of this investment was linked to service provision (principally of childcare, family support, and addiction services), whereas in the former most of the schemes relevant to this sector funded more general community development activities.

Governance of area-based interventions

The complexity of arrangements for funding ABIs, and the increasing fragmentation of these arrangements over the decade under examination here, clearly raise governance challenges. Concerns in this regard have been raised in a number of reports by government and other commentators over the last decade (most notably: Comptroller and Auditor General, 1996, 1999; National Economic and Social Forum, 1999). These have inspired governance reforms at central and local level.

At central level the Cabinet Social Inclusion Committee has been assigned ultimate responsibility for setting priorities in relation to the area-based measures. Until 2011, responsibility for policy development and programme design was concentrated in one ministry – the Department of Community, Rural and Gaeltacht Affairs – which was established in 2002 for this purpose, and responsibility for the administration of many, but not all, area-based programmes has been transferred to a government agency called Pobal. In 2006 the Department of Community, Rural and Gaeltacht Affairs held responsibility for nine of the 23 area-based measures in operation that year, responsibility for the remainder was distributed among six other ministries, and seven intermediate agencies (if local government is classified as a single agency) played a role in the management of these measures. Whereas Teague (2006) estimates that in 2000 area-based measures were managed by eight ministries and 13 government agencies. Despite these reforms, central responsibility for the area-based programmes remains fragmented and the research evidence indicates that the associated governance challenges are heightened by the lack of cross-ministry agreements regarding the coordination of the area-based measures, the failure to allocate coordination responsibility to any single ministry, and the failure to evaluate the effectiveness of existing coordination structures before new programmes are introduced (NDP/CSF Evaluation Unit, 2003b).

At local level, two significant reforms to the governance of area-based interventions have been introduced in recent years. Between 2003 and 2007 some Partnerships and Community Groups were amalgamated in an effort to reduce the number of service delivery bodies, to ensure that a single body was responsible for delivering these functions in a given geographical area and to improve service coordination (Comptroller and Auditor General, 2007). Second, efforts have been made to integrate local government and the area-based interventions. However, despite ambitious objectives, this process is characterised by false starts and limited meaningful progress. Its origins can be traced to 1994 when County Strategy Groups were established in each of the major local authorities to coordinate the area-based measures. The 1996 white paper on local government reform recommended that these should be developed into Community and Enterprise Groups tasked with promoting coordination between the local government and the area-based measures and also planning for the integration of the two sectors (Department of the Environment, 1996). However, this was overtaken by the publication of the Task Force on the Integration of Local Government and Local Development Systems report (1998), which proposed the establishment of County and City Development Boards tasked with the coordination of all public services at local government level, including the area-based measures. These were set up in 1999 and afforded statutory recognition by the Local Government Act of 2001. The

Task Force on the Integration of Local Government and Local Development Systems (2001) envisaged that the CDBs would implement their mandate by reviewing local service provision and planning for their coordination and that their work would be underpinned by coordination protocols agreed between service providers at the national and local levels.

The available evidence indicates that the local government-related governance reforms have had limited impact. Research on the CDBs, published in 2003, acknowledged that they are efficiently run, they have provided a valuable networking forum and their service coordination strategies fulfil an important planning function. But it concluded that 'they have failed to effect greater co-ordination and integration' of area-based social inclusion measures (NDP/CSF Evaluation Unit, 2003b, p. iv). The lack of robust local-level data on the provision and funding of services, including area-based measures, contributed to this outcome. A far more significant driver was the lack of authority underpinning their coordination function, coupled with the multiplicity of area-based measures, responsible ministries, and government agencies, and the underdevelopment of national-level arrangements for their coordination. In view of these arrangements the report concludes that 'The task that the CDBs ... were set was extremely ambitious and perhaps even unrealistic in some respects' (NDP/CSF Evaluation Unit, 2003b, p. iv). Due to its recent completion, any attempt to assess the impact of the rationalisation of the Local Partnership Companies would be premature, however, the relatively modest scope of this reform merits comment. Its failure to further integrate the Partnerships with the local government runs counter to the thrust of public policy on this issue and the rationale behind the decision not to do so is not clear.

Targeting area-based interventions

The review of the rationales for the establishment of area-based interventions set out in Chapter 5 concludes that efficiency and rationing are central among these. Measures of this type are regarded as the most effective way to ensure that the limited available public resources reach poor households. In addition, there is growing (but still contested) evidence that spatially concentrated poverty has cumulative and qualitatively different effects on individuals, organisations, and infra-structure than less concentrated poverty. These 'area effects' are now increasingly prominent among the arguments in favour of area-based interventions.

In view of the importance of these rationales, the underdevelopment of arrange-ments for targeting area-based investment in Ireland is striking. As mentioned above, among the 24 ABIs under examination here only half are strongly spatially targeted. Furthermore, the targeting mechanisms employed by these 12 programmes have been widely criticised. For instance, although the CLÁR programme has broad local development objectives, target areas are selected solely on the grounds of population decline rather than any other indicators of disadvantage and the Rural Renewal Scheme was targeted using similar criteria. An assessment of the four measures to support disadvantaged primary schools in operation in 2004 raised a number of fundamental criticisms of targeting arrangements, including:

1 different qualifying criteria were used for each scheme, with the result that some schools qualified for some types of support, but not others;
2 some targeting decisions were based on information supplied by principal teachers, which raises concerns about the accuracy of this information; and
3 targeting decisions were rarely reviewed, so schools remained eligible for additional funding, even if their socioeconomic profile improved, while there was no mechanism for including those schools whose profiles deteriorated after initial targeting decisions were reached.

(Comptroller and Auditor General, 2006)

However, these concerns were largely addressed when the various supports for disadvantaged schools were amalgamated into the DEIS scheme in 2005 and were therefore subject to the same targeting criteria (Department of Education and Science, 2005).

By contrast, decisions regarding the spatial focus of the Partnerships were reached using significantly more robust methodology – a multi-variate deprivation measure called the Pobal HP Deprivation Index, which is detailed in Chapter 2 (Haase, 1993; Haase and Pratschke, 2005). More recently this index has also been used to target the Local Employment Service and RAPID.

Despite the technical sophistication of the present version of PHDI, the effectiveness of the targeting it allows for is hampered by the limitations of the underlying data. It examines electoral divisions – the smallest geographical area into which census data can be disaggregated. However, these 3,340 units include varying numbers of residents and their boundaries, which have not been comprehensively updated for decades, no longer reflect contemporary settlement patterns, particularly in urban areas (Haase and Pratschke, 2005). Although this issue has recently been addressed by the relevant authorities, and more robust small-area census data was made available in 2012.

In Table 6.3 the Pobal HP Deprivation Index is used to assess the effectiveness of arrangements for targeting the most strongly spatially targeted ABIs. The data presented here indicate that targeting arrangements are problematic on two grounds. First, a number of the measures examined here target a large proportion of the national population. These include: the urban Partnerships, the operational area of which encompasses 78.4 per cent of the national population, the rural Partnerships (78.4 per cent), and the Local Employment Service (56.9 per cent). Second, analysis of the mean Pobal HP Deprivation Index scores of the ED targeted by these measures indicates that several do not target the most disadvantaged neighbourhoods. A high score in this index indicates low levels of disadvantage, while low and declining (over time) scores point to high and rising disadvantage. These data indicate that the least effectively targeted area measures are: the urban Partnerships (mean score of 9.0 in 2006, compared to 10.4 for the country as a whole and −3.3

TABLE 6.3 Targeting and impact of strongly spatially targeted area-based interventions, 1996–2006

Intervention	Targeting criteria	Share of national population (%)	Mean PHDI score of target neighbourhoods		Change in PHDI score of target neighbourhoods
		2006	1996	2006	1996–2006
CLÁR (Ceantair Laga Árd-Riachtanais)	Severe population decline between 1926 and 1996, averaging 50%	18.1	−0.9	7.0	7.8
DEIS (Delivering Equality of Opportunity in Schools)	Primary schools: % of pupils from large families (5 or more children); who are eligible for free school books and whose parents are unemployed, social housing tenants, lone parents; members of the Traveller community. Second level schools: % of Junior Certificate candidates (exam completed after three years at second level) eligible for free medical care; retention rates after completion of Junior Certificate; Junior Certificate results	Nav	Nav	Nav	Nav
Partnerships and Employment Pacts (urban)	Pobal HP Deprivation Index	74.9	3.4	9.0	5.6
Partnerships and Employment (rural)	Pobal HP Deprivation Index	78.4	6.2	11.4	5.2
Local Drugs Task Forces	Drug treatment data (especially on opiate dependency); police crime statistics; data relating to school attendance/drop-out and data on social and economic disadvantage	17.7	0.1	6.3	6.2
Local Employment Service (LES)	Pobal HP Deprivation Index	56.9	5.9	10.5	4.6
RAPID (Revitalising Areas by Planning, Investment and Development)	Pobal HP Deprivation Index Levels of social housing; designated disadvantaged schools	15.3	−3.8	4.0	7.8

(Continued)

TABLE 6.3 (*Continued*)

Intervention	Targeting criteria	Share of national population (%) 2006	Mean PHDI score of target neighbourhoods 1996	Mean PHDI score of target neighbourhoods 2006	Change in PHDI score of target neighbourhoods 1996–2006
Rural Renewal Scheme	Long-term population and economic decline, lack of urban centres	3.0	0.5	7.2	6.6
Urban Renewal Scheme	Population and economic decline, social problems, dereliction	12.2	–1.3	4.6	6.0
Urban Project	Bidding from 10 most disadvantaged areas	Nav	Nav	Nav	Nav
Village and Town Renewal Scheme	Population and economic decline, social problems, dereliction	5.2	0.4	6.5	6.0
Young Peoples' Facilities and Services Fund	Drugs Task Force target areas and three additional cities and one town	21.9	1.1	6.6	5.5
Comparators					
Ireland as a whole		100	5.2	10.4	5.2
Decile 1 (least disadvantaged)		23.1	21.0	19.7	–1.3
Decile 10 (most disadvantaged)		11.0	–15.2	–3.3	11.9

Note: PHDI means Pobal HP Deprivation Index. The neighbourhoods designated under the area-based measures all refer to 2006, with the exception of: Local Development Partnerships (rural) – 2008 designation; RAPID – 2005 designation and the Urban Renewal Scheme – refers to all neighbourhoods designated under the lifetime of this programme (i.e. 1985–2006). The Dormant Accounts Fund is not included because all of its funding is channelled through other ABIs. The DEIS programme is not included because it targets individual schools rather than entire neighbourhoods for the most disadvantaged decile of the population), the rural Partnerships (mean score of 11.4 in 2006), and the Local Employment Service (10.5).Whereas the most effectively targeted measures are: RAPID (4.0); the Urban Renewal Scheme (4.6), and the Local Drugs Task Force (6.3).

Design of area-based interventions

Most of the area-based interventions under examination have been subject to extensive evaluation and research – indeed significantly more than mainstream public spending programmes. At the same time, as is outlined further below, this evaluation is limited in two important ways: it has generally focused on each programme separately, without any cross-cutting analysis of area-based programmes as a collective, and it has concentrated on examining programme inputs and throughputs (for instance, money spent, clients trained) to the neglect of impact assessment (change in the socioeconomic profile of target areas and the extent to which ABIs contributed to this). Drawing on this literature, it is possible to draw some broad conclusions about the quality of the design of the area-based measures, but as is discussed below, not to definitively assess their effectiveness.

Unsurprisingly, in view of the multiplicity and diversity of the area-based measures in operation, this research indicates that their achievements have been mixed. The early reviews of the Local Drugs Task Forces were negative, however, more recent analysis is much more positive (PA Consulting Group, 1998, 2001; Ruddle, Prizeman, and Jaffro 2000; National Drugs Strategy Team, 2002; Goodbody Economic Consultants, 2006) and research on the Springboard programme, the Community Development Programme, and the Family and Community Services Resource Centres Programme has reached similarly positive conclusions (Family Support Agency, 2007; Motherway, 2006; McKeown, Haase, and Pratschke, 2002). Research on the Partnerships is also largely positive about the impact of their local development planning and the interventions in disadvantaged neighbourhoods that they fund, but is less enthusiastic about their wider role as a form of 'deliberative governance' (Motherway, 2006; Teague, 2006).

By contrast Fitzpatrick Associates' (2006) evaluation of RAPID indicates that its early years were dominated by detailed local development planning, and the target communities were disappointed when the funding provided failed to match the expectations generated. Similarly an evaluation of the Equal Opportunities Childcare Programme (EOCP) attributed disappointing progress in the provision of new childcare places to the lengthy planning required for programme set-up and building capacity among the community sector providers of these services (NDP/CSF Evaluation Unit, 2003a). The extensive literature on the Community Employment Scheme indicates that it has not improved participants' success in accessing mainstream employment (Denny, Harmon, and O'Connell, 2000; Indecon International Economic Consultants, 2002; O'Connell, 2002), although limited evidence on its role in supporting local development activities proffers more positive conclusions (WRC Social and Economic Consultants, 2003).

Research on the early years of the Urban Renewal Scheme found that it achieved very positive results in combating dereliction and increasing the population of target areas but few tangible socioeconomic benefits for existing low-income local residents (KPMG, 1996). However, research on its impact since 2000 and on the Rural Renewal Scheme has reached more negative findings. Although the take up of these incentives was significant, in the context of a property market boom, they were associated with significant deadweight (investment that would have occurred without the incentives) and oversupply of housing (Goodbody Economic Consultants, 2005). The available evidence on social housing regeneration schemes, such as the Remedial Works Scheme, indicate that where the problems of target neighbourhoods relate primarily to the built environment, these interventions have been successful. However, because they only provide capital funding, social landlords face significant difficulties in raising funding for regeneration programmes that aim to address social and economic decline (Treadwell Shine and Norris, 2006).

In terms of the causes of the success or failure of ABIs, four issues are raised repeatedly in the evaluation literature. First, the timeframe for implementation of these measures is significant, as combating complex socioeconomic problems often requires lengthy intervention. On this basis, the longevity of many of the Irish ABIs, highlighted in the preceding discussion, could be regarded as a positive attribute. Second, in view of the importance of longitudinal intervention, the literature highlights the importance of mainstreaming the funding for some projects. However, arrangements of this type are relatively rare in the Irish case. Only the Local Drugs Task Force has well-developed mainstreaming procedures. Most other area-based interventions provide only short-term funding for pilot projects and service providers are forced to reapply for funding repeatedly in order to maintain their service. The third prominent theme in the evaluations of area-based measures relates to the nature of the interventions they provide for. During the early 1990s the bulk of area-based investment was for non-mainstream measures such as community development or 'once-off' interventions such as inner city and social housing estate regeneration. By 2006, however, services such as childcare provision (funded under the EOCP) and environmental improvement (funded by RAPID and CLÁR), which would be regarded as mainstream government responsibilities in most Western European countries, accounted for a significant proportion of area-based investment. This raises a number of important questions, such as: should this investment be mainstreamed and should these services have been provided by mainstream agencies in the first place? Finally, the evaluations of the area-based interventions, and the wider good practice literature on this field, highlight the importance of addressing the particular needs of disadvantaged neighbourhoods, which in turn requires flexibility in programme design. In this regard, many of the area-based measures are problematic because they fund a very restricted range of projects and the decisions regarding their terms and the allocation of this investment are generally made by central government. This tendency is particularly strong in the area-based programmes established since the mid-1990s such as RAPID, CLÁR, and the EOCP, but it is not confined to programmes of this vintage. Teague's (2006,

p. 438) review of the Partnerships highlights 'a fair degree of uniformity across local partnerships in terms of what they do and how they go about doing it'. For this he blames central government, which, he claims, failed to provide 'substantial or sustained support to local stakeholders that would have enabled them to launch genuinely experimental interventions'.

As was alluded to above, despite the huge volume of evaluation research on area-based measures and the very stringent reporting requirements generally imposed on grant beneficiaries (NDP/CSF Evaluation Unit, 2003a), this material does not provide an adequate basis for assessing the effectiveness of programmes. This view is shared by Haase and McKeown (2003, p. 37), who called for 'a fundamental rethinking of the whole monitoring framework', and by Fitzpatrick and Associates (2007), who note that although 2.6 per cent of funding for the Partnerships in the 2000–6 period was allocated to performance monitoring, it was still difficult to identify what had been achieved by this programme. They argue:

> [T]he greatest weakness of the Partnership experiment is lack of ability to state definitively in an evidence-based manner, after 15 years of implementation, what impact they have had as a programme on the communities in which they are established. Evaluators have generally concluded that, while there is no doubt that the areas have developed over time, it is more difficult to demonstrate what the Partnership's distinct contribution has been over and above what might have occurred anyway because of economic growth or other interventions.
>
> *(Fitzpatrick and Associates, 2007, p. 23)*

A fundamental reason for the inadequacy of this body of evaluation literature is because the vast majority of studies examine a single area-based intervention and, to date, no comprehensive cross-cutting analysis of the full suite of these programmes has been produced. Furthermore, the monitoring data refers mainly to pro-gramme throughputs rather than outcomes. Calculating the latter would be difficult to do retrospectively because few projects conducted baseline assessments of social conditions in target neighbourhoods prior to project commencement – an oversight that is regularly criticised in the evaluation literature (for instance: Comptroller and Auditor General, 1996, 1999). Like the external evaluations of area-based measures, ongoing monitoring is also organised separately for each programme, there is no mechanism for collating the results of these processes to assess the collective impact of all of these measures on the target neighbourhoods, and doing so would raise significant challenges because the data generated for different programmes are not generally comparable (NDP/CSF Evaluation Unit, 2003b).

In an effort to assess the impact of the ABIs in a more robust fashion, Table 6.3 details the change in the mean Haase Deprivation Index score of EDs targeted by the strongly spatially targeted programmes of this type between 1996 and 2006. During this decade the mean score of the Irish population as a whole increased by 5.2 – which indicates that social exclusion levels in the country decreased during this period. However, the mean score of the EDs targeted by only five of the ten area-based measures under examination increased by significantly more than this – which indicates that only half of these ABIs had a significant impact in practice. The measures in question are: CLÁR, RAPID; the Local Drugs Task Forces and the Rural, Urban and Village, and Town Renewal Schemes. Notably, the five schemes in this category share a number of key features in common that may have helped to increase their impact. First, Table 6.3 also reveals that these measures were strongly targeted at poor EDs and their operational areas encompass a relatively small proportion of the total national population. Thus the associated investment per household was higher than in the case of less effectively targeted measures. Second, many of the neighbourhoods targeted under these five measures were also targeted by other area-based programmes. For instance, Dublin's inner city was targeted by all of the measures listed in Table 6.3, with the exception of CLÁR and the Rural Renewal Scheme. Thus, the total volume of area-based investment in these areas was significantly above the norm. The particularly strong performance of the Urban and Town Renewal Schemes in decreasing the mean levels of disadvantage in the target neighbourhoods is also striking. As mentioned above the methods employed by these Schemes are distinctive among the ABIs under examination, insofar as they focus on attracting affluent residents to move to poor areas. The data presented in Table 6.3 indicates that this strategy has been succesful but other research on these schemes (KPMG, 1996; Goodbody Economic Consultants, 2005) indicates that this is largely due to 'dilution effects' associated with the entry of new, wealthier residents, as they have yielded few direct benefits for the existing poor population of target areas.

Conclusions

This chapter has examined the collective scale, significance, and impact of area-based interventions in Ireland since the mid-1990s. It has highlighted a marked expansion in the number of these measures over this period. Between 1996 and 2006 expenditure also increased by 51.1 per cent in absolute terms though it fell concurrently as a share of GDP from 0.8 per cent to 0.5 per cent. Although these measures have yielded many positive benefits, analysis of the available evidence on their targeting, design, and governance indicates that their impact has been less than would be expected considering their scale and the associated public investment.

Many of the factors that have lessened the impact of the area-based measures mirror those that have reduced the effectiveness of the broader Irish welfare state and public services. A recent review of the latter by the OECD (2008, p. 12) argues: 'While it has created structures and systems to enable horizontal co-ordination, the [Irish] Public Service remains segmented overall, leading to sub-optimal coherence in policy development, implementation and service delivery'. Similarly an evaluation of arrangements for coordination of ABIs links inefficiencies in this regard to factors 'inherent to the organisation of the public administration system in Ireland such as the vertical nature of departmental organizational cultures and the lack of flexibility to adjust spending programmes to local circumstances' (NDP/CSF Evaluation Unit, 2003b, p. iii). The OECD (2008) report also suggests that the problems associated with the segmentation of the public service have been further reinforced by the absence of meaningful outcome measures and indicators of performance and the dispersal of responsibility for policy making and service provision through a plethora of agencies. The preceding analysis demonstrates that these same factors have undermined the impact of the area-based interventions.

The structural nature of these factors and the limited impact of the minor reforms to the governance of area-based social inclusion measures attempted to date implies that radical reform of the focus and design of the entire ABI programme is required to improve its impact, although, in this process, its more successful elements must be protected. The evidence from the numerous evaluations of ABIs, summarised in this chapter, indicates that funding for the family support, education, and addition services that have been positively evaluated should be continued but arrangements for disbursement of this funding and service planning and policy development at central and local level should be reformed. In particular, the duplication between the local development planning remit of the Partnerships and the City and County Development Boards should be eliminated. A logical method of achieving this would be to assign responsibility for the administration and local-level design of most ABIs to the local government sector, whilst retaining the associated high-level policy-making function at central level. This would eliminate the intermediate layer of bureaucracy in programme administration and help to ensure that programme design is more effectively tailored to meet local needs. Reform of local government funding arrangements is a further logical step in this process. Irish local authorities rely heavily on central government for funding, and, unlike the United Kingdom for instance, decisions regarding its spatial distribution take no account of spatial variations in the distribution of disadvantaged households. If local government funding allocation systems were reformed to take account of the spatial distribution of poverty, funding for area-based anti-poverty measures could be distributed via this route in a far more streamlined fashion than is achieved by the large number of separate funding streams currently employed. This reform programme should also be under-pinned by more robust, comprehensive, and outcomes-orientated performance monitoring arrangements.

References

Area Development Management (2000) *The interface between community development and local development*. Dublin: Area Development Management.

Callanan, M. (2003) The role of local government. In M. Callanan and J. Keogan (eds) *Local government in Ireland: Inside out* (pp. 3–13). Dublin: Institute of Public Administration.

Comptroller and Auditor General (1996) *Report on value for money examination: Regional development measures*. Dublin: Comptroller and Auditor General.

— (1999) *Report on value for money examination: Local development measures*. Dublin: Comptroller and Auditor General.

— (2006) *Report on value for money examination: Department of Education and Science – Educational disadvantage initiatives in the primary sector.* Dublin: Comptroller and Auditor General.

— (2007) *Special report: Improving performance: Public service case studies.* Dublin: Comptroller and Auditor General.

Cousins, M. (1997) Ireland's place in the worlds of welfare capitalism. *European Journal of Social Policy,* 7(3), 223–35.

Denny, K., Harmon, C., and O'Connell, P. (2000) *Investing in people: The labour market impact of human resource interventions funded under the 1994–1999 Community Support Framework in Ireland.* Dublin: Economic and Social Research Institute.

Department of Education and Science (2005) *Moving beyond educational disadvantage: Report of the Educational Disadvantage Committee, 2002–2005.* Dublin: Department of Education and Science.

Department of Finance (1994) *Local Urban and Rural Development O.P. (1994 – 1999) Final report.* Dublin: Department of Finance.

— (2007) *National Development Plan 2007–2013: Transforming Ireland.* Dublin: Stationery Office.

Department of the Environment (1996) *Better local government: A programme for change.* Dublin: Stationery Office.

Donnelly-Cox, G. and Faffro, G. (1999) *The voluntary sector in the Irish Republic: into the twenty-first century.* Coleraine: Centre for Voluntary Action Studies.

Esping-Andersen, G. (1990) *The three worlds of welfare capitalism.* Princeton, NJ: Princeton University Press.

Family Support Agency (2007) *Family and community resource centres programme: resources, activities, partners & achievements, 2007.* Dublin: Family Support Agency.

Fitzpatrick Associates (2006) *Evaluation of the RAPID (Revitalising Areas Through Planning, Investment and Development) programme.* Dublin: Department of Community, Rural and Gaeltacht Affairs.

Fitzpatrick and Associates (2007) *Value-for-money review of the Local Development Social Inclusion Programme 2000–06. Final report.* Dublin: Department of Community, Rural and Gaeltacht Affairs.

Geoghegan, M. and Powell, F. (2006) Community development, partnership governance and dilemmas of professionalization: Profiling and assessing the case of Ireland. *British Journal of Social Work,* 36(4), 845–61.

Goodbody Economic Consultants (2005) *Review of area-based tax incentive renewal schemes.* Dublin: Goodbody Economic Consultants.

— (2006) *Expenditure review of the Local Drugs Task Forces,* Dublin: Goodbody Economic Consultants.

Government of Ireland (1998, 2008) *Revised estimates for public services.* Dublin: Stationery Office.

Haase, T. (1993) *Identifying prospective areas for inclusion in the Local Development Programme.* Dublin: Combat Poverty Agency.

Haase, T. and McKeown, K. (2003) *Developing disadvantaged areas through area-based initiatives.* Dublin: Area Development Management Ltd.

Haase, T. and Pratschke, J. (2005) *Deprivation and its spatial articulation in the Republic of Ireland: New measures of deprivation based on the Census of Population, 1991, 1996 and 2002.* Dublin: Area Development Management.

Indecon International Economic Consultants (2002) *Review of active labour market programmes.* Dublin: Department of Enterprise and Employment.

Kautto, M. (2002) Investing in services in West European welfare states. *Journal of European Social Policy,* 12(1), 53–65.

KPMG (1996) *Study on the Urban Renewal Schemes.* Dublin: Department of the Environment.

Lee, A. (2003) Community development in Ireland. *Community Development Journal,* 38(1), 48–58.

McKeown, K., Haase, T., and Pratschke, J. (2002) *Springboard: promoting family well-being through family support services.* Dublin: Department of Social and Family Affairs.

Motherway, B. (2006) *The role of community development in tackling poverty in Ireland: A literature review for the Combat Poverty Agency*. Dublin: Combat Poverty Agency.

Muir, J. and Rhodes, M.L. (2008) Vision and reality: Community involvement in Irish urban regeneration. *Policy and Politics*, 36(4), 497–520.

National Drugs Strategy Team (2002) *Review of the Local Drugs Task Forces*. Dublin: National Drugs Strategy Team.

National Economic and Social Forum (1999) *Local development issues*. Dublin: National Economic and Social Forum.

National Economic and Social Council (2005) *The developmental welfare state*. Dublin: National Economic and Social Council.

NDP/CSF Evaluation Unit (2003a) *Evaluation of the Equal Opportunities Childcare Programme 2000–2006*. Dublin: NDP/CSF Evaluation Unit.

— (2003b) *Evaluation of social inclusion co-ordination mechanisms*. Dublin: NDP/CSF Evaluation Unit.

Ó'Cinnéide, S. and Walsh, J. (1990) Multiplication and divisions: Trends in community development in Ireland since the 1960s. *Community Development Journal*, 24(4), 326–36.

O'Connell, P.J. (2002) Are they working? Market orientation and the effectiveness of active labour market programmes in Ireland. *European Sociological Review*, 18(1), 65–83.

O'Connor, S. (2003) Welfare state development in the context of European integration and economic convergence: situating Ireland within the European Union context. *Policy and Politics*, 31(3), 387–404.

OECD (2008) *OECD public management reviews: Ireland, 2008 – towards an integrated public service*. Paris: OECD.

PA Consulting Group (1998) *Evaluation of the Drugs Initiative: final report*. Dublin: Department of Tourism, Sport and Recreation.

— (2001) *Operations and management study of the National Drugs Strategy Team and Drugs Strategy Unit*. Dublin: Department of Tourism, Sport and Recreation.

Pobal (2007) *Annual report 2006*, Dublin: Pobal.

Powell, F. and Geoghegan, M. (2004) *The Politics of community development: reclaiming civil society or re-inventing governance*. Dublin: A&A Farmer.

Ruddle, H., Prizeman, G., and Jaffro, G. (2000) *Evaluation of Local Drugs Task Force projects: experiences and perceptions of planning and implementation*. Dublin: Policy Research Centre, National College of Ireland.

Sabel, C. (1996) *Ireland: local partnerships and social innovation*. Paris: OECD.

Task Force on the Integration of Local Government and Local Development Systems (1998) *Task Force on the Integration of Development Systems report*. Dublin: Stationery Office.

— (2001) *Guidelines on the co-ordination of social inclusion measures at local level by CDB social inclusion measures (SIM) working groups*. Dublin: Department of the Environment and Local Government.

Taylor, G. (2005) *Negotiated governance and public policy in Ireland*. Manchester: Manchester University Press.

Teague, P. (2006) Social partnership and local development in Ireland: The limits to deliberation. *British Journal of International Relations*, 44(3), 421–43.

Treadwell Shine, S. and Norris, M. (2006) *Housing policy discussion series: regenerating local authority estates – review of policy and practice*. Dublin: Centre for Housing Research.

Walsh, J., Craig, S., and McCafferty, D. (1998) *Social partnerships for social inclusion?* Dublin: Oak Tree Press.

Watson, D., Whelan, C., Williams, J., and Blackwell, S. (2005) *Mapping poverty: National, regional and county patterns*. Dublin: Combat Poverty Agency.

WRC Social and Economic Consultants (2003) *Evaluation of the Social Economy Programme*. Dublin: WRC Social and Economic Consultants.

7

A NEIGHBOURHOOD-LEVEL VIEW OF AREA-BASED INTERVENTIONS

Des McCafferty and Eileen Humphreys

Introduction

The rapid increase in the number and range of state-funded area-based interventions (ABIs) in recent years has been documented in Chapter 6. These interventions and the associated funding streams are mixed and matched in various ways at local level, as community and voluntary organisations, as well as local statutory bodies, deploy them to tackle poverty and social exclusion. In addition to the national programmes described earlier, neighbourhood-level organisations are able to draw also on a number of localised measures, so that the picture of area-based interventions at the point of delivery is even more complex than at national level. The proliferation of ABIs, differences in the strength of their spatial targeting, and the adoption of different targeting mechanisms for different programmes, together mean that the 'density' of these interventions varies considerably from locality to locality, even amongst the seven neighbourhoods covered in this study. This in turn suggests, *prima facie*, that there are likely to be significant differences across localities in the amount of area-based funding received, and that in certain instances there may be a considerable concentration of support channelled through these mechanisms.

However, in large part because of the complex pattern of area-based interventions, to date there has been no structured attempt to gather and report the information that would allow an assessment of the overall level of funding in particular localities. At the most basic level, we have been unable to answer the question: is it a little or is it a lot? This chapter represents a first attempt to fill this gap in our knowledge of the local significance of ABIs, by examining the detailed pattern of interventions 'on the ground', in four of the case study neighbourhoods with different demographic and socioeconomic profiles. The objectives are, first, to indicate the range and scope of area-based interventions in each of the selected neighbourhoods by compiling an 'inventory of interventions', and, second, to estimate the level of funding channelled into the neighbourhoods via area-based interventions over a specified period of time, in an attempt to get some impression of the overall commitment of financial resources. Third, we identify a number of issues arising with area-based measures, their funding and implementation, at the local level.

As detailed in Chapter 1, the four neighbourhoods selected for this exercise comprise two relatively high-intervention neighbourhoods, Moyross in Limerick and Fatima Mansions in Dublin, and two relatively low-intervention neighbourhoods, Cranmore in Sligo and Deanrock in Cork. All four neighbourhoods have been the subject of regeneration initiatives in recent years, though these vary considerably in scale, sources of funding, and stage of development. The Fatima Mansions regeneration programme, which began in 2004, is the most advanced, and also the most reliant on private funding through a public–private partnership. The Moyross regeneration programme is the most recent, the masterplans for which were launched in October 2008. However, the area has a long history of ABI activity extending back to the EU Poverty 3 programme introduced in 1989. The neighbourhoods also vary in terms of the severity of their problems, and recent development trends. Moyross and Fatima Mansions were among the most distressed of the seven neighbourhoods in 1996, and indeed ranked among the most disadvantaged localities nationally, as indicated by the Pobal HP Deprivation Index (see Chapter 2).[1] Although the latter improved in terms of liveability and disadvantage during the ensuing decade, liveability in the former declined (see Chapter 3). In contrast, Cranmore and Deanrock were among the least disadvantaged neighbourhoods of the seven in 1996. However, whereas Cranmore showed a degree of stabilisation to maintain its position as one of the less problematical of the neighbourhoods, the wider Togher area, containing Deanrock, deteriorated in terms of its score on the PHDI.[2] As well as being the most disadvantaged of the neighbourhoods in 2006, Moyross is also distinguished from the other three neighbourhoods that are of interest in the present chapter by virtue of its considerably larger size. In 2006 it contained an estimated 1,014 households, roughly double the number in the next largest neighbourhood, Cranmore (511). Fatima Mansions, where the re-housing programme was not yet complete, was by far the smallest neighbourhood with just 150 households (see Chapters 1, 2, and 3).

The remainder of the chapter is structured as follows. The next section describes some of the challenges involved in accessing and collating data on area-based interventions at local level, and outlines the protocols and methodology used in order to construct the inventory of interventions for the four neighbourhoods, and to appraise the overall financial commitment. The results of this exercise are then presented, in the form of an overview of the number and range of interventions across the four neighbourhoods, and an inter-neighbourhood comparison of the levels of funding per household. To help interpret these data and form an impression as to the overall significance of the funding involved, we provide a comparison with mainstream social welfare spending. The penultimate section identifies and discusses a number of issues arising from the funding of area-based interventions, and more generally the deployment of these measures in the four neighbourhoods. This discussion is based on information gathered from interviews with representatives of community, voluntary, and statutory organisations active in the neighbourhoods, as well as on insights gained in the course of compiling the data for the inventory of interventions. Some general conclusions are set out in the closing section.

Methodology

The difficulties inherent in the identification of area-based interventions at national level have been outlined in Chapter 6, where a wide-ranging definition was employed, encompassing measures that are relatively weakly targeted spatially, as well as those with a stronger and more explicit focus on designated areas of disadvantage. When we shift our focus to the local level the task of identifying and accurately accounting for area-based interventions is even more complex. This is because, as noted above, not all spending in the four neighbourhoods that comes under the heading of special or area-based interventions is sourced from national funding programmes; some of it may come from local or city-based sources. In addition, the link between national ABIs and local interventions is not always clearly traceable. For instance we came across cases where a statutory body draws funding from a national funding mechanism and channels it through a local voluntary body operating in a neighbourhood, or across a group of neighbourhoods, which in turn combines that funding with monies received from other sources, to deliver a service or range of services to the local community. In such situations, national funding bodies were often unable to provide a detailed geographical breakdown of the final disbursement of funding, a problem that is exacerbated by the absence, in most instances, of an appropriate spatial framework for doing so in terms of the actual neighbourhoods targeted, as opposed to the spatial units employed for administrative purposes.

Because of these difficulties, it was decided to adopt a local, neighbourhood-specific approach to the identification and costing of ABIs in this strand of the research. Instead of attempting to trace each national funding programme through to local level, we followed a bottom-up methodology, by trying to identify all locally based organisations that draw funding through area-based interventions. One consequence of this decision was that, despite our best efforts, it was not possible to adhere rigidly to a common methodology across all four neighbourhoods. The methodology described hereunder was therefore adapted to the needs of each local situation.

Before the local delivery projects could be identified, it was necessary to decide on a working definition of area-based interventions. For consistency with the broadly based approach at national level, we included local projects funded via both strongly and weakly spatially targeted programmes. The most important of the latter group, in terms of the level of spending across all four neighbourhoods, are the community employment projects.

The starting point in building the inventory of interventions for each neighbourhood was the national list of ABIs set out in Chapter 6, on which the local knowledge of team members was brought to bear in order to produce a preliminary list of activities funded through ABIs in the neighbourhood. Next, local directories of services were consulted where available, including those compiled by bodies such as the Partnerships and City/County Development Boards. The lists derived from these sources were then added to, and proofed, using documentary information obtained from some of the larger funding bodies, as well as information collected in field surveys of the neighbourhoods. Interviews with key informants (primarily representatives of community, voluntary, and statutory organisations working in the neighbourhoods) were used as a further means of identifying active and relevant area-based projects in the four neighbourhoods. Based on the wide range of sources consulted, and the cross-checks that we put in place, we are confident that, while we cannot claim to have identified every single area-based initiative or project, we have captured all those that made a significant contribution to the neighbourhoods.

Once the local interventions were identified, information on their activities in the neighbourhoods was requested from them for the calendar year 2006, which, at the time of the fieldwork, was the most recent year for which they were likely to have final accounts. Where full annual accounts were obtained these provided information on both the income and expenditure of the organisation or project. Our preference was to use expenditure data where possible, since this relates more closely to the impact of the project in the neighbourhood than data on income (which might not be fully disbursed in the year in which it is received). However, it did not prove possible to focus exclusively on expenditure, as the required information was not always forthcoming. The need to mix income with expenditure data gave rise to some problems in the collation of the data, and in particular the danger of overstating the level of area-based interventions by double counting expenditure and income data for the same activity. In order to deal with this issue, detailed information was sought from all the local organisations (in particular those that acted as 'umbrella bodies' that employed staff or ran a community employment scheme on behalf of smaller agencies) about their relationships with other bodies, and about what precisely was included in their annual accounts. While this helped avoid double counting, variations across neighbourhoods in the way information on expenditure and resource inputs was attributed to individual projects made it impossible to present a reliable comparison across estates of expenditure data disaggregated by project.

Gaps in the data collected at local level meant that expenditure had to be estimated in a number of instances. The two most important cases where some degree of estimation was required are the community employment/jobs initiative and DEIS schemes. Expenditure under the CE and JI schemes was adjusted (deflated), to exclude the social security payments that would have been incurred in the absence of the schemes (see Chapter 6). For Cranmore, Deanrock, and Fatima this adjustment was based on the national estimate that 34.1 per cent of total expenditure under CE is additional to the imputed social security payments. In the case of Moyross, however, detailed information on CE scheme expenditure was available, on the basis of which the 'net' or additional CE/JI scheme expenditure was calculated at 24.3 per cent of the total. The variation of this figure from the adjustment factor for the other neighbourhoods may be attributed to differences in the nature of the schemes, and to the atypical balance between CE and JI schemes in this neighbourhood.[3] With regard to DEIS expenditure, detailed information was available for Moyross and Deanrock only. Expenditure for Cranmore and Fatima was therefore estimated from the number of children living there and the average expenditure per child in the other two neighbourhoods. It should also be noted that, because none of the four neighbourhoods under examination contained a secondary school, DEIS expenditure was calculated for primary schools only.

A further problem to be overcome in trying to arrive at an accurate picture of the overall level of intervention in the neighbourhoods is that in many cases the operational boundaries of the projects (often only vaguely defined) were not coterminous with the boundaries of the neighbourhoods. Thus, projects based in the four neighbourhoods in some instances dealt with clients from neighbouring areas, and conversely area-based initiatives and services located outside (but close to) the case study neighbourhoods were often availed of by residents of these neighbourhoods. In general the approach adopted was to allocate expenditure by a project to each neighbourhood according to the proportion of total users/clients resident in the neighbourhood. This information was obtained from the projects themselves.

Finally, it should be noted that the neighbourhood-level data collected relate to the current or revenue spending of activities, not to their capital spending. The omission of capital spending is due to the fact that it tends to be rather 'lumpy' and sporadic, occurring sometimes at a very high level in a particular year and then not for a period of several years. We also omitted private and philanthropic expenditure from the comparative analysis since our focus, as in Chapter 6, is on public funding. However, we managed to generate reasonably comprehensive estimates of funding from private and philanthropic sources for Fatima Mansions – the neighbourhood in which it is most significant – and these data are given below.

Area-based interventions in the case-study neighbourhoods

Number and function: The results of the inventory of interventions for the four neighbourhoods are summarised in Table 7.1, and reported at neighbourhood level in Tables 7.2 to 7.5. These tables reveal a wide range of local 'on the ground' interventions, and funding sources associated with them.

The number of ABI-funded services in 2006 is large: 23 in Moyross (including an education bursaries programme), 17 in Fatima Mansions, and 14 in Cranmore. Deanrock is somewhat of an outlier in this regard with only six relevant services in operation in this neighbourhood in 2006. Reflecting differences in the nature of local problems and needs, there was some variation across neighbourhoods in the type of activities present. All neighbourhoods had projects focused on community

TABLE 7.1 Number and funding sources of area-based interventions by estate

Estate	No. of area-based interventions	Average no. of funding sources per project
Cranmore	14	2.6
Deanrock	6	2.0
Fatima Mansions	17	2.1
Moyross	23	2.5
All Four Estates	60	2.4

development as well as on family support and childcare, but concentrations of projects with particular focuses were evident. In the largest and most disadvantaged neighbourhood, Moyross, there was a concentration evident in the areas of youth work and community development (see Table 7.5). Childcare and family support initiatives featured prominently in Cranmore, and adult education and training in Fatima (Tables 7.2 and 7.4 respectively). In the smaller and less disadvantaged Deanrock neighbourhood four of the six projects were focused mainly on children and youth (Table 7.3).

Source and level of funding: The funding sources that neighbourhood-level organisations drew on were also numerous. Twenty-one of the 60 organisations and projects listed drew on three or more sources of funding in 2006 and, on average, projects drew on 2.4 sources of funding across all four neighbourhoods (see Table 7.1). Funding arrangements for area-based services in Cranmore and Moyross appear particularly complex – the average number of funding sources per project was 2.6 in the former and 2.5 in the latter. In both Cranmore and Fatima Mansions a significant proportion of funding for neighbourhood-based services was derived from the neighbourhood regeneration programme, but whereas in Cranmore this was public money channelled through the local authority, in Fatima Mansions the source was the 'community dividend' contributed by the developer who was the private-sector partner in the public–private partnership that implemented the regeneration programme (see Chapter 4). As indicated earlier, this private funding is not included in our estimates of the overall level of publicly funded ABI spending on the neighbourhoods.

All of the voluntary services in the neighbourhoods relied to a considerable degree on Community Employment and Jobs Initiative schemes for staff. In Cranmore, Deanrock, and Moyross, several different community-based services employed staff under these schemes. In Fatima Mansions, a single umbrella body for community-based services (Fatima Groups United) employed all of the CE/JI staff and assigned them to the various community services operating in the area. However, these workers accounted for a smaller share of staffing in community services in Fatima Mansions than in the other neighbourhoods.

Table 7.6 presents our estimates of the level of public revenue expenditure on all area-based interventions in the four neighbourhoods in 2006. This table reveals a

TABLE 7.2 Services funded by area-based interventions in Cranmore, 2006

Service	Function	Vocational Education Committee	Special Projects to Assist Disadvantaged Youth	RAPID	Remedial Words Scheme	Programme of grants for locally based community and voluntary organisations	Private and philanthropic sector	Other statutory source (area based)	Local employment service	Partnership	Local Authority	Health Services Executive	Equal Opportunities Childcare Programme	Dormant Accounts Fund	Delivering Equality of Opportunity in Schools (DEIS)	Community Employment Scheme
Abbey Quarter Community Centre	Youth work, childcare					X		X				X				X
Abbey Quarter Community Employment scheme	Education for adults															X
Cranmore Community Co-op	Community development			X										X		
Cranmore Regeneration Project	Estate regeneration				X						X			X		
Foroige the CRIB	Youth work											X				
Jobs club/Jobs Initiative/Back to Work Enterprise Scheme	Employment								X	X						
Mercy College School	Education for children, sports			X											X	X
North Connacht Youth and Community Services	Youth work		X					X								

Service / Function / Funding programme/agency

Funding programme/agency	Resource House Project (Family support, childcare)	Sligo Family Support Ltd. (Family support, childcare)	Sligo Leader Partnership (Community development, youth work, recreation)	Sligo Sports and Recreation Partnership (Sport and recreation)	Sligo Social Service Council Ltd. (Family support, childcare)	St Anne's/Avalon Centre (Youth work, eldercare)
Vocational Education Committee	X					
Special Projects to Assist Disadvantaged Youth						
RAPID						X
Remedial Words Scheme						
Programme of grants for locally based community and voluntary organisations						
Private and philanthropic sector	X					
Other statutory source (area based)	X				X	
Local employment service						
Partnership	X		X			
Local Authority				X		
Health Services Executive	X	X		X	X	X
Equal Opportunities Childcare Programme	X	X				
Dormant Accounts Fund						
Delivering Equality of Opportunity in Schools (DEIS)						
Community Employment Scheme	X			X	X	X

Table 7.3 Services funded by area-based interventions in Deanrock, 2006

Service	Function	Delivering Equality of Opportunity in Schools (DEIS)	Family and Community Services Resource Centres Programme	Community Employment Scheme	Health Service Executive	Local Drugs Task Force	Ogra Corcai	Other statutory source	Pobal	Vocational Education Committee	Young Peoples' Facilities and Services Fund	Youth Diversion programme
School	Education for children	X										
TACT (Youth Diversion Programme)	Youth work			X								X
Togher Community Centre	Community development			X								
Togher Link Up	Drug misuse					X						
Togher Family Centre	Family support / Childcare		X		X			X	X		X	
Togher Special Youth Project (SPY)	Youth work						X			X		

TABLE 7.4 Services funded by area-based interventions in Fatima Mansions, 2006

Service	Function	Private / philanthropic sector	Other statutory source (area based)	National Childcare Investment Programme	Local Partnership Company	Local Authority	Local Drugs Task Force	Irish Youth Federation	Health Services Executive	Fatima Regeneration Board*	Delivering Equality of Opportunity in Schools (DEIS)	Combat Poverty Agency	Community Employment	Community Development Programme	Client contributions	City of Dublin Youth Services Board	Cityarts	ARK Children's Cultural Centre
Community Employment Scheme	Employment, training for adults												X					
Digital Community Project	Education, training for adults	X								X								
Equality for Women Project	Education, training for adults				X													
Fatima ArkLink	Arts, youth work							X										X
Fatima Children's Day Centre	Childcare	X	X	X											X			
Fatima Groups United	Community development						X		X			X		X				
Fatima Health Initiative	Health promotion						X			X								
Fatima Homework Club	Education for children, childcare		X	X		X					X							

(Continued)

TABLE 7.4 (Continued)

Service	Function	Private/philanthropic sector	Other statutory source (area based)	National Childcare Investment Programme	Local Partnership Company	Local Authority	Local Drugs Task Force	Irish Youth Federation	Health Services Executive	Fatima Regeneration Board*	Delivering Equality of Opportunity in Schools (DEIS)	Combat Poverty Agency	Community Employment	Community Development Programme	Client contributions	City of Dublin Youth Services Board	Cityarts	ARK Children's Cultural Centre
Fatima estate regeneration	Regeneration	X				X												
Fatima Regeneration Board	Regeneration	X				X												
Fatima Youth Initiative	Youth work								X									
Rialto Community Drug Team	Drug misuse						X		X									
Rialto Family Centre	Family support, childcare						X		X									
Rialto Learning Community	Education, training for children																	
Rialto Youth Project outreach project in Fatima	Youth work	X							X							X	X	
Schools	Education for children										X							
Towersongs	Arts, culture					X		X										

Note: *funded by the private sector via the public–private partnership project for the regeneration of the estate

TABLE 7.5 Services funded by area-based interventions in Moyross, 2006

Service	Function	Community Development Programme	Community Employment Scheme	Delivering Equality of Opportunity in Schools (DEIS)	Dept of the Environment	Local Authority	Health Service Executive	Local employment service	Local Partnership Company	Other statutory source (area based)	Other statutory source (non-area based)	National Childcare Investment Programme	Private/philanthropic sector	Vocational Education Committee	Youth Diversion Programme	Young People's Facilities and Services Fund
Adult and community education	Education for adults		X											X		
Barnardos	Family support, childcare		X								X					
Blue Box Creative Learning	Education for children			X			X						X			
Bursaries and Scholarships	Education for adults						X		X				X			
CCYDG/Youth Diversion Project	Youth work, support for ex offenders		X												X	
Céim ar Chéim (probation service)	Training, support for ex offenders									X				X		X

(Continued)

TABLE 7.5 (Continued)

Service	Function	Community Development Programme	Community Employment Scheme	Delivering Equality of Opportunity in Schools (DEIS)	Dept of the Environment	Local Authority	Health Service Executive	Local employment service	Local Partnership Company	Other statutory source (area based)	Other statutory source (non-area based)	National Childcare Investment Programme	Private/philanthropic sector	Vocational Education Committee	Youth Diversion Programme	Young People's Facilities and Services Fund
Community Development Programme	Community development	X	X													
Corpus Christi Parish Community Employment Scheme	Access to employment, training for adults, service provision		X													
Limerick Youth Service Youth Intervention Project	Youthwork		X				X				X			X		X
Moyross Action Centre	Welfare rights, community development								X							

Funding programme/agency

Service	Function	Young People's Facilities and Services Fund	Youth Diversion Programme	Vocational Education Committee	Private/philanthropic sector	National Childcare Investment Programme	Other statutory source (non-area based)	Other statutory source (area based)	Local Partnership Company	Local employment service	Health Service Executive	Local Authority	Dept of the Environment	Delivering Equality of Opportunity in Schools (DEIS)	Community Employment Scheme	Community Development Programme
Moyross Community Development Network	Community development															X
Moyross Community Enterprise Centre	Community development, estate management						X		X		X	X			X	
Moyross Development Company	Community development and enterprise support				X		X									
Moyross Estate Management	Housing management, resident participation, regeneration							X	X			X	X			

(Continued)

TABLE 7.5 (Continued)

Service	Function	Community Development Programme	Community Employment Scheme	Delivering Equality of Opportunity in Schools (DEIS)	Dept of the Environment	Local Authority	Health Service Executive	Local employment service	Local Partnership Company	Other statutory source (area based)	Other statutory source (non-area based)	National Childcare Investment Programme	Private/philanthropic sector	Vocational Education Committee	Youth Diversion Programme	Young People's Facilities and Services Fund
Moyross Integrated Childcare	Childcare, education for children						X		X			X				
Moyross Obair	Assess to employment, training							X								
Moyross Partners*	Coordinating community groups									X						
Northside Learning Hub	Education for children, youth work								X				X			X
Respond! Childcare	Childcare										X		X			

Service	Function	Community Development Programme	Community Employment Scheme	Delivering Equality of Opportunity in Schools (DEIS)	Dept of the Environment	Local Authority	Health Service Executive	Local employment service	Local Partnership Company	Other statutory source (area based)	Other statutory source (non-area based)	National Childcare Investment Programme	Private/philanthropic sector	Vocational Education Committee	Youth Diversion Programme	Young People's Facilities and Services Fund
Respond! Housing Initiative	Housing for vulnerable families				X	X	X				X					
School	Education for children			X					X		X					
Suaimhneas	Homelessness				X		X									
We're OK (Northside youth initiative)	Youthwork								X							X

Funding programme/agency

Note: *received no significant funding in 2006

TABLE 7.6 Current public expenditure on area-based initiatives in four estates, 2006

Estate	Total expenditure (€)	Estimated no of households[1]	Expenditure per household (€)	Expenditure per household as percentage of overall average
Cranmore	1,337,892	511	2,618	84
Deanrock	309,370	336	921	29
Fatima Mansions	536,679	150	3,578	114
Moyross	4,114,042	1,014	4,057	130
All Four Estates	6,297,983	2,011	3,132	100

Note: [1] Because estate boundaries do not correspond to the small areas used for the census of population, and there is no definitive information available from other sources, the number of households had to be locally estimated for each estate

wide range of inter-neighbourhood variation, not just in total spending but also in spending per household, with the latter varying from a low of €921 in Deanrock to a high of €4,057 in Moyross. Deanrock again appears as an outlier in the data, with spending per household that is less than one-third of the average for all four neighbourhoods. The estimates for Fatima Mansions (14 per cent above average) and Cranmore (16 per cent below average) are both closer to the Moyross estimate (30 per cent above average). The results bear out our expectations, in that Moyross and Fatima Mansions were chosen for inclusion in this exercise as two high-intervention neighbourhoods, compared with the relatively low level of intervention in Deanrock and Cranmore. Furthermore, per household spending in Moyross, Fatima Mansions, and Cranmore is in line with the illustrative national expenditure estimates set out in Chapter 6, which are based on the assumption that all spending from national ABI programmes is concentrated on the most disadvantaged 10 per cent of households. However, per household ABI spending in Deanrock is considerably below what would be expected from these national expenditure estimates.

As mentioned above, the table does not include funding supplied to ABIs by private and philanthropic agencies. We estimate that the contribution made by these sources was modest in Cranmore, Deanrock, and Moyross. In the case of Fatima Mansions, however, private funding (from the community dividend paid by the private developer involved in the regeneration PPP) and, to a lesser extent, philanthropic funding, were substantial. We estimate that these sources contributed approximately €4,500 per household in ABI expenditure to that neighbourhood in 2006.

There are several possible explanations for the wide inter-neighbourhood variation in public revenue spending on ABIs. First, variation may be in part the result of differences in the sizes of the neighbourhoods. While the calculation of spending per household facilitates comparison of resource input across neigh-bourhoods by adjusting for the number of households, the effects of size may not be entirely removed by this calculation. This is because larger and more self-contained neighbourhoods, such as Moyross and Cranmore, are more likely to contain area-based interventions within their boundaries. We tried to allow for this in the data collection by taking into account on a *pro rata* basis the spending of projects located outside a neighbourhood if they were availed of to a significant degree by residents of the neighbourhood. However, projects located outside the neighbourhood are more difficult to identify, so the account may be incomplete. Second, in both Cranmore and Deanrock lower ABI expenditure reflected the greater reliance on the community employment scheme for the staffing of projects in these neighbourhoods. In contrast, comparatively more expensive salaried staff was more commonly employed to implement ABIs in Moyross and, particularly, Fatima Mansions.

A third, and more obvious, explanation for differences in ABI spending is that they reflect differences in needs, as measured by the severity of poverty and related social problems. There is some evidence to support this explanation in the fact that Moyross, with the highest level of expenditure per household, was also the most dis-advantaged, not just of these four, but of all seven neighbourhoods in the wider study (see Chapter 2). Thereafter, however, the association between expenditure and need is weak: Deanrock, with by far the lowest level of spending, ranked as the second most disadvantaged area in 2006 and the relative rankings of Fatima Mansions and Cranmore on the HP Deprivation Index (third and fourth respectively) are reversed in terms of spending per household (second and third respectively). How-ever, as noted in Chapter 2, accurate comparisons between neighbourhoods in terms of their relative disadvantage are difficult to make, because of the non-coincidence of neighbourhood boundaries with the spatial units for which disadvan-tage is measured. As a consequence, we lack the kind of data that would enable us to properly assess the relationship between spending and needs.

A fourth possible explanation is that variations in ABI activities across the neighbourhoods derive from differences in the local capacity to access and attract funding. This capacity depends to a great extent on the density and quality of local community and voluntary organisations. The relatively high levels of spending in both Moyross and Fatima Mansions may well be explained by this factor, at least in part, as both neighbourhoods have notably strong community development infrastructures (see Chapter 3).

Leaving aside the issue of inter-neighbourhood variation in spending levels, a more fundamental question is: how should we regard the overall level of spending on area-based interventions, amounting to €3,132 per household on average across the four neighbourhoods? In terms of the query raised in the introduction: is it a little or is it a lot? In order to help answer this we can use as a benchmark data related to spending on mainstream social security benefits. This information was generated as part of an analysis of the 2004 rent assessment records of Limerick City Council (McCafferty and Canny, 2005), which indicated that social security payments in 2004 to tenants in local authority rented housing in Moyross amounted to €7,204,604. The estimated €4,114,042 spent on area-based interventions in 2006 therefore amounted to 57 per cent of social security payments (including insurance-based benefits, means-tested benefits, and universal benefits such as child benefit). Inflating the latter forward to 2006 in line with increases in social welfare rates would obviously reduce this proportion, as would grossing up the social security expenditure to account for tenant households for whom information was unavailable in the 2004 study, as well as non-tenant households (owner occupiers and those in the process of purchasing their homes via the local authority tenant purchase scheme) albeit that the latter are likely to depend less on benefits as compared to tenant households. We can improve the accuracy of the comparison to some extent by comparing expenditure levels on a per household basis. This reveals that spending per household under area-based initiatives in Moyross in 2006 (€4,057) had a value equivalent to 47 per cent of social security transfers per household (€8,618) in 2004.

Issues with the funding of area-based interventions at neighbourhood level

The analysis set out above has provided some insights into the overall level of funding through area-based initiatives on four of the seven neighbourhoods in our study, as well as into the range and complexity of such interventions. The complexity of the funding environment also emerged prominently in the key informant interviews; indeed in general it was commented on more than the overall level of funding. This section summarises some of the main issues in relation to funding and related matters as they arose in these interviews, beginning with the issue of complexity.

The complexity of funding arrangements: The representatives of the local organisations engaged in promoting and managing interventions on the ground identified both advantages and disadvantages arising from complexity in funding arrangements. One of the perceived advantages is that the need to fund local projects from multiple sources (often a mix of local, regional, and national funding programmes) requires working in partnership and a lot of networking, which in turn helps bring cohesion and integration to the delivery of local services. Thus, one interviewee (voluntary organisation) commented 'good inter-agency cooperation is vital to the work of [named organisation]'. It can also promote certain efficiencies in organisational roles and service delivery. This is evident in the way that organisations like the Partnerships increasingly operate at a more strategic level, tapping into local knowledge and evidence to target the funding effectively, and providing information and support services to more localised organisations. In this vein, a representative of a small local ABI in one of the case study neighbourhoods told us:

> The [named Partnership] operates a number of development programmes . . . [with] funding provided through the Exchequer and the EU. The [named

Partnership] adapts the funding to the local needs. They are well-placed to do this as they understand the local groups, and have the baseline information and statistics to ensure that the funding is appropriate.

In some areas, the establishment of regeneration programmes based on new structures has brought 'cohesion of services within the area'. For instance, one service provider (voluntary sector) commented:

> [P]rior to the regeneration many people felt there was a dearth of funding in [named area] coupled with a lack of services, but an audit of services in the area showed that there was a good deal of funding and service delivery ... the process acted as a catalyst for cohesion for these services ... there is room for further cohesion.

The demands of funding arrangements are also seen to have resulted in improved local organisational capacity, and funding relationships that are better structured in terms of formal contracts that link service delivery to funding:

> 'In recent years there has been growing recognition of the competence of [named organisation] by the major funding bodies, and there is now better, more structured, engagement with the funders, involving service level agreements etc.'

Another significant advantage of the funding environment for local initiatives, as identified by respondents, is the transfer of good practice to local organisations. This can result in improvements in the quality of services provided to clients, and in the overall level of performance. Examples here include requirements to have policies on health and safety and child protection in place in local organisations in order to qualify for funding support, requirements for staff engaged in service delivery to be appropriately qualified, and the need to have policies on confidentiality and informed consent for those accessing support services:

> Because [named organisation] works very closely with the social work service of the HSE. ... It has a strict policy of not sharing information without the permission of the family ... Some agencies don't always report to social workers because of lack of response ... and perhaps for fear of losing the engagement of families. However, [the named organisation's] experience is that families won't stop engaging provided an up-front, honest approach is adopted.

The perceived disadvantages of complexity in the funding environment relate primarily to the administrative burden of preparing funding applications and meeting accountability requirements (reporting and monitoring), and the fact that organisations lacking the necessary capacity are effectively excluded. For instance, a manager of one voluntary sector agency commented:

> 'To sustain its activities [named organisation] has to put together a patchwork quilt of funding from different agencies. There are different application procedures for each agency, and different reporting schedules and requirements'.

A representative of another relatively large-scale voluntary organisation noted that, whereas in the past the organisation received most of its funding from EU sources, it now receives support from multiple sources, such as the Office of the Minister for Children and Youth Affairs, the Department of the Environment, Heritage and Local Government, the local council, and the local regeneration project. This interviewee describes the funding process as a 'maze' with 'no system of uniformity in application and reporting requirements', while the bureaucracy attached to the funding process is seen as tedious and increasingly complex. It was noted that separate financial reports are required for their own organisation, the revenue commissioners, and all the individual funders.

Even with the support of intermediaries such as the Partnerships, some smaller-scale neighbourhood-based organisations reported that they cannot successfully manage the administrative side of funding applications and monitoring and reporting requirements, and some have faced difficulties linked to their lack of capacity (e.g., interruption of project delivery, and inability to pay staff because of cash flow problems). A small voluntary organisation operating projects targeted at vulnerable young people referred to 'haphazard' funding arrangements and difficulties it had encountered with cash flow and deficits in its accounts. These problems were eventually resolved by a larger scale organisation taking on the contractual and financial management aspects of a group of projects (as described above):

> 'So ... just in the last year they negotiated with a youth organisation ... to take over the project ... and since then the funding, I presume, still comes through the justice department, but ... goes to a bigger organisation and then they pay for everything'.

The fact that some sources of funding are not managed directly by the organisations responsible for implementing the interventions further amplifies the complexity of funding arrangements and adds to the difficulty of accurately accounting for spending under specific ABIs.

Lack of clarity and certainty: A general problem identified by interviewees in programmes like RAPID, and even the newest wave of neighbourhood regeneration programmes, is that local actors do not know what funding is actually available for the local plan. This is because these initiatives are not structured as programmatic interventions that have dedicated funding available, but rather as funding access and coordination mechanisms, drawing on existing national public spending programmes. Therefore, local groups cannot be confident that the funds are actually available to their area for plan implementation. This lack of clarity can be problematic, and the issue becomes highly politicised in local environments, negatively affecting inter-organisational cooperation and relationships with residents in neighbourhoods. Often residents do not understand how the system works, and when expected monies do not flow, local organisations can be heavily criticised, sometimes unfairly.

The lack of clarity was mentioned in particular in relation to the RAPID programme. According to our interviewees, the scope of RAPID is often articulated in such a way that it is unclear whether there are dedicated funds available through the programme, and, if so, what amounts of funds are involved. Methods of accessing funds for local action are complex and uncertain:

> [T]here isn't really any funding [associated with RAPID]. ... It can vary every year. You might get €300,000 one year, you might get €200,000 the next year ... we have ... a scheme which is around estate enhancement and ... a lot of that comes from the Department of the Environment, and ... that is basically once every two years, I think, and it is around things like traffic calming.... RAPID itself does not have a budget ... the idea ... is that the [statutory] agencies should be prioritising RAPID within their own budget ... sometimes that happens and sometimes it doesn't ... it is very difficult.

Bias towards capital as opposed to revenue funding: Several key informants identified what they considered to be a bias towards capital as opposed to revenue funding in ABIs. Local organisations perceive this bias in the unwillingness of state agencies to agree recurrent or revenue funding, which is less easy to 'contain' than one-off capital funding. This unwillingness creates uncertainty regarding the continuity of local projects and service provision, and a need to continuously 'chase' funding (which diverts time and energy from core activities). A further problem concerns staff contracts of employment, especially in ABIs where, although funding is not formally time-limited, there is no guarantee it will continue. In these situations it is not possible to offer permanent employment contracts to staff and, during the Celtic Tiger boom, when alternative employment opportunities were plentiful, this resulted in a high turnover of staff in some areas, and a loss of experienced, highly trained, and skilled staff. This is a significant problem because it tends to be people-based services rather than buildings that are needed most in disadvantaged neighbourhoods, and they are needed on an ongoing basis.

A further aspect of the bias towards capital funding is that the benefits of expenditures on the management of construction projects and related services (design, engineering, fitting) generally leak from disadvantaged areas, since professional staff employed in service provision typically do not live in the neighbourhoods. Indeed it is often the case that employment even in basic construction work does not benefit local people. Moreover, while the types of facility that are provided through capital investment projects (e.g., housing improvements and community infrastructure such as community centres and crèches) are needed, they do not support the development of private/commercial services that are typically needed to generate local employment opportunities and to retain expenditure of local income within the areas.

Rigidity in the rules of funding programmes: Among the key actors involved in the implementation of ABIs in the case study neighbourhoods there is a strong perception that the rules of the national funding programmes for ABIs are often both too narrow, and applied in an excessively rigid, inflexible manner. In some cases, local organisations report difficulties in trying to get projects to 'fit' with objectives specified nationally, and with reporting frameworks that, sometimes, do not reflect what they are actually trying to achieve. In other words, programme objectives are not necessarily responding well to local need.

Rules and requirements of funding programmes are also seen to place new demands on small, often poorly resourced, organisations, resulting in the exclusion of certain types of individuals from involvement with the organisations. One interviewee in a youth organisation referred to the many changes to relevant regulations, particularly in the area of child protection, and their effects on youth services. While the need for guidelines is acknowledged, the interviewee highlighted a 'downside' in the strain these have placed on voluntary sector services, where the traditional involvement of volunteers in service is becoming increasingly difficult to maintain due to the necessity to implement the guidelines. For instance, the system for Garda clearance involves a lengthy process, and excludes many with previous offences, even if these offences were committed in the distant past and would appear to bear little relevance to an individual's suitability for the current situation. While Garda clearance is acknowledged as extremely important, it excludes people or 'writes them off'.

Proliferation and duplication of interventions: The preceding discussion noted the gains that arise from local organisations drawing together supports from several different sources or funding bodies. Local projects acting in this way are often the primary means of achieving integration across national or regional/local funding programmes in areas such as health, education, and housing. However, the key informants also identified a proliferation of projects, and of ABI funding programmes to support them, as a problem resulting in the duplication of effort between different local projects. Such duplication can occur even when the projects operate under the umbrella of a single organisation.

> On access funding ... we have been contracted by a number of agencies to provide ... projects and services in the [named] area ... they all tend to come under the name of [named organisation] but technically they are separate stand alone projects. As a result ... we have a youth information centre which is funded through the Department of Education and Science, we have five Garda Youth Diversion Projects ... we have the local drugs task force funded project ... one of the cafés ... is funded through the Crisis Pregnancy Agency and one of the cafés is funded through the ... local drugs task force. I am

trying to remember all the different projects. We have a project that is another local drugs task force funded project. And so you can see our funding comes from a range of different sources. And then within [named area] there is up to 14 different services and projects all under the banner of [named organisation].

Often the problem of duplication arises between single-purpose, stand-alone initiatives focused on specific target groups. For example, in one of the case study neighbourhoods there were three different projects with a stated remit of dealing with 'children at risk', all of which engaged in similar work, often with the same clients. As reported by a representative of one of the organisations involved:

> There is little cooperation or day-to-day contact between the agencies [named agencies working in the same field], and no formal sharing of information about the children and families they are working with. When one learns of the other's activities it tends to be by accident.

Another informant reported that:

> There are good relations with the [named project] ... the [organisation] manager sits on the board of the [named project] ... and manages three of the other [similar projects] in the city ... However, cooperation between agencies is more problematical at the operational level with, for example, a considerable area of overlap and waste on the ground, which often results in hitting the same [clients] twice.

The key actor interviews highlight a lack of decision-making power on the part of agency personnel involved in partnerships and a similar lack of local autonomy in the regional/local structures of mainstream funding agencies as reasons for the perceived duplication of activities, because these deficits militate against integrated working on the ground. For instance, one service provider in a voluntary organisation commented:

> I don't really know whether cooperation has improved. People working for organisations in the community have a very tight remit. Most of them working in structures with other agencies have seniors to answer to, and can't make decisions about things.

Importance of active labour market programmes to ABI implementation: The process of preparing the inventory of actions and accounting for total ABI expenditure highlighted the importance of community employment (CE) and to a lesser extent job initiative (JI) schemes. They account for a significant proportion of area-based local spending that, in turn, underscores their significance for the viability of local projects, as well as their importance to the delivery of local services. Several service providers in the voluntary sector stressed the importance of CE, with one large voluntary organisation drawing attention to the role of 'the large and vital CE scheme', which provides 24 workers in five areas: security, housekeeping, driving, reception, and childcare. A voluntary organisation in one of the neighbourhoods mentioned that, over the years, the training element of the CE programme had become more sophisticated, with accredited courses in childcare, computers, health and safety, first aid, and manual handling being provided to participants. Some interviewees from the ABIs based in the case study neighbourhoods highlighted how CE schemes had evolved over time to create capacity and new projects and services:

> [W]e inherited the Community Employment project and I suppose my analysis at the time was you build slow and you build up. ... [T]he Community Employment project became a kind of vehicle for ... residents' training and ... participation through education ... community development training ... meetings ... and the arts ... because some interested parties that got involved ... who had an arts background ... we attracted people in who were very committed people ... very creative and very strong willed ... then the project began to roll itself out.

Nominally, both CE and JI are active labour market programmes (ALMPs), that is, a means to support the long-term unemployed and lone parents to gain skills, develop networks relating to employment, and make the transition back into the mainstream labour market. Evaluations of CE have shown that it has not been effective in these terms, even at times of buoyant demand in the labour market (e.g., Indecon International Economic Consultants, 2002; O'Connell, 2002). As a result, calls have been made for it to be scaled back or abolished, and it has been argued that the numbers employed on CE schemes should have fallen to low levels when overall employment growth was strong in the first half of the 2000s (Grubb *et al.*, 2009). However, in times of recession the case for CE-type employment schemes becomes stronger, and they can be viewed as a useful means to add value to the social protection system. With a modest additional expenditure over and above that which clients would receive in any event as benefit recipients, they provide two significant social benefits: first, they give a valuable role in their communities to CE workers, many of whom otherwise would be marginalised and economically inactive; and, second, they help sustain valuable social services and community organisations in disadvantaged areas. Viewed in these terms, the justification for these schemes becomes stronger, and there is a strong case that the terms under which they are evaluated should not be restricted to considerations that arise under ALMPs in the strict sense.

Conclusions

Despite the increasing number, scale, and scope of area-based interventions in Ireland there has remained a considerable information deficit in relation to their local impact. This chapter has attempted to redress this deficit by assembling and costing an inventory of interventions for four of the seven case-study neighbourhoods that are the focus of this book. Our research in the neighbourhoods of Cranmore, Deanrock, Fatima Mansions, and Moyross has highlighted the wide range and variety of local projects that can be regarded as area-based interventions. These ABIs are located in public policy areas ranging across health, education and training, employment support, childcare, youth work, family support, drugs treatment and prevention, housing, and community development. Both the number and the types of initiatives vary across the neighbourhoods, reflecting differences in the social composition of neighbourhoods and their needs. However, a notable feature is the large number of projects with a focus on issues where the area-based approach represents a relatively recent policy development, such as 'at-risk' youth and multi-problem families. These are now comparable both in number and in scale to projects in traditional, more established domains of area-based activity, such as employment support and community development. In part, this trend may reflect the time at which the exercise was undertaken – after a sustained period of economic growth and falling unemployment. In part too, though, it reflects the increasing incidence of social pathologies in disadvantaged areas.

The research reveals that government expenditure in 2006 on area-based initiatives averaged over €3,000 per household across the four neighbourhoods under examination in this chapter. While this level of funding is certainly not insignificant, nevertheless it is put in context by the fact that it represents less than half of social security benefit expenditure per household in the neighbourhood with the highest level of spending. Perhaps more significant than the overall level of ABI funding is the marked variation in the funding received by the different neighbourhoods under examination, with the spending per household ranging from over 70 per cent below the average to 30 per cent above it. Given the differences in the nature and severity of problems faced in the neighbourhoods, variation in funding levels is to be expected, but we do not have the kind of data needed to establish whether there is a close relationship between resource input and level of need. While there is some evidence that spending is related to need, it would appear that need alone does not fully explain the variation in expenditure. Among the other explanatory factors, the most likely candidate is variation in the capacity of neighbourhoods to access and to effectively deploy funding. This points to the importance of high quality, locally based organisations that are well administered and well connected to funding agencies and programmes, and ultimately serves to emphasise the continuing importance of community development.

The importance of local capacity has increased in recent years in line with an increase in the complexity of the funding environment. One aspect of this is that three-quarters of local projects are funded through more than one source, and almost one-third draw their support from three or more sources. A second aspect is the increasing emphasis placed on value for money and accountability in the use of public funds, which has led to more onerous requirements in applying for funding, and in ongoing monitoring and reporting of expenditure. Together with increased regulation (in areas such as child protection) the complexity of the funding environment has increased the burden of administration for local activities. This was a prominent concern of the key informants we spoke to, who highlighted the waste of resources in administrative work. Indeed this issue generated more adverse comment than, for example, the amount of funding available, as did a number of other issues such as lack of certainty about monies available, and about the long-term funding base for projects, inflexibility in the rules governing the eligibility of activities for funding, and the duplication of initiatives. In general it would appear that, at the time our analysis was undertaken, concern about the resourcing of area-based initiatives had been replaced by concern about inefficiencies in the design, management, and administration of funding programmes.

Finally, one of the most significant findings arising from the exercise described here is the difficulty in carrying it out. The attempt to build a comprehensive picture of area-based initiatives encountered major problems in acquiring the necessary data. At national level, bodies such as government departments were unable to provide a breakdown of area-based spending at a sufficient level of detail as to permit the data to be collated for the neighbourhoods. At local level, projects were often unable to identify the ultimate source of funding channelled through intermediary organisations. If the focus of area-based measures is to improve the position of communities suffering particularly acute social problems then it is vital that they work together, and be monitored and evaluated not individually but on an area-wide basis. At present the information to do this is not available, and nor is the institutional framework.

Notes

1 As indicated in Chapter 2, these comparisons are affected by differences in the degree to which the boundaries of the electoral division reflected those of the individual neighbourhoods.
2 However, as noted in Chapter 3, this deterioration was not reflected in the picture emerging from the interviews conducted in Deanrock.
3 JI scheme expenditure in Moyross is more significant than on the other estates, and expenditure on the non-wage elements under this scheme is significantly less in proportionate terms than under CE.

References

Grubb, D., Singh, S., and Tergeist, P. (2009) *Activation policies in Ireland*. Paris: OECD Publishing, OECD Social, Employment and Migration Working Papers, No. 75.
Indecon International Economic Consultants (2002) *Review of active labour market programmes*. Dublin: Department of Enterprise and Employment.
McCafferty, D. and Canny, A. (2005) *Public housing in Limerick city: A profile of tenants and estates*. Limerick: Limerick City Council.
O'Connell, P. (2002) Are they working? Market orientation and the effectiveness of active labour market programmes in Ireland. *European Sociological Review*, 18(1), 65–83.

8

DRUG USE, DRUG MARKETS, AND AREA-BASED POLICY RESPONSES

Aileen O'Gorman

Introduction

In the decade since the first phase of our fieldwork was conducted, patterns and trends in drug use have changed substantially in Ireland. Here, as elsewhere, the consumption of an assortment of licit and illicit substances has become *normalised* and embedded into the social and cultural practices of many different social groups (Parker, Aldridge, and Measham, 1998; Measham, Aldridge, and Parker, 2001; Parker, Williams, and Aldridge, 2002). Drug use is now much less the covert sub-cultural practice it was in the 1980s and 1990s, and the (typically combined) use of alcohol, cannabis, cocaine, and amphetamine-type substances (ATS such as: amphetamine/'speed', methamphetamine, MDMA/ecstasy, etc.) has become a regular feature of weekend and festive socialising among many social groups in Ireland.

At the time of our 2007–9 fieldwork, a national drug prevalence survey reported that one in four (24 per cent) of the Irish population had ever used an illegal drug (National Advisory Committee on Drugs and Drug and Alcohol Information and Research Unit, 2008). The vast majority of these were cannabis users (22 per cent), with a significantly smaller level of ecstasy and cocaine users (between 5 and 6 per cent each). Cocaine use had increased significantly in the 2000s to the extent that Ireland had one of the highest rates of use within the EU by the middle of this decade (European Monitoring Centre for Drugs and Drug Addiction, 2004, 2008), and rates of heroin use had also risen, most notably outside of the Dublin region, where use of this drug had not previously been prevalent (Kelly, Carvalho, and Teljeur, 2009).

Public discourse on 'drug use' invariably revolves around illegal drug use, though our consumption of legal drugs is far higher, and arguably more harmful (see Nutt, King, and Phillips, 2010). Almost three-quarters of the Irish population

(73 per cent) report being current drinkers, i.e. had taken alcohol in the previous 30 days (National Advisory Committee on Drugs and Drug and Alcohol Information and Research Unit, 2008). Irish people consume more alcohol per capita than almost all of their European counterparts, and 54 per cent of the Irish population binge drink (drink six or more standard drinks in any drinking occasion) at least once weekly compared to 28 per cent of all Europeans (TNS Opinion and Social, 2007). In addition, other legal drugs such as prescription and over-the-counter medications are widely taken in quantities and/or for purposes other than for what they were prescribed (O'Gorman, Doyle, and Crean, 2007).

These macro-level prevalence rates, however, capture drug use as a rather atomised and individualised undertaking and do not reflect the complex and situated nature of drug-using behaviour, or the extent of drug use and drug-related harms at a community level, which is the key issue under discussion here. Epidemiological studies of drug use illustrate a distinct socio-spatial concentration of drug-related problems in marginalised communities where residents experience an unequal burden of multiple and interconnected deprivations such as poverty, unemployment, early school leaving, homelessness, and social exclusion (Buchanan, 2006; Foster, 2000; O'Gorman, 2005). These life experiences have been identified in the drugs research literature as risk factors for 'problem drug use' (namely dependent levels of use, ill-health, criminalisation, and fractured family and community relations) as distinct from 'drug use' (Advisory Council on the Misuse of Drugs, 1998; Fountain, 2006; Health Advisory Service, 2001; Lloyd, 1998). When these risk factors cluster spatially, and are situated in their structural and policy contexts, a 'risk environment' that facilitates the development of community drug problems is observed (O'Gorman, 2005; Rhodes, 2002). As with many social phenomenon – space matters (Massey, 1995). So too, as we shall see, does 'structure' in terms of the opportunities, constraints, and policy contexts that shape people's life experiences, including their drug-using behaviour.

This chapter traces continuity and change in drug use, drug markets, and drug-related concerns on the seven neighbourhoods over the past decade, and situates this analysis within the broader socioeconomic and risk environment contexts. It examines the impact and challenges drug use poses at a community level, and documents and assesses the policy responses implemented locally and nationally.

Recalling drug trends in the case-study neighbourhoods in 1997–8

In the mid-1990s, epidemic levels of heroin use had been identified among young people in many of Dublin's marginalised, inner-city, and suburban social housing neighbourhoods. In the communities most affected, residents shared a common history of structural exclusion manifest in long-term unemployment, poverty, educational disadvantage, and a large population of young people with limited social, economic, and recreational opportunities (O'Gorman, 1998; O'Higgins 1999). The first phase of fieldwork on the seven case-study neighbourhoods in

1997–8 revealed that several were classic risk environments for problem drug use. However, not all of the areas were equally affected as drug markets, and the consequent availability and accessibility of drugs had not penetrated many areas outside of Dublin at that time.

In two of the Dublin neighbourhoods – Fatima Mansions and Fettercairn – the 1997–8 fieldwork found that the public sale and use of heroin, and the accompanying health and social order concerns, had impacted detrimentally on everyday life in the neighbourhoods. Of these two neighbourhoods, Fatima Mansions was then the most severely affected by the sale and use of drugs. What Natarajan and Hough (2000) term an 'open' drugs market (i.e. one open to any buyer, without need for a prior introduction to the seller) was in operation at that time. This market attracted users and dealers from around the city and drew many young people living in the flats complex and the neighbouring community into the drugs economy. Adult and young residents in the neighbourhood described how their daily routines involved negotiating paths through fractious drug sales; through users injecting in the courtyards and open stairwells; and through discarded syringes and blood-stained debris. They described too the less frequent but deeply traumatic witnessing of overdoses and fatalities. Experiences were exacerbated by harsh living conditions in the poorly maintained local authority flats by the 'cauldron-like' layout of the neighbourhood, where central courtyards surrounded by blocks of flats intensify the impact of anti-social activity in the public spaces on the ground.

Back then, Fettercairn was one of the many disadvantaged suburban local authority neighbourhoods in Dublin affected by epidemic levels of heroin use among its young people and was a greatly troubled area. The neighbourhood shared a similar structural position to Fatima in terms of the high levels of poverty, unemployment, and educational disadvantage experienced by residents as well as a poorly maintained environment with uncollected refuse and abandoned burnt out cars. Frequent bouts of young people 'joy riding' through the streets and the large tracts of undefensible green areas ('prairie lands') surrounding the neighbourhood added to the residents' difficulties. At the time of our 1997–8 fieldwork a community mobilisation initiative, instigated by mothers in the neighbourhood, held nightly vigils and street patrols to try to halt the open sale of drugs and quell the drug-related disturbances.

In the other neighbourhoods, the picture was somewhat different. In Finglas South, heroin use was less evident in 1997–8 and there was no visible heroin market in operation. Dealing and use were routed through a prolific drugs market operating in an adjacent neighbourhood. The high level of covert use at that time is now evidenced by the numbers of people from the area receiving drug treatment in 2007–9 who were active heroin users at the time of our original study.

In the neighbourhoods outside of Dublin, drug concerns at that time were more related to the use of cannabis and ecstasy, and the individuals and groups perceived to be involved in their trade. Public drug scenes were not identified as a problem except for those associated with alcohol use.

Drug issues in the case-study neighbourhoods in 2007–9

Compared to the intolerable situation a decade earlier, at the time of our 2007–9 fieldwork the situation regarding drug issues had improved greatly in both Fatima Mansions and Fettercairn. In both areas, drug use and drug markets were less visible than they had been previously. As a Fatima Mansions resident related, drug dealing and use is 'not in your face like it used to be' when the calls of sellers asking: 'Are you looking? Are you looking [to buy drugs]?' reverberated around the complex.

The demise of the intrusive public drug-dealing scenes that had proliferated in both Fatima and Fettercairn was attributed to a combination of intensive community development work, policy and practice initiatives (such as the Local Drug Task Forces and community drug treatment services, which will be discussed later), as well as improved tenancy and neighbourhood management (including eviction of tenants in some cases), and community policing (see Chapter 9). In addition, in Fatima Mansions, a holistic regeneration process had resulted in the demolition and spatial reconfiguration of the neighbourhood so that the secluded central squares, open stairwells, and balconies that had facilitated the open drug scenes were removed (see Chapter 4). At the same time, an extensive community-led social regeneration process that focused on improving the education, health, and employment well-being of the residents had been put in place (see Chapter 7 and O'Gorman, 2000). This two-pronged regeneration process, involving both physical and social regeneration contributed very significantly to addressing problems related to drugs. As one of the younger residents described:

> [B]ack in the flats [prior to the regeneration] you know, we seen people OD-ing [over dosing] on drugs, we were around people that took drugs, you don't see that now. People that are on drugs are living in the area but they do their own thing in their own home, like no one is hanging outside your door and drinking and no robbed cars are flying around at all hours of the morning.

Similarly in Fettercairn, the situation regarding drugs had improved and was described by a resident to be 'not as bad as it used to be', and a member of the Gardaí reported 'it is not out of control'. Both views were echoed by a long-standing community worker:

> It wouldn't be like it was in the Nineties, definitely not. We had major drug dealing problems on the streets then – the drugs are still there, without a doubt, but you don't see it the way that we used to see it. It was on every street corner.

The reduced visibility of drugs in public spaces was a recurring theme in the narratives of change on these two neighbourhoods with the view that 'drugs are not gone, just less open' common across both neighbourhoods. As one drugs worker suggested:

> I don't think it has changed, but people are not standing around anymore, I think that is what has changed. Most of the drug trade now would be done by mobile phone so you are not going to have the crowds – the technology has changed that. People are not knocking on doors because they have a mobile phone and can call and say – I'll meet you in such and such a place.

However, the decreased visibility was more an indicator that drug-related problems had been contained and rendered private, rather than that they had been fully resolved. Many of the residents that had once been active in the drug scene and use had moved away (sometimes voluntarily, sometimes as a result of eviction or the threat of eviction), others had died prematurely of drug-related illnesses and incidents, were imprisoned, or were stabilised in drug treatment provided by community drug services. Furthermore, the legacy of that time has left a palpable imprint on the communities' psyche, most notably evident when the litany of names of the deceased are called out at annual commemoration services. And a new generation of drugs, drug users, and drug markets had emerged presenting a different set of challenges and drug-related harms to the residents and service providers working on all seven neighbourhoods.

In our 2007–9 fieldwork, the increased drug consumption rates in the general population, noted earlier, were mirrored in the case study neighbourhoods, though with varying levels of intensity and visibility. Whereas the key drug-related concerns in 1997–8 were with heroin and open drug markets, now 'drugs' were perceived by interviewees as 'being everywhere' and as being the root cause of the neighbourhoods' difficulties. On closer investigation, however, the situation was found to be more differentiated and complex than these observations suggest. In effect, two distinct, albeit overlapping, cohorts of drug users were identified across the neighbourhoods. These groups were demarcated by their drug-using behaviour and their relationship to the drugs economy, and who, for the purposes of exploring the situation in the neighbourhoods, are best described as 'recreational' and 'habitual' drug users. As we shall see, these groups had a differential impact on everyday life in the neighbourhoods, which was relative to the overall levels of drug use and the size and nature of the drugs markets in each neighbourhood.

The normalisation of recreational drug use: recreational drug use practices in the neighbourhoods were seen to revolve around the consumption of combinations of alcohol, cannabis, cocaine, amphetamine-type stimulants, and various 'tablets' (i.e. prescription medications) in a variety of social settings – a park, house party, pub, or club. This type of normalised 'illegal leisure' had become an integral part of (predominantly young) people's recreational activities with the belief that the occasional use of these drugs is not habit forming or addictive (Parker *et al.*, 2002) – a process noted by residents and service providers in all of the seven neighbourhoods as the following quotations reveal:

> [I]t's very normalised to take drugs … it's just so in their face and so normalised, it's automatic, you take drugs.

> The drug of choice is hash and coke – and alcohol which has come back in a major way interspersed with coke and hash, and coke is so accepted as a recreational drug, it's not associated with problem drug use.

> The amount of people that come to [the neighbourhood] at the weekend for cocaine parties – there's a lot, a lot of cocaine. House parties, pubs as well, but predominantly house parties, binges going right the way through the weekend, from Friday to Sunday.

Part of the normalisation process of these drugs is that they are regarded as 'clean' and 'safe', a view unintentionally reinforced by the health and addiction services who at the time had few services to offer the users of these drugs. In addition, these recreational users were rarely involved in the type of acquisitive crime, such as handbag snatches and robberies, that had been a contentious issue in the neighbourhoods where drug use was prevalent in 1997–8. These drug users were seen to have sufficient disposable income to cover their use, or they traded and shared drugs within their peer network to minimise costs. In addition, these recreational drug users further distinguished themselves from habitual users by maintaining some level of boundary between their illegal leisure activities and their everyday lives and remaining 'linked in' with school, work, sporting activities, etc. (see Parker *et al.*, 2002).

However, residents and service providers in the seven neighbourhoods had many concerns raised in relation to this group including the negative effect of their drug-using behaviour on the trajectory of their development and life chances, and on their social relations with their families and community and, in particular, a 'law and order' concern regarding their public behaviour and its perceived impact on community safety and social order (this latter issue is addressed further in Chapter 9).

The situated context of habitual drug use: in contrast to recreational drug users, drug consumption was fully integrated into the everyday lives of habitual users. Though some level of overlap between the drugs consumed by habitual and recreational drug users was noted, for the most part heroin, cocaine, 'tablets', and/ or, if available, affordable crack cocaine were reported to be the drugs of choice for the habitual users. Their drug use was further differentiated from recreational drug users, by being accompanied by high-risk behaviour *vis-à-vis* the quantity, frequency, and method of drug use, the latter often including injecting drug use practices. This group was also seen to be more engaged in acquisitive crime and the drugs economy as a means of funding their drug use. In contrast to the mainly 'linked in' recreational users, the habitual drug users were described as more chaotic, as experiencing more risk factors for problem drug use, and, as Buchanan (2006, p. 6) noted in a similar UK study, with less mainstream opportunities to fashion an identity, purpose, and meaning in their lives, drug use was seen to take on a deeper significance in their lives.

Compared to a decade earlier, almost all of the neighbourhoods reported clusters of habitual drug users in their midst, part of the nationwide trend noted earlier regarding the diffusion of the sale and use of heroin, and other high-risk drug practices, to areas outside of Dublin. In Muirhevnamore, there had been very little talk of drugs impacting on the neighbourhood ten years ago. However, in 2007–9, the Gardaí reported that 'there is a heroin problem, a cocaine problem, and a tablet problem'. In Deanrock, a number of interviewees reported an influx of heroin into the Cork area and that 'heroin has become widely available which it hasn't been in previous years', and a very small cluster of residents of this neighbourhood were reported to be using this drug. In Cranmore, drugs were not raised as a major concern, though a number of murders in the area were under investigation at the time of our fieldwork (there was conflicting evidence as to whether these were related to the drug trade or not), and the ongoing police investigation and increased surveillance on the neighbourhood was considered to have displaced drug-related activities for the time being. As noted earlier, in Fatima Mansions and Fettercairn, a less intrusive but nonetheless persistent cluster of habitual use had remained and continued to be reproduced. However, it was Moyross and Finglas South, where there have been little outward signs of a drug problem in 1997/8, that were now the most severely affected neighbourhoods.

Of all seven neighbourhoods, the level of deprivation in Moyross had risen most significantly since 1997/8 (see Chapter 2) and its residents experienced high levels of disadvantage that were even more pronounced in comparison to the affluence in other parts of this highly segregated and polarised city (see Fitzgerald, 2007). High-risk drug-using practices (mainly cocaine and heroin related) were seen to have become embedded in parts of the neighbourhood that contributed to Limerick city having both the highest level of offences against the Misuse of Drugs Act and the highest number of drug users in treatment outside of the Dublin area (Howley, 2009). In Finglas South, though the levels of disadvantage were not so severe and most neighbourhoods were settled, many young people experienced a host of risk factors for problem drug use. As a Finglas-based drug worker observed: '[W]hen you start to unpack a heroin addiction, you unpack a load of issues, of social issues'. Arising from the socioeconomic aspects of these high-risk environments, the growth of a local drugs market was seen to have contributed to the worsened drug situation on these neighbourhoods.

The uneven impact of the drugs economy: In the late 1990s the drugs economy in Ireland underwent a radical transformation. Though cannabis remained the most widely used and traded drug, cocaine use surged. By 2004, the number of cocaine seizures outstripped those of heroin for the first time to become the second most seized drug after cannabis (Garda Síochána, various years). These changes in the drugs economy can be traced to a convergence of national and international events including changes in drug production trends and consumer preference, which saw an increased demand for drugs, and particularly for cocaine, during the Celtic Tiger economic boom (O'Gorman, 2010). The infrastructural requirements for this rapidly expanding new drugs economy were seen to have dovetailed into the prevailing conditions in Moyross and, to a lesser extent, Finglas South and by 2007–9 the first neighbourhood in particular had gained national reputations as drug distribution centres and for the drug-related harms and social disorder that accompany this trade.

These locally based high-level drug markets ushered in a wide range of drugs to the neighbourhoods, particularly those associated with higher risk behaviour, which in both neighbourhoods were described as being readily available; as an interviewee from Finglas South described:

> I can get any drug I want within three minutes without a problem and nobody would question that I would ask for it. It is that level of blatant availability; they won't question the asker . . . anything you want you can get.

In both neighbourhoods, interviews with local authority officials, police, community workers, and residents described how 'major dealers' (members of organised crime groups involved in drug importation and the nationwide distribution of cannabis, cocaine, and heroin) had established operational bases there, in effect, colonising these districts. Local authority letting policies and procedures for vetting tenants were seen to be inadequate for preventing or addressing this situation. Moreover, the policy of enabling tenants to purchase social housing inadvertently provided the drug traders with the opportunity to bypass local authority vetting procedures by buying dwellings or renting dwellings from private owners in the neighbourhood. An interviewee based in Moyross related:

> [Y]ou get groups moving in trying to sell [drugs] and they don't rent off the local authority, they will rent off a landlord. Or the big boys who are trying to run the estate, they own their own houses so the local authority has no control over them.

The establishment of organised crime groups in these neighbourhoods heightened the level of the 'risk environment', as did the ready supply of labour. Research studies internationally have demonstrated how marginalised young people with aspirations for status and financial success, but with little opportunity to achieve these through the formal economy, can provide a steady supply of labour for local drugs markets (Nightingale, 1993; O'Gorman, 2005). Storing, bagging, and distributing drugs and money requires space, anonymity, and a large workforce, and these physically as well as socially marginalised neighbourhoods provided the space and the cohorts of young unemployed men to carry out this work. Young people were reported to be drawn to the opportunities offered for accessing some of the 'huge, ostentatious wealth' seen to be enjoyed by the high-level dealers, as pointed out by some Dublin-based community workers, who told us: '[T]he risks are high but so too are the rewards' and 'you see a kid who doesn't work, doesn't do anything, no income and next minute is driving a BMW'.

Families and community workers in the neighbourhoods expressed concerns about teenagers recruited as 'runners' by older mid-level dealers. Many were paid (in money and/or supplies of drugs) or intimidated into storing and transporting drugs, money, and occasionally firearms. One Dublin-based youth worker reported that:

> [T]hey know the consequences for an under-16 year old caught with drugs is minimal, and they make it attractive to them. They might offer them €300 a week, and any 14 or 15 year old getting €300 a week will certainly take a chance.

In addition, all of the case study neighbourhoods shared a common experience of a thriving local licit ('legal') drugs market with the sale and use of alcohol identified as a key concern on all the neighbourhoods (this is examined in more depth in Chapter 9). In the decade since the first round of fieldwork, the deregulation of licences to sell alcohol had led to a significant expansion of alcohol outlets (Butler, 2009). For example, in the immediate vicinity of Fatima Mansions, in addition to four public houses, there were six off-licences, four of them in the local grocery stores – only one small food store in the area did not sell alcohol.

The diversion of prescription medication and their circulation within family and peer networks was reported to be widespread also, and concerns were expressed about the prescribing practices of family doctors (general practitioners or GPs).

These concerns are apt reminders that policy contexts, as well as socioeconomic and structural contexts, are influential components of the risk environment that residents in the neighbourhoods inhabit. The adequacy of policy responses in addressing the dynamics of these community drug problems will be examined in the next section of this chapter.

Policy responses to the drugs problem

Until the mid-1990s, the dominant paradigm shaping drugs policy and drug services in Ireland was an abstinence-based medical model that positioned dependent drug use as an outcome of an individual's psycho-social characteristics. These concepts were found wanting in light of the heroin epidemics, rooted in profound marginalisation, that had developed in many of the social housing neighbourhoods in Dublin in the 1980s and 1990s (O'Gorman, 1998). By 1996, government concerns about drug use and drug-related crimes, the rise in drug-related infections (HIV and Hepatitis C, etc.), and a voluble civil society mass movement demanding services and policy responses led to a marked shift in drugs policy (O'Gorman, 1998). The two reports published by a ministerial task force attached to the prime minister's office, in 1996 and 1997, reframed the drugs problem by acknowledging the evidence linking problem drug use with poverty and disadvantage (Ministerial Task Force on Measures to Reduce the Demand for Drugs, 1996, 1997). The reports recommended addressing the concentration of problem drug users in marginalised communities through an area-based response (known as Local Drug Task Forces), underpinned with the structures, resources, and community 'buy-in' necessary for its swift implementation.

Local and national drug strategies: At the time of our 1997–8 tranche of fieldwork, 14 of these multi-sectoral Local Drug Task Forces (LDTFs) had been established in the areas identified as being most affected by the heroin epidemic. Each of the three Dublin-based case study neighbourhoods, Fatima Mansions, Fettercairn, and Finglas South, as well as Deanrock in Cork, were covered by the LDTF initiative (the Canal Communities, Tallaght, Finglas–Cabra, and Cork LDTFs respectively). Regional Drug Task Forces (RDTFs) were established later, in 2003, and covered much larger areas, including the remaining three case study neighbourhoods.

The LDTFs were tasked with assessing the nature and extent of the drug problem within their area, and, on the basis of this evidence, developing action plans and subsequently implementing, coordinating, and monitoring a series of community initiatives (mainly in the fields of education, prevention, and treatment) that would add value to existing statutory services. Or, as was more likely at that time, to fill the gaps where little or no services existed. Membership of the task forces was drawn from the community and voluntary organisations involved in service provision for drug users, young people, and families; representatives from local branches of state agencies such as the health service, local government, and development bodies; the police and probation services; the state training agency (FÁS); as well as representatives from a number of government ministries, namely education, health, and justice.

This spatially targeted initiative was subsequently followed by an over-arching National Drugs Strategy, *Building on Experience 2001–2008* (Department of Tourism, Sport and Recreation, 2001), which outlined an integrated, 'cross-cutting' response at national level, incorporating a number of ministries and agencies, which mirrored the inter-agency approach at the local level and also the local focus on four 'pillars' – supply reduction, education, and prevention, treatment, and research – which in turn reflected wider European drugs policy trends at the time.

The overall coordination and funding for both the LDTFs and the National Drug Strategy was assigned to a newly established Drug Strategy Unit, staffed by public servants and, for the most part, located within a community affairs ministry under the direction of a minister responsible for the Drugs Strategy. The Drugs Strategy Unit appointed an intermediary multi-sectoral agency, the National Drug Strategy Team, to assess, review, and make funding recommendations for the individual LDTFs, and monitor the implementation of the overall National Drugs Strategy. In turn both the Drugs Strategy Unit and the National Drug Strategy Team reported to a group of senior civil servants representing a number of relevant

TABLE 8.1   Implementation arrangements for national drugs strategy

Structure	Members	Role
Cabinet Committee on Social Inclusion	Senior government ministers, chaired by the Taoiseach (prime minister)	Provides a strategic focus on tackling cross-cutting issues relating to social inclusion; has a specific remit in relation to the National Drugs Strategy
Inter Departmental Group	Senior civil servants (Assistant Secretaries) from the relevant ministries, representatives of the Drug Strategy Unit and the National Drugs Strategy Team; chaired by the Minister of State responsible for the Drugs Strategy	Advises the Cabinet Committee on drug-related matters and the implementation of the National Drugs Strategy; approves LDTF's plans and evaluates and monitors outcomes; oversees departmental input to the drugs strategy
Drug Strategy Unit (located in the communities ministry)	Minister of State responsible for the Drugs Strategy and public servants from the Drug Strategy Unit	Coordinates the overall implementation of the NDS; advises and supports the minister of state with responsibility for the NDS; drives the implementation of the NDS – particularly through the IDG; monitors implementation and is financially accountable for the NDS
National Drugs Strategy Team	Representatives of government departments, state agencies, community and voluntary sector	Ensures effective coordination of departments, state agencies, community and voluntary sector; addresses policy issues arising from the LDTFs; evaluates LDTF action plans, makes recommendations regarding their funding and monitors same
14 Local and ten Regional Drugs Task Forces	Partnership of statutory, community, and voluntary sector agencies	Develop evidence-based action plans on local drug-related needs; coordinates and monitors implementation and funding of multi-agency response to drugs in their areas

Sources: Department of Tourism, Sport and Recreation, 2001; Department of Community, Rural and Gaeltacht Affairs, 2004, 2005

ministries who in turn advised a cabinet committee responsible for social inclusion that was chaired by the Taoiseach (see Table 8.1).

Impact of the Drug Task Force area-based initiative

Local Drug Task Forces: The LDTF model represented an innovate policy response to a spatially situated social problem in terms of its mode of governance and as a model of participatory democracy – it was unique in terms of the extent to which the target communities were involved in developing and implementing policy at a local level, and influencing policy at a national level.

With regard to funding, the LDTFs received approximately €1 million each per annum and, by 2006, the ministry with responsibility for the Drugs Strategy estimated that approximately €125 million had been allocated to the 14 LDTF areas since 1997, leading to the establishment of over 400 community-based projects that employed more than 300 staff (Ahern, 2006). These projects provided local information, advice, and support centres for drug users and their families, and produced drug awareness materials and drugs training programmes for community groups, teachers, youth workers, etc. The LDTFs also supported Community Drug Teams – non-profit services providing harm reduction treatment as part of a holistic programme for drug users, their families, and community – such as those operating in Fatima and Fettercairn; rehabilitation programmes; family support projects; counselling services; and special projects aimed at those at risk of being involved with drugs. The community development ethos of many of these projects enabled the interrelated social issues at the root of these community drug problems to be addressed. As a Dublin community drugs worker noted of their clients: '[I]t's not a group of people that are on a buzz [high on drugs]. It's mostly people struggling, you know, struggling with pretty ordinary, basic problems, employment, housing, relationships etc.'.

In this context, harm reduction *realpolitik* became not just about reducing the harm caused by drugs to drug users but also about reducing the social harms they experience. As described by a doctor working in addiction services in Dublin:

> [T]he majority of clients come in for treatment for harm reduction reasons – they're there to reduce their [criminal] charges, to avoid jail, to avoid debt, to avoid threats, to avoid throw-outs [from home], to avoid illness, to avoid hospitalisation, avoid homelessness, avoid problems with their families, any of those things.

The provision of the community-based harm reduction treatment services (often by non-profit agencies in community drug teams but sometimes by statutory addiction services), particularly in the form of prescribing the substitute drug methadone for problem opiate users, was seen by interviewees as one of the positive outcomes of drug policy, and one that had a beneficial impact on a number of the case study neighbourhoods. For example, a national longitudinal study of opiate users found that this treatment resulted in significant reductions in drug use, injecting-related risk behaviour, criminal behaviour, as well as the health and social functioning of drug users (Cox, Kelly, and Comiskey, 2008). In 2009, almost 10,000 people were receiving methadone treatment in Ireland mostly in the greater Dublin area, and most of these were living in risk environment LDTF areas. Though the development of these treatment services was at times tortuously slow, with opposition from a wide range of opinion, treatment brought habitual drug users into a more stable lifestyle to replace the 'ripping and running' of their drug scoring years, as a community worker related:

> I've seen more and more people getting clean [not using high-risk drugs] and I'm working fifteen years in this field and I can remember at one point knowing nobody clean . . . and now I know a huge amount of people that are clean and are sustaining their recovery, and that is a big plus. People are doing great, they're coming out at the other end.

Among the seven neighbourhoods under examination, Fatima Mansions, Fettercairn, and Finglas South, by virtue of being situated in LDTF catchment areas, benefited most from this area-based initiative. Outside of the Dublin area, the initiative appeared to have been less successful. Despite the fact that a LDTF operated in Cork since 1997 and widespread reports of an influx of heroin into the city since the first round of fieldwork was conducted in 1997–8, services were described as being poorly resourced. It was reported that there was only one addiction counsellor and one GP who prescribed methadone treatment in the city and drug workers reported a year-long wait for treatment with heroin users having to travel to Dublin to access services. In the Regional Drug Task Force areas, as noted below, treatment services, particularly for harm reduction, were similarly slow to develop.

Regional Drug Task Forces: Regional Drug Task Forces (RDTFs) were established in 2003 with a similar structure and remit to the LDTFs, but they covered a much larger area (regions, rather than city neighbourhoods or towns) and were substantially less well resourced. Three case study neighbourhoods were covered by RDTFs – Moyross, Cranmore, and Muirhevnamore. However, interviews conducted with residents and service providers during the 2007–9 fieldwork indicate that the neighbourhoods included in the RDTFs benefited less from this initiative than their counterparts that were included in the LDTFs. This outcome was attributed to a number of factors such as: the large size of the RDTF operational area and the ensuing difficulty in targeting drug interventions with sufficient intensity at dispersed clusters of risk environments. The RDTFs also had to contend with reportedly difficult local political sensitivities when attempting to deal with a number of local authorities and health services operating within their area. Funding was also limited with approximately €500,000 being made available to each RDTF area initially. These administrative and resource difficulties were further compounded by a lack of support for, and subsequent provision of, harm reduction services in the regions. As was the case in Cork, interviewees related stories of drug users from the neighbourhoods having to travel to Dublin to avail of methadone treatment and needle exchange services that were either not available, or insufficiently available, in their locality. For example, in Dundalk, where Muirhevnamore is located, a local Garda reported that 'there are 42 people on the methadone programme and there is a waiting list of another 40 but there is only one doctor who can administer methadone'.

The paucity of harm reduction treatment services in the regions is difficult to comprehend at a time when state resources were plentiful. As noted earlier, evidence points to the beneficial impact of such services, not only for the individual user but their community also, particularly in terms of their capacity to contain and minimise the diffusion of a drug trend (Cox *et al.*, 2008). The impasse regarding this issue appears to be both ideological as well as structural.

Workers in the regional drug services, similar to their counterparts in the Dublin area, also described the need for social policy initiatives to deal with drug-related problems: 'A lot of care with families is more about social services, liaising with the Vincent de Paul [prominent charity in Ireland] and MABS [Money, Advice and Budgeting Service] – it's more social services they need'.

To meet the needs of the regions, members of the National Drugs Strategy Team recommended that a more focused RDTF structure be established in urban areas outside of Dublin that had been identified as having acute drug problems coupled with high levels of disadvantage. However, their recommendations were not adopted – a policy decision that had particular repercussions for Limerick city.

As reported earlier in this chapter, Moyross was a high-risk environment for drug problems. However, it was not until 2008 that the Mid-Western RDTF was allocated an additional €1.3 million to address drug use in the city – a delay further aggravated by the funding being provided to establish and develop a 'Limerick city sub-group' of the RDTF rather than a more autonomous and focused LDTF. A case of too little too late for the drug use and drugs markets that had become entrenched in the meantime in the city and in the Moyross neighbourhood.

Financial support for the Drug Task Force initiative: The less generous support for the RDTF initiative was one of many indicators that government support for the overall (local and regional) Drug Task Force initiative had begun to wane. From 1997–2001, prior to the implementation of the National Drug Strategy, the LDTFs were seen to enjoy a rather protracted honeymoon period at a time when they were the key drug policy delivery mechanism, and drugs were a highly prioritised social policy issue. In retrospect, however, the origins of the policy shift away from this initiative may be traced to the change in the parties in government in 1997, and to the decision of the new government to transfer responsibility for dealing with the drugs issue from the Taoiseach's office to the tourism, sport, and recreation ministry. This decision was justified at the time on the grounds that the latter ministry was a neutral location and could join up the disparate policy pillars of supply reduction, education, and treatment; and that it already had existing responsibility for local development and a number of social inclusion programmes (Department of Tourism, Sport, and Recreation, 2001; Pike, 2008). However, the tourism, sport, and recreation ministry had considerably less power and influence and a considerably smaller budget for the Drugs Strategy than the Taoiseach's office. In the years that followed, the Drug Strategy Unit was again moved to another similarly low-profile ministry, responsible for community affairs, and the brief of the responsible minister was stretched to cover yet more additional areas of responsibility: another signal of the reduced priority for this brief.

An additional shift in policy is discernible in the National Drug Strategy itself, published in 2001, which proposed a highly centralised drugs policy redressing the process of decentralisation that had begun with the establishment of the LDTFs. In this strategy document, one hundred actions were listed with responsibility for leading and implementing each one assigned to a ministry and/or statutory agency, which effectively side-lined the role of the Local and Regional Drug Task Forces and heralded the gradual diminution of their influence.

As detailed further in Chapter 6, area-based initiatives have been subject to extensive evaluation research – significantly more than mainstream public spending programmes – and the Drugs Task Forces are no exception. For example, in addition to ongoing internal monitoring, the Drugs Task Force initiative has been the subject of five separate major external reviews since their establishment in 1997 (Goodbody Economic Consultants, 2006; National Drugs Strategy Team, 2002; PA Consulting Group, 1998, 2001; Ruddle, Prizeman, and Jaffro, 2000). Even though the reviews have been largely supportive of their work, this intense focus on the Drugs Task Forces is disproportionate to the role they play in the overall drugs strategy.

In financial terms, though it is difficult to fully disaggregate expenditure on the drugs strategy within ministry budgets, overall government expenditure on drugs-related issues was estimated to be approximately €215 million in 2006 (Alcohol and Drug Research Unit, 2007) (see Table 8.2). Approximately 40 per cent of this funding was allocated to the health services (largely for the provision of addiction treatment services), 25 per cent to criminal justice services, and 20 per cent to the Drugs Strategy Unit, which covers the Local and Regional Drugs Task Forces as well as a host of capital intensive programmes. These funding allocations further evidence the lesser priority being placed on the area-based drugs initiatives.

TABLE 8.2   Drugs programme expenditure, 2006

Government ministries/agencies	€000s
National Drugs Strategy Unit	43.000
Department of Health and Children	0.978
Health Service Executive	85.053
FÁS [state training agency]	18.600
Department of Education and Science	12.140
Department of Environment, Heritage and Local Government	0.461
Department of Justice, Equality and Law Reform	9.530
Prison Service (estimate)*	5.000
Police	33.400
Revenue's Customs Service	6.525
Total	214.687

Source: Department of Community, Rural and Gaeltacht Affairs, 2007; Alcohol and Drug Research Unit, 2007, p. 31

The DTF initiative in context: In addition to examining spending on the Drugs Task Force initiative as part of the overall expenditure on drug policy, it is useful to look at the initiative in the context of drugs policy and social policy more broadly in Ireland. For example, notable gaps in mainstream social and health care services were observed in the case study neighbourhoods. Several of the neighbourhoods lacked adequate primary healthcare facilities. Finglas South and Fettercairn, in particular, were described by interviewees as being 'under-doctored' and residents had to travel considerable distances, or pay for a private appointment, in order to access primary healthcare. Given the strong relationship between ill-health and disadvantage, this has farreaching implications for the well-being of the residents, including those struggling with, and impacted by, drug use.

The effectiveness of education policies can also be seen to impact on drug problems in the case study neighbourhoods. Shortcomings in education policies, which contributed to high levels of early school leaving in the neighbourhoods, place young people out of school at an increased risk of drug use during adolescence and their later marginalisation and exclusion from society in adulthood (McCrystal, Higgins, and Percy, 2007). This combination of risk factors, as described earlier, exacerbates the likelihood of young people developing problematic patterns of drug use and engaging with the drugs economy.

The national drug policy (as outlined in the National Drug Strategy) itself also has a number of shortcomings, in terms of addressing neighbourhood drugs problems, as highlighted in the mid-term review of the strategy concluded in 2005 (Department of Community, Rural and Gaeltacht Affairs, 2005). A key limitation identified was the strategy's strong focus on one specific drug – heroin. As new drug-use trends emerged in the early 2000s, particularly relating to cocaine and poly-drug use (use of a number of drugs), projects by the Drug Task Forces found themselves locked into specific service-level agreements that required them to focus on heroin use with little flexibility to respond to new drug-use patterns. The need for a generic rather than a substance-specific drugs strategy was unfortunately only learned in hindsight. The exclusion of alcohol from the remit of the National Drugs Strategy stymied the capacity of the Drug Task Forces to address the alcohol issue at a community level. Furthermore, a focus on the treatment pillar in the strategy, albeit to deal with the chronic shortage of drug treatment places, had the unanticipated effect of underestimating the rehabilitation needs of the drug users, and in 2007 rehabilitation was added to the treatment pillar of the strategy to address this gap (Department of Community, Rural and Gaeltacht Affairs, 2007).

The future of drug policy: When the first National Drug Strategy drew to an end, its successor – the *National Drugs Strategy (Interim) 2009–2016* – was launched in 2009 (Department of Community Rural and Gaeltacht Affairs, 2009). The interim status of the new strategy reflects the fact that the government are awaiting the deliberations of the National Substance Misuse Strategy Steering Group, which was established to advise on the integration of a joint drug and alcohol policy. Nonetheless, the Interim Strategy marks a discernible shift in policy, heretofore largely inferred. Most notably, the Interim Strategy frames the increase in drug use in the general population as a universal, rather than a predominantly space- and context-specific, phenomenon. By failing to make a distinction between individuals' drug use and the dynamic of community drug problems played out in a context of social and economic exclusion, the new strategy is unlikely to provide an adequate response to the types of drug problems that have been identified in the seven case study neighbourhoods.

Furthermore, the strategy prioritises responses to anti-social behaviour and public disorder associated with drug and alcohol use, and the organised criminal groups involved in the illegal drugs industry. Though these issues were noted in the first section of this chapter as a major concern to the communities affected, this focus signals a shift towards the criminalisation of drugs policy, whereby the drugs problem is prioritised on the policy agenda because of its propensity to cause crime and disorder, rather than as a substantial social problem meriting attention in itself (see Duke, 2006; Rodger, 2008). This policy focus inevitably leads to an almost exclusive focus on reforming individual behaviour – whether through drugs education, treatment, or the criminal justice system – without addressing the broader social context in which this behaviour occurs (MacGregor, 1996; Shiner *et al.*, 2004). As with other area-based initiatives, accompanying structural changes are required to maximise their potential for success (Haase McKeown, 2003).

In addition to these marked changes in policy emphasis, the Interim Drug Strategy proposed a significant restructuring of the institutional mechanisms for its implementation. These involve disbanding the National Drugs Strategy Team and establishing a new Office for the Minister of Drugs to centralise policy formulation within the communities ministry. The Interim Strategy further suggests that the responsibility for the coordination of the Local Drug Task Forces be moved to either the Partnerships or the local authorities. This recommendation has inspired concern that it would result in the loss of specialised knowledge accumulated by Drugs Task Force staff and a dilution of their holistic, participatory community development approach.

Conclusions

In the period since our first study of the seven neighbourhoods, drug use had become a much more common phenomenon nationwide and become a concern on all case study neighbourhoods, though not uniformly so. The level of these concerns was seen to be influenced by the extent to which drug use impacted on the day-to-day lives of residents, on the well-being, behaviour, and life chances of the drug users, and on their social relations with their families and community.

The nature of the drugs economy had changed considerably too during the decade under examination to meet the increased demand for drugs, particularly cocaine. Among our case study neighbourhoods, the locus of drugs markets had shifted from the Fatima Mansions and Fettercairn in 1997–8. By 2007–9, the public visibility of the drugs markets in these neighbourhoods had been reduced greatly and they have benefited *inter alia* from the area-based Local Drugs Task Force Initiative and its support for community and harm reduction projects. The other neighbourhoods, in contrast, have been heavily affected by a burgeoning high-level drugs economy operating from within the neighbourhoods and the disorderly social relations that underpin drug consumption, trade, and distribution at a neighbourhood level.

Using a risk environment framework of analysis, this chapter has demonstrated how marginalisation, structural forces, and policy responses shape the development of drug problems at neighbourhood level, as does the related availability and use of high-risk drugs and the extent to which a local drugs economy operates. Though the area-based Drugs Task Force Initiatives established in 1997 are by themselves insufficient to address the complexity of these inter-related issues, they provided much needed services to address the impact of drug problems on drug users, families, and communities. The ensuing incremental shift from this micro-policy focus, which has taken place over the study period, does not augur well for the future of these neighbourhoods and other communities susceptible to drug-related harms.

References

Advisory Council on the Misuse of Drugs (1998) *Drug misuse and the environment.* London: HMSO.

Ahern, N. (2006) *Parliamentary Debates Dáil Éireann Official Report: Unrevised*, Vol. 621, No. 5, col. 1244-1245, www.oireachtas-debates.gov.ie (accessed 4 July 2013).

Alcohol and Drug Research Unit (2007) *2007 National Report (2006 data) to the EMCDDA by the Reitox National Focal Point. Ireland: new developments, trends and in-depth information on selected issues.* Dublin: Health Research Board.

Buchanan, J. (2006) *Understanding problematic drug use: A medical matter or a social issue?* Wrexham: Glyndwr University Research.

Butler, S. (2009) Obstacles to the implementation of an integrated national alcohol policy in Ireland: Nannies, neo-liberals and joined-up government. *Journal of Social Policy*, 38(2), 343–59.

Cox, G., Kelly, P., and Comiskey, C. (2008) *Results from the national drug treatment outcome study (ROSIE).* Dublin: National Advisory Committee on Drugs.

Department of Community, Rural and Gaeltacht Affairs (2004) *National drugs strategy 2001–2008: Critical implementation path.* Dublin: Government Stationary Office.

— (2005) *Mid-term review of the National Drugs Strategy 2001–2008: Report of the steering group, March 2005.* Dublin: Stationery Office.

— (2007) *Report of the Working Group on Drugs Rehabilitation.* Dublin: Stationery Office.

— (2009) *National Drugs Strategy (Interim) 2009–2016.* Dublin: Stationery Office.

Department of Tourism, Sport and Recreation (2001) *Building on experience: National drugs strategy 2001–2008.* Dublin: Stationery Office.

Duke, K. (2006) Out of crime and into treatment? The criminalization of contemporary drug policy since Tackling Drugs Together. *Drugs: Education, Prevention and Policy*, 13(5), 409–15.

European Monitoring Centre for Drugs and Drug Addiction (2004) *The state of the drugs problem in Europe, Annual report.* Lisbon: European Monitoring Centre for Drugs and Drug Addiction.

— (2008) *The drugs situation in Europe.* Lisbon: European Monitoring Centre for Drugs and Drug Addiction.

Fitzgerald, J. (2007) *Addressing issues of social exclusion in Moyross and other disadvantaged areas of Limerick city, Report to the Cabinet Committee on Social Inclusion.* Limerick: Limerick City Council.

Foster, J. (2000) Social exclusion, crime and drugs. *Drugs: Education, Prevention and Policy,* 7(4), 317–30.

Fountain, J. (2006) *An overview of the nature and extent of illicit drug use amongst the Traveller community: an exploratory study.* Dublin: Stationery Office.

Garda Síochána (various years) *Annual reports 2000–2005.* Dublin: Stationery Office.

Goodbody Economic Consultants (2006) *Expenditure review of the Local Drugs Task Forces.* Dublin: Goodbody Economic Consultants.

Haase, T. and McKeown, K. (2003) *Developing disadvantaged areas through area-based initiatives: Reflections on over a decade of local development strategies.* Dublin: Area Development Management.

Health Advisory Service (2001) *The substance of young needs: Review.* London: HMSO.

Howley, D. (2009) *Strategic plan for Limerick city 2009–2013.* Limerick: Mid-West Regional Drugs Task Force.

Kelly, A., Carvalho, M., and Teljeur, C. (2009) *Prevalence of opiate use in Ireland 2006:* a *3-source capture recapture study.* Dublin: Stationery Office.

Lloyd, C. (1998) Risk factors for problem drug use: identifying vulnerable groups. *Drugs: Education Prevention and Policy,* 5(3), 217–32.

MacGregor, S. (1996) *Drugs policy, community and the city.* Middlesex: Occasional paper, School of Sociology and Social Policy, Middlesex University.

Massey, D.B. (1995) *Spatial divisions of labor: Social structures and the geography of production,* second edition, New York: Routledge.

McCrystal, P., Higgins, K., and Percy, A. (2007) Exclusion and marginalisation in adolescence: The experience of school exclusion on drug use and antisocial behaviour. *Journal of Youth Studies,* 10(1), 35–54.

Measham, F., Aldridge, J., and Parker, H. (2001) *Dancing on drugs: Risk, health and hedonism in the British club scene.* London: Free Association Books.

Ministerial Task Force on Measures to Reduce the Demand for Drugs (1996) *First report of the Ministerial Task Force on Measures to Reduce the Demand for Drugs.* Dublin: Government Stationery Office.

— (1997) *Second report of the Ministerial Task Force for Measures to Reduce the Demand for Drugs.* Dublin: Government Stationery Office.

Natarajan, M. and Hough, M. (eds) (2000) *Illegal drug markets: From research to prevention policy.* New York: Criminal Justice Press/Willow Tree Press.

National Advisory Committee on Drugs and Drug and Alcohol Information and Research Unit (2008) *Drug use in Ireland and Northern Ireland; Drug prevalence survey bulletin 1: First results from the 2006/2007 Drug Prevalence Survey.* Dublin and Belfast: National Advisory Committee on Drugs and Drug and Alcohol Information and Research Unit.

National Drugs Strategy Team (2002) *Review of the Local Drugs Task Forces.* Dublin: National Drugs Strategy Team.

Nightingale, C. (1993) *On the edge.* New York: Basic Books.

Nutt, D.J., King, L.A., and Phillips, L.D. (2010) Drug harms in the UK: a multicriteria decision analysis. *The Lancet,* 376(9752), 1558–65.

O'Gorman, A. (1998) Illicit drug use in Ireland: An overview of the problem and the policies. *International Journal of Drug Issues,* 28(1), 155–66.

— (2000) *Eleven acres: Ten steps.* Dublin: Fatima Groups United.

— (2005) *Drug use and social exclusion: the development of heroin careers in risk environments. PhD Thesis.* London: School of Health and Social Sciences, Middlesex University.

— (2010) *From boom to dust: an analysis of the rise and fall of the Irish cocaine market during the Celtic Tiger era.* Paper presented at the European Society for Social Drugs Research, June, Lisbon.

O'Gorman, A., Doyle, M., and Crean, D. (2007) *National drug trend monitoring system. Results from a feasibility study.* Dublin: NACD.

O'Higgins, K. (1999) Social order problems. In T. Fahey (ed.) *Social housing in Ireland: A study of success, failure and lessons learned* (pp. 149–72). Dublin: Oak Tree Press.

PA Consulting Group (1998) *Evaluation of the Drugs Initiative: final report*. Dublin: Department of Tourism, Sport and Recreation.

— (2001) *Operations and management study of the National Drugs Strategy Team and Drugs Strategy Unit*. Dublin: Department of Tourism, Sport and Recreation.

Parker, H., Aldridge, J., and Measham, F. (1998) *Illegal leisure: The normalisation of adolescent recreational use*. London: Routledge.

Parker, H., Williams, L., and Aldridge, J. (2002) The normalization of 'sensible' recreational drug use: Further evidence for the North West England Longitudinal Study. *Sociology*, 36(4), 941–64.

Pike, B. (2008) *Development of Ireland's drug strategy 2000–2007. HRB Overview Series 8*. Dublin: Health Research Board.

Rhodes, T. (2002) The 'risk environment': a framework for understanding and reducing drug related harm. *International Journal of Drug Policy*, 13(2), 85–94.

Rodger, J.J. (2008) *Criminalising social policy: Anti-social behaviour and welfare in a de-civilised society*. London: Willan.

Ruddle, H., Prizeman, G., and Jaffro, G. (2000) *Evaluation of Local Drugs Task Force projects: Experiences and perceptions of planning and implementation*. Dublin: Policy Research Centre, National College of Ireland.

Shiner, M., Thom, B., MacGregor, S., Gordon, D., and Bailey, M. (2004) *Exploring community responses to drugs*. York: Joseph Rowntree Foundation.

TNS Opinion and Social (2007) *Attitudes towards alcohol. Special Eurobarometer 272*. Brussels: European Commission.

9

SOCIAL (DIS)ORDER
AND COMMUNITY SAFETY

Aileen O'Gorman

Introduction

Social Housing in Ireland, the book that described our original study of the seven neighbourhoods in 1997–8, noted the centrality of social order in discussions about liveability and the quality of life on the seven neighbourhoods and, in its conclusion, suggested that the presence or absence of social order marked the distinction between housing 'success' and 'failure':

> The prevalence of anti-social behaviour and the absence of a sense that order and civility can be taken for granted is the single biggest problem in troubled local authority estates. Most settled estates are characterised by the absence of this problem.
>
> *(Fahey, 1999, p. 257)*

This chapter revisits the theme of social (dis)order a decade later and examines the views and experience of residents, community leaders, and service providers in the seven case-study neighbourhoods on this issue. Following on from this, the role and capacity of the two statutory agencies – the local authorities and the Gardaí – tasked with the responsibility for maintaining social order in the neighbourhoods are discussed and assessed. A number of themes raised in the preceding chapter on Drug Use and Drugs Markets are explored further in this chapter, which revisits the theme of the drugs economy/violence nexus.

The nature and context of social (dis)order

In our 2007–9 fieldwork, the topic of social (dis)order and anti-social behaviour was central to discussions on liveability in the seven neighbourhoods, as it had been a decade earlier. In many respects, this is not surprising. These discussions mirror media, political, and public concerns about the increased rates of violent assaults, public order offences, and homicides since the late 1990s (Mulcahy and O'Mahony, 2005). However, despite the in-depth explorations of the complex relationship between these trends and wider social forces (including growing inequality, anomie as well as increased alcohol consumption and the drugs trade) available in the research literature (see O'Donnell, 2005), media discourses have been predominantly sensationalist and focus almost exclusively on the disorderly activities of particular age and social groups in urban 'hot spots', including some of the seven case study neighbourhoods (this issue is explored in more depth in Chapter 10). This social construction of anti-social behaviour as a problem relating mainly to young working-class men was further reinforced by legislative treatment of this issue. The first legislative action on anti-social behaviour – in the form of the Housing (Miscellaneous Provisions) Act 1997 – applied only to tenants of local authority housing in Ireland. It was not until the enactment of the Criminal Justice Act 2006 that the offence was extended to include the rest of the population (Kenna, 2006).

The unequal power relations embedded in this legislation reinforce and re-produce the disadvantaged position of the seven case-study neighbourhoods relative to the general population (as discussed in Chapter 2) and reflect the multidimensional relationship between marginalisation, powerlessness, economic and social inequality, and crime and social order (see Grover, 2008; MacDonald, Shildrick, Webster, and Simpson, 2005; Shildrick, 2006; Wilkinson and Pickett, 2009).

In addition to the inequitable application of the term anti-social behaviour, varying definitions of what constitutes such behaviour were employed by the residents and service providers interviewed for this study. In our fieldwork interviews a wide range of problems and behaviours were conflated under the rubric of anti-social, including manifest signs of physical disorder (such as boarded-up houses, abandoned cars, and refuse-littered streets) and symbols of social disorder (ranging from young people hanging out in the area, noisy and belligerent neighbours, harassment and intimidation, horse and car racing through the streets, and drink- and drug-related public nuisance). These interpretations contrast somewhat with the legal definition of anti-social behaviour that is set out in the Housing (Miscellaneous Provisions) Acts 1987 and 2009 – namely violence, threats, intimidation, coercion, harassment, etc., which are of a 'significant or persistent' nature. Consequently, many of the social order issues raised by residents of the seven neighbourhoods and associated service providers as problematic (those relating to young people's nuisance behaviour), were not, legally speaking, 'anti-social behaviour' under the terms of the 1987 and 2009 Acts.

Noting how social (dis)order is constructed, defined, and contextualised helps clarify how these processes feed into contested notions of public space and concerns about community safety and links this exploration of order/disorder in the case study neighbourhoods to the relevant social, economic, and policy contexts.

The trajectory of social order in the seven case study neighbourhoods

As noted above, social order was central to discussions on liveability in the seven neighbourhoods in 2007–9, as it had been ten years previously. Though then, as now, perceptions on the nature and level of order on each of the neighbourhoods differed. Over time too, the trajectory of each of the seven neighbourhoods, in social order terms, proved to be rather different than might have been expected. Some of the more 'troubled' neighbourhoods experienced an improvement in community safety while some previously 'settled' neighbourhoods experienced a deterioration (see Table 9.1).

The 1997–8 study concluded that Deanrock was considered the most successful and settled of the seven neighbourhoods in terms of social disorder, and was found to be similarly settled during the research team's revisits in 2007–9, though there were some difficulties in the intervening period. On the two estates considered most troubled a decade ago, Fettercairn and Fatima Mansions, social order was seen to have improved substantially though difficulties remained. In Muirhevnamore little had changed between 1997–8 and 2007–9, some difficulties were identified then and the situation remains similar now, a similar situation to that of Cranmore, though there social order problems were perceived to be concentrated in micro-areas within the larger estate and in neither case were social order problems as serious as those found in the Dublin case studies. In our 1997–8 fieldwork, Finglas South was identified as having high levels of anti-social behaviour related to the operations of gangs of young people in parts of the neighbourhood (McAuliffe and Fahey, 1999). According to some interviews conducted during the latest round of fieldwork, this situation was seen to have worsened in the past decade, particularly with regard to the involvement of organised crime in the expanding drugs economy. The drugs trade was viewed as having impacted severely on Moyross too (an issue discussed in more depth later), an area perceived as having a lot of potential in our original study but which was deeply troubled now with residents experiencing a drastic deterioration in their quality of life over the past ten years.

TABLE 9.1 Level of social order in the seven case study neighbourhoods 1997–8 and 2007–9

	1997/8	*2008*	*Change*
Cranmore	Medium	Medium	Stable
Deanrock	High	High	Stable
Fatima Mansions	Low	Medium	Improved
Fettercairn	Low	Medium	Improved
Finglas South	Mixed	Mixed	Mixed
Moyross	Medium	Low	Worsened
Muirhevnamore	Medium	Medium	Stable

In seeking to comprehend the social order trajectories of these seven neighbourhoods two particular difficulties were identified – the public presence of groups of young people and the impact of the sale and use of drugs and alcohol on behaviour and on the community.

Activities of young people

The activities of young people were a shared concern across all seven neighbourhoods. Devlin (2006) has suggested that society's tendency to demonise youthful behaviour has led to a wariness of young people and a heightened intolerance for youth street life, and many youth workers interviewed for this study were concerned about the negative labelling of young people in public spaces, contending that congregating in groups is a typical phase of youthful behaviour, as one described: 'It's important that teenagers are allowed to be teenagers, to stand at their garden gate, talk to whoever – their friends, etc., etc. Not all teenagers are drug-taking, drink-fuelled louts'. Nonetheless, the sometimes destructive dynamic associated with groups of young people in some neighbourhoods created difficulties for those having to pass by or live near the public spaces they inhabited. As one youth worker noted: '[I]f you have 20 or 30 young people gathered in the same spot every night that brings some energy with it'.

Congregational sites were seen to change with the season, the level of local tolerance and policing, and the topography of each area. The gardens of gable-end houses, the shelter of bridges and stairwells, remote spaces by nearby railway or tram tracks, isolated fields and parks, as well as derelict houses and 'free gaffs' (i.e. homes where no supervising adult was present) were particularly favoured for their 'ecological advantage' (St. Jean, 2007), meaning that they were hidden from view or had multiple exits for rapid dispersal. This spatial pattern of youth congregation contributed to the differentiation in social order at a micro-level within the case study neighbourhoods.

For young residents of the seven neighbourhoods, the transition from youth to adulthood was seen to be a fraught exercise involving the negotiation of complex local social relations and high-risk activities. Local youth workers observing the common rites of passage on this journey noted that a warning sign for a shift to more problematic behaviour was when hanging out on the street became the main form of social interaction. As one youth worker noted:

> [W]hen I see young people get involved in anti-social behaviour – I ask where are they hanging in? Are they hanging in at work, are they hanging in with the groups with us, are they hanging in with the football teams? Are they hanging in anywhere? Because if they're hanging in you have some chance but if they jump ship from all the social structures that exist and if their primary activity is drinking and smoking, and abusing people going past, if that's their primary activity well then they're in trouble.

In this context, the provision of supervised social and developmental activities for young people was seen to act as a protective factor in minimising the risk of becoming involved in anti-social behaviour. Yet, in all of the case-study neighbourhoods (with the exception of Fatima Mansions, which had an intensive social, cultural, and educational programme for young people in place), the community and youth workers, teachers, and the Gardaí interviewed noted the lack of such services for young residents. Youth services reported that they had insufficient capacity to respond to the level of need, particularly in the more marginalised neighbourhoods where families had less economic resources to access the type of extra-curricular (and costly) activities available to more affluent families, as a youth worker told us:

> [I]f you don't play soccer or if you don't play Gaelic [football] or if you don't do Irish dancing, then really there's nothing locally for you. And then as well there are young people that wouldn't be able to fund any type of private enterprise, like the gym, be it a fiver a week or whatever.

Funding for youth services increasingly comes through the justice ministry (such as for the Garda Youth Diversion Programmes) and is targeted at those who are already 'at risk' and have come into contact with the criminal justice system, are out of school, or otherwise 'disengaged' – rather than young people in general and marginalised youth in particular. As one youth worker related: '[T]he biggest criticism [we get] is does my son or daughter have to be in trouble before anybody takes notice and puts a bit of work in with them?'

In the midst of restricted service provision, youth workers reported extreme levels of need among the young people they encountered: needs that required additional and more wide-ranging responses. They described young people struggling to cope with ill, absent, imprisoned, or deceased family members and coping with drug, alcohol, and/or gambling addiction in the family, often acting in *loco parentis* to raise younger brothers and sisters. Many of the youth in the more troubled neighbourhoods had witnessed serious assaults or gangland shootings, in some cases involving a family member, and had experienced intimidation themselves. The severity of these difficulties was seen to be related to increased levels of death by misadventure and suicide on the more troubled neighbourhoods. The challenges faced in trying to support these young people is illustrated by the following quotations from interviews with youth workers in two of the case study neighbourhoods where social order problems were particularly prevalent:

> There is no point in just bringing those lads out sailing or snorkelling out every week, if there are problems in the home ... and the crime aspect of it is usually a symptom of something else, you know. Probably a lot of people, their fathers would be in prison or their father mightn't be known to them or leaving school early or there might be alcohol problems, drug problems in the house. They'd be coming from tough enough backgrounds, you know.

> You identify that these problems can cause the crime as opposed to them deciding one day, listen I am going to go and break into a car – so it would be trying to identify those issues and trying to give support.

> Young people in here have witnessed gangland shootings, they've been running for the criminals and doing all sorts of stuff . . . How do we deal with someone who's seen their Dad being shot, how do we deal with someone who's running drugs and they're ten? We're not social workers, we're not counsellors, we're youth workers, but we seem to be picking up a lot of pieces that a lot of other agencies should be doing.

It is clear that addressing such difficulties is beyond the capacity of youth services alone. Furthermore, the situation calls into question the adequacy of existing social service provision in meeting, or preventing, such a high level of need.

National education policies and programmes aimed at tackling educational disadvantage, as detailed in Chapter 6, had limited effect in practice on the problems of young people in the seven case study neighbourhoods because these were largely targeted at schools. Students with high levels of absenteeism from school were seen to 'stay below the radar' as there were insufficient personnel to address this issue. For example, there was one officer of the National Education Welfare Board (which is responsible for addressing school non-attendance) responsible for the whole of Limerick city, whereas interviewees claimed that one officer would be needed to address the issue in Moyross alone. School leaving exam completion rates in Ireland have remained unchanged since the late 1990s with boys and working-class pupils faring least well (Smyth, McCoy, Darmody, and Dunne, 2007), and pupils in schools designated as disadvantaged have significantly lower literacy and numeracy skills (Eivers, Shiel, and Shortt, 2004). Staff from schools serving the neighbourhoods described a high level of unmet need among its pupils and detailed innovative programmes they had introduced to improve attendance, exam completion rates, etc. Yet, this work had been stymied by cutbacks in funding and resources.

Deficits in the capacity of social and educational services to address educational disadvantage in these neighbourhoods have far-reaching implications. One outcome, which is of particular relevance to this discussion, is that educational disadvantage is a key risk factor for young people becoming engaged in problematic drug use and with the criminal justice system, and for their potential to get involved in anti-social behaviour, as both perpetrator and victim.

Drivers of social disorder in troubled neighbourhoods

Drug (and alcohol)-related violence: In addition to the perceived problems generated by the public presence of young people across all of the case study neighbourhoods in 2007–9, a key concern identified in the more troubled neighbourhoods was the level of alcohol use and 'street drinking' they engaged in, especially at weekends, 'calendar events' (such as public holidays, Halloween and St Patricks' Day festivals), and during the school holidays. Street drinking in high-risk unsupervised settings brings additional complications and potential for difficulties by being unfettered by the traditional codes of behaviour that regulate more formal drinking locations, such as pubs, and can often escalate into disorderly behaviour and Garda intervention.

A deregulatory alcohol policy (as set out in the Intoxicating Liquor Act 2000) resulted in a notable increase in alcohol outlets between 1997–8 and 2007–9 in, or nearby, most of the seven neighbourhoods. Residents and service providers in these neighbourhoods viewed these additional outlets, and a laxity in monitoring their activities, including selling alcohol to those under the legal age of consumption, as contributing to order-related problems.

In discussing drug- and alcohol-related violence, many interviewees focused on the psycho-pharmacological effects of alcohol and drugs (particularly cocaine and other stimulants) on young people's behaviour. Nonetheless, the research evidence clearly demonstrates that the drugs themselves are just one aspect of a complex web of possible effects and outcomes of drug use and at least two other issues need to be taken into consideration – economic and systemic factors (see Zinberg, 1984 and Goldstein, 1985 among others).

The link between violence and acquisitive crime to fund drug purchases had been raised as an issue in the 1997–8 fieldwork. However, a decade later this economic-related violence was scarcely mentioned and then just in relation to the activities of a few long-term habitual drug users. Now, respondents were more likely to raise instances of systemic drug-related violence arising from the operation of the drugs economy and local drug markets, in particular in the troubled parts of Finglas South and Moyross, but also sporadically in Cranmore, Fatima Mansions, and Muirhevnamore (see Chapter 8).

A key aspect of the social disorder/drugs economy nexus in the troubled neighbourhoods related to the activities of organised crime groups involved in large-scale drug distribution. By establishing enclaves within the neighbourhoods by renting privately or buying up clusters of houses, either directly or through their associates, these crime groups maintain a subtle but firm control over public space in the neighbourhoods and surrounding areas so as to create a safe haven from where to run their businesses. Intermittent threats and intimidation of other residents, and occasional outbreaks of orchestrated violence, are aimed at deterring people and services from the areas and engendering a state of fear so that other residents do not challenge or 'rat' on them (report them to the authorities). As a consequence, while everyday life in the more troubled neighbourhoods can appear relatively peaceful on the surface, for those who lived there the underlying tension was palpable.

According to one community worker: '[T]he culture of threatening people is now very pervasive in the area, residents are constantly being told that they will be burned out if they fall foul of certain families or individuals'. Residents also spoke of their concerns that calls to the police could be detected and so were reluctant to call for assistance. According to an interviewee from Finglas South:

> [T]here would still be quite a high level of public order offences and they tend to rear their heads like when we had the St. Patrick's Day riots [2008] ... we would suspect that there is a very subtle level of quite dangerous criminal gangland activity in [the area] that fuels a lot of this public order stuff, a lot of availability of drugs, a lot of availability of alcohol and that kind of thing.

As mentioned in Chapter 8, the increased demand from within the general population for illicit drugs, and particularly for cocaine, led to an exponential growth in the drugs economy during the early 2000s. Many interviewees from the case study neighbourhoods where cocaine use was prevalent suggested it was responsible for the increased levels of aggression and violent behaviour locally. However, this explanation strays into the territory of what Reinarman and Levine (1997) term 'pharmacological determinism' and overlooks the persuasive evidence that such violence is also a systemic outcome of the illegal and unregulated, multi-million euro drugs industry. In this hidden economy, without recourse to a legal means to police itself, disputes over territory, suspected informants, and stolen or seized consignments of drugs are liable to be resolved by violent means (Hammersley, 2008).

Reports of harsh punishment being meted out to enforce the servicing of drug-related debts, including severe beatings, murder, and suicides by those unable to cope with their situation, were recounted by interviewees from very troubled neighbourhoods. Parents, particularly female-headed lone-parent families, were reported as being threatened and intimidated to repay the debts their sons and daughters had accumulated, often for sums much larger than the original amount owed. A youth worker in one of the Dublin neighbourhoods under examination told us: 'We'd a young person who owed €1,800 and a note came to the house, to the mother saying the house would be burned if the money wasn't paid'.

At the distribution end of the trade, the complexity and volatility of inter- and intra-crime group relations (often kinship based, sometimes with various splinter groups of former allies now foes) was reported to generate a mercurial atmosphere in the neighbourhoods with disputes liable to flare over intercepted consignments, suspected informants, and contested sales territories. Police reports, parliamentary debates and newspaper articles report that an estimated 127 'gangland killings' took place in the country as a whole in the decade between the two study periods (1998–2008). These have been disproportionately linked to the drugs trade in Finglas and Limerick/Moyross. Approximately half occurred in Limerick (the city had the highest per capita levels of homicide in Europe in 2008) and around 15 per cent in Finglas (Dáil Éireann, 2003, 2008; *Sunday Independent*, 2008; *Sunday Tribune*, 2009). Not all these victims were involved in the drugs trade, some were innocent bystanders in the wrong place at the wrong time and were mistaken for or in the company of the intended victim. In these two neighbourhoods, the fear and tension on the streets was palpable after such incidents, with young men in the aftermath of a shooting walking the streets in bulletproof vests to avoid the next strike.

The impact of the drugs industry on the broader community, not just those involved in its operations, had been noted by Ghodse (2008) who outlined its destabilising effect on civil society, in terms of the loss of community cohesion and the erosion of social capital and the impact on people's freedom of movement due to fear. These issues were tangible in residents' expressed fears of walking through the neighbourhoods at night, attending community events, etc. As one interviewee described: 'At night-time I wouldn't go near the place. A lot of violence, a lot of intimidation, people are afraid to leave their houses in the night time'.

Community leaders seen to be threatening the power balance in very troubled neighbourhoods, by mobilising around local issues, had experienced intimidation by others wishing to preserve the *status quo*. One community worker told us:

> [T]here is certainly a serious problem of gangland activity in certain areas and it probably also undermines in no small way the willingness of people to maintain their contact with residents associations or to be community representatives or to put themselves out there in the community because they can end up being targeted and they're afraid.

In this context, the difficulties in engaging in community development activities, or mobilising social capital, cannot be underestimated. Residents reported being fearful of engaging in community events, attending public meetings, or being perceived as colluding with the authorities leading to even further isolation of individuals and the continued atomisation of the community. These barriers to community organising have further ramifications as a high level of community development and capacity building is seen to be beneficial in a multitude of ways including acting as a protective barrier against social-order problems in a neighbourhood. For example, in Fatima Mansions, strong community leadership and a high level of community participation in the regeneration process was seen to be a key contributory factor to the improved liveability of the neighbourhood. Nonetheless, community responses by themselves (as demonstrated by the preceding discussion on youth services) cannot redress underlying problems of inequality and marginalisation that are inherently structural in origin (MacGregor, 2003).

Local authorities' role in addressing social order

The book describing our 1997–8 tranche of fieldwork identified an unwillingness to address social order problems 'as one of the greatest weaknesses of "traditional" local authority housing management' (Fahey, 1999, p. 257). In the intervening decade, the organisational restructuring of local authorities (as outlined in Chapter 4) has enhanced the range of administrative and legislative tools available to their officials to address social order problems. These tools relate to: neighbourhood maintenance and management; remedial and regeneration work; tenancy support and enforcement; as well as the capacity for bilateral inter-agency work (such as with the police force) and multi-agency partnership approaches under the auspices of area-based initiatives.

Neighbourhood maintenance: The decentralisation of housing departments, and the consequent establishment of area-based offices, as part of an overall restructuring process, was seen to have improved accountability at the local level. As explained in Chapter 4, in Fettercairn and Fatima Mansions in particular, improved levels of estate management were reported – a task undertaken in a partnership arrangement with local community services.

However, the abolition of traditional 'on the ground' posts (such as rent collectors and maintenance workers), as part of the restructuring process, was perceived to have had a negative impact on awareness of residents' concerns and on levels of neighbourhood maintenance. An increase in the physical signs of disorder (such as uncollected litter and fly-tipping, broken street furniture and high level of 'voids' [empty, boarded-up houses]) were reported in Muirhevnamore, Finglas South, and Moyross. These, amplified by poor lighting, and inadequate transport links, heightened the residents' sense of insecurity. In response, local authority officials cited the prohibitive cost and length of time it took to retro-fit vacant dwellings and bring them up to current health and safety, accessibility, and environmental standards, and reported a reluctance of ground-level staff to work on the more troubled neighbourhoods for fear of intimidation from organised crime groups.

Designing out anti-social behaviour: Our 1997–8 fieldwork found that aspects of the built environment and a lack of defensible public spaces impacted on social order in the neighbourhoods (Norris, 1999). Since then, local authorities have embarked on a strategy of 'designing out' anti-social behaviour through improvement and regeneration works. Four of the seven neighbourhoods (Finglas South, Fatima Mansions, Fettercairn, and Deanrock) have experienced various levels of redesign with a major focus of the work being the removal of congregational and undefensible spaces, described by one of the local authority officials interviewed as 'causing' anti-social behaviour. At the time of the 2007–9 fieldwork the three remaining neighbourhoods – Muirhevnamore, Cranmore, and Moyross – were undergoing or planning regeneration work.

Of all three, the situation in Moyross was the least satisfactory and both the social landlord (Limerick City Council) and the Regeneration Agency (tasked with the rebuild at the time of writing) attracted much criticism from interviewees. Ongoing delays in the regeneration process were a source of deep anxiety and frustration among residents. Conditions in the neighbourhood were deplorable with sections boarded up, without street lighting and refuse uncollected, contributing to a major decrease in their quality of life since 1997–8.

Tenancy management: The first round of the research coincided with the enactment of the Housing (Miscellaneous Provisions) Act 1997 (outlined earlier), which enabled local authorities to issue an exclusion order against a member of a household or secure the eviction of the entire household in cases where tenants (or their children) were engaged in persistent or significant anti-social behaviour – defined in the 1997 Act as drug dealing, serious violence, and intimidation (Kenna, 2006).

As mentioned earlier, this legislation has a number of anomalies and limitations. These include the fact that it is applicable only to the behaviour of the registered tenants or their children under the age of 18, thereby excluding non-registered inhabitants such as undeclared partners, visitors, etc. In the case of adult children engaged in anti-social behaviour, the authority may seek, or request the parent seek, an exclusion order requesting the person to leave the house and prohibiting him/her from entering or being in the vicinity of the house or neighbourhood. Reports of local authorities putting pressure on families to initiate the exclusion order as a means of retaining their tenancy was regarded as placing them in an almost impossible situation. A number of local authority personnel acknowledged that they were uncomfortable with this approach and its capacity to displace the problem and create homelessness by 'pushing the problem out on to the streets', as one community worker remarked:

> I think people have come to recognise that that Act goes more to putting young people homeless. If a young person now gets a letter and is invited down to speak to the council, there's a lot of misunderstanding around it and what it means, it's definitely put fear into a lot of the parents they aren't prepared to put their house on the line, so out they go, and it's put more young people on the street than anything.

Under the same housing legislation, offences within the remit of the Misuse of Drugs Acts (1977 and 1984) can be used to inaugurate eviction proceedings. However, this aspect of the legislation was seen to be inconsistently applied across the neighbourhoods with some personnel reporting a 'zero tolerance' of drug charges while others expressed a reluctance to proceed when the offence is for the possession of drugs. The latter response was seen to be based both on an empathy and a pragmatic acceptance that this would be nigh on impossible to enforce. For example, officials from two different local authorities told us:

> [I]t's different where you might have people caught for personal use ... the tendency is to hang on we'll give the benefit of the doubt there because if someone's son or daughter is a heroin addict or whatever, it's not easy for them, eviction is the last thing you want to be honest with you ... we do tend to just give warnings, we do try to work with them and find a solution.

> If it is a conviction for somebody dealing drugs from the house, you go to court, you are excluded, no problem. Now if you are going to take drugs for your own consumption, well you wouldn't go for that, everybody is doing that nowadays so you wouldn't, but supply is the more serious one.

A further anomaly of the legislation – and an unanticipated effect of the Irish government's policy of facilitating tenants to buy their homes – is that local authority neighbourhoods do not have jurisdiction over private residents, much to the frustration of, and an aggrieved sense of injustice to, neighbouring tenants who reported having to endure uncivil behaviour from neighbours in 'purchase houses'.

A lack of human resources to deal with complaints, and a fear-based reluctance to take action against tenants involved in 'hard-core' anti-social behaviour, were also seen to hamper responses to disorder. For example, in Louth county (the region where Muirhevnamore is located) there was one official responsible for investigating (over 250) anti-social behaviour cases. In Limerick city, there were two such officers, again dealing with a similar number of cases ranging 'from dogs barking to drug dealing'. A community worker in the Louth region remarked that this was:

> [T]otally insufficient for the amount of anti-social that goes on in the county – one worker for the whole of the county for such a serious issue. Like that issue is in the headlines all the time and it causes so much hassle for everybody so to employ one worker for the whole county means that the local authorities are not taking it seriously. Because his job would be to deal with a lot of anti-social things, not just the gangs and all that but, dumping, burning of cars, dumping of cars, neighbours fighting and kids out of control.

Though the legislation provides anonymity for a complainant the accused has a right to know the nature of the complaint against him/her and consequently may discover or suspect the identity of the person who has made the complaint. As a result, when this became known to them, complainants sometimes withdrew their complaints.

As an alternative, in recent years local authorities have increasingly used Section 62 of the Housing Act 1966 (which enables them to evict tenants for any breech of their tenancy agreement including anti-social behaviour) as a lesser requirement for evidence is required in order for a court to grant an order for eviction. However, this approach has been suspended because recent court rulings (*Donegan* v *Dublin City Council* and *Dublin City Council* v *Gallagher*) found this process to be incompatible with the provisions of the European Court of Human Rights Act 2003 (Kenna, 2006).

Despite the fact that many interviewees expressed reservations about this legislation, the termination of tenancies for anti-social behaviour in Fatima Mansions was regarded as having a positive impact on overall stability and its transition from a troubled to a more settled neighbourhood. Thus a local community activist told us progress in addressing anti-social behaviour

> didn't happen until the Guards and the local authorities actually started sitting down [with community activists] talking about policies of [community]

safety ... it is the one area that kills projects and it is the one area that doesn't, let's say, require money, it requires trust, it requires ourselves to sit with the Guards and the officials to say, we are sitting here and we are ... able to talk in confidence ... It took us three years to get to that point ... and [then] Dublin City set up a pilot project on anti-social behaviour and that was a very significant development because it really focused in on [anti-social] families ... but we were at a point where some families had to go.

However, it is noteworthy that these evictions did not occur in isolation and were accompanied by a broad range of other interventions aimed at effecting the social regeneration of the neighbourhood and all of these activities took place within a wider framework of partnership between the Gardaí, the local authority, and the community.

The focus of local authorities on addressing anti-social behaviour through legislation and remedial works reflects what Burney (2009) terms their conversion from housing managers to behaviour managers and raises concerns that a lesser emphasis is placed on effective neighbourhood management practice as a result. Interviewees suggested that poor housing management practices, particularly in relation to allocations, facilitated anti-social behaviour in the neighbourhoods. For example, practices resulting in the clustering of households with a high level of (unmet) need, particularly those with a number of young children, were seen to be problematic for social order. Inadequacies in the tenant vetting process and in the organisation of pre-tenancy courses were flagged and it was reported that tenants were offered these courses retrospectively when there was no longer an incentive or an enforceable obligation to attend. Or, as in the case of Moyross, where the vetting of tenants was viewed to have been short-circuited under an unstated policy, which one interviewee described as 'letting at all costs' in order to avoid vacant units.

In addition, the allocation of 'quasi-policing functions' to local authorities (O'Connell, 1998) [including the use of private security companies in some neighbourhoods], raises questions as to whether this has detracted from the Gardaí's responsibility for social order in the neighbourhoods.

The role and capacity of the Gardaí in addressing social order

Historically, there has been a legacy of poor relations between the Gardaí and marginalised communities (Committee of Inquiry into the Penal System, 1985; Browne, 2008). This issue was noted by McAuliffe and Fahey (1999). Our 1997–8 fieldwork and the 2007–9 fieldwork indicates that this situation remained unchanged in the more troubled parts of Finglas South and Moyross, some residents of which reported a range of grievances including a poor investigative response to reports of crime, and a poor response to calls for assistance with a tendency for the Gardaí to arrive after an event had calmed down or deescalated.

A frequently cited example is the 'riots' that occurred in Finglas South on St Patrick's Day 2008 and which were reported to have been allowed to run for a number of hours before the Gardaí arrived. The lack of consistency in policing received particular criticism from residents:

> [E]very second day there's a check point on every corner . . . if there's a call, they don't respond . . . they are only coming when things have quietened down.

> [Y]ou see cars going wild around here, and then they do a lot of spot checks, and that's good. There's a kind of blaze of being out on patrol for a few weeks, and then it's gone. Then you ring up, they're not here, there's no continuity.

The use of aggressive and confrontational policing styles, especially against young men, was also noted and members of the force interviewed for this study acknowledged that tactics could be harsh. Thus one resident told us: 'I wouldn't like his [the Inspector's] tactics quite frankly, quite tough, quite hard' and another claimed 'The policing may have been heavy handed'.

These elements of 'over-policing' and 'under protection' led residents and service providers to suggest that the troubled neighbourhoods were policed differently to other areas. In this vein, as one resident noted:

> The problem here as I see it is that the guards operate a policy of containment in areas like [this] and the people who live here are expected to put up with a level of anti-social behaviour that wouldn't be tolerated by the residents of other more affluent districts.

In the more troubled neighbourhoods, Gardaí were viewed as being 'out of their depth' and at best 'trying to keep a lid on things'. A lack of resources and manpower, a high turnover of personnel, and a shortage of experienced officers who were committed to staying in the areas and developing working relationships with residents and service providers were cited as affecting continuity and effectiveness, as a member of the Gardaí commented:

> I don't believe that there's been stability in the guards in X over the last few years. There's been constant changes in inspectors . . . I always thought if there's stability of a certain amount of people, they get to know the territory, they get to know the people, what works, what doesn't work, how you approach them.

Since the 1997–8 study, a number of pieces of legislation have extended the Gardaí's powers to deal with social order problems, culminating in the enactment of five new Criminal Justice Acts in 2009. Among these, the introduction of anti-social behaviour orders (ASBOs) by the Criminal Justice Act 2006 gave the Garda powers to deal with anti-social behaviour in the general population (similar to that granted to local authorities in relation to social housing tenants) including, controversially, powers to deal with the behaviour of children aged 12 to 18 years. Under this civil legislation, adults and children are issued (incrementally if the behaviour is seen to persist) with a behavioural warning; a good behaviour contract; and finally a behavioural order that, if broken, is a criminal offence punishable by fine or detention. Data on the first two-year period of the implementation of the legislation indicate that 988 behaviour warnings were issued to adults and 684 issued to children; 12 good behaviour contracts (used only for children) were agreed; and eight applications for behavioural orders were made to the courts, six of which were granted (three for adults and three for children) (O'Brien, 2009). The small number of ASBOs processed under this Act may be due to the extensive criticism of its use by children's rights groups. These groups regard the legislation as criminalising youth behaviour and providing children with an ASBO 'badge of honour', while failing to address the needs of young people who are at risk and/or vulnerable through more appropriate state interventions such as mental health services, family or educational support, and addiction treatment (cf. Children's Rights Alliance, 2005; and Squires, 2006).

A more positive approach to dealing with anti-social behaviour and community safety that had emerged since our first visit to the neighbourhoods was seen to result from ideas of restorative justice and the community policing initiative – defined by the Gardaí as a group of dedicated officers to help and work with residents, statutory, community, and voluntary agencies to prevent crime. The Gardaí working in the seven case study neighbourhoods who were involved in this initiative told us: 'It's about building a relationship between the community and the Gardaí. It's about the Gardaí being visible and seen to be visible' and 'They know their own parish, they know everyone who lives in it, the issues, the criminals, the people who might be involved in drugs and they know all the situations and they can nip it off at the bud'.

This method of working was seen to have improved relationships between residents and the Garda in a number of the case study neighbourhoods, namely, Cranmore, Deanrock, Fatima Mansions, and Fettercairn. In the last of these neighbourhoods, one interviewee claimed 'once upon a time Guards couldn't walk through the estates' but this had changed significantly by the time of the 2007–9 fieldwork. An important part of this work was seen to lie in liaison with local schools, community leaders, and community centres; involvement in summer projects; building positive relations with young people and through consistent foot and bike patrols by the community Garda assigned to the area.

In addition, each of the seven case study neighbourhoods was linked to a Garda Youth Diversion Programme that was run by local youth services and the community police. These were regarded as being successful in diverting young people from criminal activity and lowering the reoffending rate of young people at risk, out of school, or 'barely hanging in school' who had come to the attention of the juvenile liaison officer – notwithstanding the reservations noted earlier in this chapter about the focus of these programmes on youth that had already come to the attention of the criminal justice system.

Though community policing approaches were viewed as being successful by those on the ground in the case study neighbourhoods, there were concerns about the priority and value placed on this work within the Garda organisation. There appeared to be little standardised policy on the role and it was down to individual personnel to interpret how this was done. Personnel were often moved on and it was suggested that young ambitious Guards 'with degrees' sought to move out of this area of work after a short time reflecting the practice of being 'promoted out of' community relations. Community Guards remarked on how they could be pulled back into the station if there was a shortage of personnel or a major operation or investigation underway. Furthermore, they noted that there was little integration between the various units of the force and they found their work could be compromised by the activities of the other sections of the Gardaí such as the Emergency Response Unit and the Public Order Unit (which respond to serious crime and civil unrest) and the Garda National Drugs Unit.

Since the first phase of fieldwork was undertaken, closed-circuit television (CCTV) has become a crime prevention feature in a number of neighbourhoods, by and large funded through the RAPID programmes (see Chapters 6 and 7), and is by and large regarded positively. In one neighbourhood it was viewed as 'the single biggest tool against crime that they have' as it was believed that after its installation drug dealers and others involved in criminal activities had moved out of the neighbourhood. However, evidence suggests (see for example, Newburn and Hayman, 2002) that CCTV can create a false sense of security and often displaces drug dealing scenes to nearby areas and as such provides a short-term respite, rather than a long-term solution. More worryingly, the short-term reduction in anti-social behaviour and criminal activities can result in a reduction in community policing resources as was the case in Cranmore, where the number of Gardaí working the neighbourhood was reduced from two to one as a lesser level of policing was seen to be needed.

The involvement of the Gardaí in inter-agency work has expanded significantly since the 1997–8 study with their representation on a number of the coordinating committees of area-based initiatives (as described in Chapter 6), though their involvement has been hesitant. Members of the Garda expressed a wariness about working in partnership with communities around social order problems expressing a concern that 'local elements' involved in high-level criminal activities would sabotage public meetings. This reluctance was most evident in initial attempts by Local Drug Task Forces to establish Policing Fora (as advocated in the National Drugs Strategy 2001) to bring residents and the statutory, voluntary, and community sectors together to address issues of crime and social order (Bissett, 1999). More recently, however, a substantial improvement has been noted in the willingness of the Garda to be involved in inter-agency working relationships. Such progress was noted by a coordinator of one of the Local Drug Task Force areas:

> [T]hat would have been a big change over the last couple of years since that last book was written, the whole change in Garda policy towards becoming involved with the community and participating in Drugs Task Forces now compared to back in 1998 and having experienced that sort of evolution, it's absolutely amazing where they've come.

This type of partnership approach has been furthered again through the establishment of Joint Policing Committees (proposed under An Garda Síochána Act 2008) in each local authority administrative area with the aim of developing cooperation between the Gardaí, local authorities, and elected local representatives on the management of policing and crime issues. The legislation also provided for Local Policing Fora and Community Safety Fora at a smaller neighbourhood level, which are intended to have a more direct and frequent level of community engagement. There is tepid optimism that these measures will have a positive impact on social order problems. However, the Gardaí's ability to develop a greater level of accountability towards residents and other agencies is crucial, especially for residents with poor previous experiences of community consultation with the Garda. As one Garda acknowledged:

> [T]here is a real level of nervousness around people feeling that they might be intimidated, targeted or otherwise if they work too closely with us and the guards basically. You would hear people saying I'll say hello to you at the meeting but if you pass me in the street, don't pretend to know me.

Conclusions

Both rounds of fieldwork on the seven case study neighbourhoods concluded that the level of social disorder had a negative impact on their liveability. During the 2007–9 fieldwork social disorder in these neighbourhoods was seen to be related to two main difficulties – the public presence of groups of young people and the impact of the sale and use of drugs and alcohol. These issues were, however, more complex than appeared on the surface. A parallel process by which social (dis)order is constructed, defined, and contextualised was seen to feed into contested notions of public space and concerns about community safety. The subsequent emphasis by interviewees on the disorderly behaviour of (mainly young) individuals tended to obfuscate the role policy can play in creating the space for social disorder to flourish, and in its failure to respond to the high level of needs identified.

In assessing the trajectories of social order in the seven neighbourhoods, the situation was found to have changed in some places for the better, in others for the worse. A number of factors influenced these changes. Negative outcomes were associated with deepening levels of inequality, deficits in social policy, the impact of the drugs economy, and an over-reliance on civil and criminal justice approaches in lieu of good practice in housing allocation policies and estate management practices. Positive outcomes were seen to result from a combination of improvements in the built environment; strong community and youth work activities; and good estate management and community policing practices – though the crucial issue was that these were seen to have little impact in isolation from each other. Overall, social order improved where the policy response was adequate and implemented appropriately.

References

Bissett, J. (1999) *Not waiting for a revolution: Negotiating policing through the rialto community policing forum.* Dublin: Rialto Community Policing Forum.

Browne, C. (2008) *Garda public attitudes survey 2008. Garda Research Unit research report No. 1/08.* Templemore: Garda Research Unit.

Burney, E. (2009) *Making people behave: Anti-social behaviour, politics and policy,* second edition. Devon: Willan.

Children's Rights Alliance (2005) *The case against Anti Social Behaviour Orders – coalition against ASBOs.* Dublin: Children's Rights Alliance.

Committee of Inquiry into the Penal System (1985) *The Whitaker Report.* Dublin: Stationery Office.

Dáil Éireann (2003) *Dáil debate, Vol. 574 No. 5 col. 1509.* Dublin: Stationery Office.

— (2008) *Dáil debates, Vol. 668, No. 1, col. 107.* Dublin: Stationery Office.

Devlin, M. (2006) *Inequality and the stereotyping of young people.* Dublin: The Equality Authority.

Eivers, E., Shiel, G., and Shortt, S. (2004) *Reading literacy in disadvantaged primary schools.* Dublin: Educational Research Centre.

Fahey, T. (1999) Summary of findings. In T. Fahey (ed.) *Social housing in Ireland: A study of success, failure and lessons learned* (pp. 249–70). Dublin: Oak Tree Press.

Ghodse, H. (2008) *International drug control into the 21st Century.* London: Ashgate.

Goldstein, P.J. (1985) The drugs/violence nexus: A tripartite conceptual framework. *Journal of Drug Issues,* 21(2), 143–74.

Grover, C. (2008) *Crime and inequality.* Devon: Willan.

Hammersley, R. (2008) *Drugs and crime: Theories and practices.* Cambridge: Palgrave.

Kenna, P (2006) *Irish housing law and policy.* Dublin: Clarus Press.

MacDonald, R., Shildrick, T., Webster, C., and Simpson, D. (2005) Growing up in poor neighbourhoods: the significance of class and place in the extended transitions of 'socially excluded' young adults. *Sociology,* 39(5), 873–91.

MacGregor, S. (2003) Social exclusion. In N. Ellison and C. Pierson (eds) *Developments in British social policy* (pp. 57–74). Basingstoke: Palgrave MacMillan.

McAuliffe, R. and Fahey, T. (1999) Responses to social order problems. In T. Fahey (ed.) *Social housing in Ireland: A study of success, failure and lessons learned* (pp. 173–90). Dublin: Oak Tree Press.

Mulcahy, A. and O'Mahony, M. (2005) *Policing and social marginalization.* Dublin: Combat Poverty Agency.

Newburn, T. and Hayman, S. (2002) *Policing, surveillance and social control: CCTV and police monitoring of suspects.* Portland: Willan.

Norris, M. (1999) The impact of the built environment. In T. Fahey (ed.) *Social housing in Ireland: a study of success, failure and lessons learned* (pp. 101–24). Dublin: Oak Tree Press.

O'Brien, C. (2009) Government to review effectiveness of Asbos. *The Irish Times,* 29 June.

O'Connell, C. (1998) Tenant involvement in local authority housing: A new panacea for policy failure? *Administration,* 46(2), 25–46.

O'Donnell, I. (2005) Violence and social change in the Republic of Ireland. *International Journal of the Sociology of Law*, 33(2), 101–17.

Reinarman, C. and Levine, H.G. (1997) *Crack in America: Demon drugs and social justice.* Berkeley: University of California Press.

Shildrick, T. (2006) Youth culture, subculture and the importance of neighbourhood. *Young: Nordic Journal of Youth Research*, 14(1), 61–74

Smyth, E., McCoy, S., Darmody, M., and Dunne, A. (2007) Changing times, changing schools? Quality of life for students. In T. Fahey, H. Russell, and C.T. Whelan (eds) *Best of times? The social impact of the Celtic Tiger.* Dublin: Institute of Public Administration.

Squires, P. (ed.) (2006) *Community safety: Critical perspectives on policy and practice.* Bristol: Policy Press.

St. Jean, P. (2007) *Pockets of crime: Broken windows, collective efficacy, and the criminal point of view.* Chicago: University of Chicago Press.

Sunday Independent (2008) Limerick is now official 'murder capital' of Europe. *Sunday Independent*, 20 April.

Sunday Tribune (2009) Grisly tale of murder mile. *Sunday Tribune*, 8 March.

Wilkinson, R. and Pickett, K. (2009) *The spirit level: Why more equal societies almost always do better.* London: Allen Lane.

Zinberg, N. (1984) *Drug, set and setting: The basis for controlled intoxicant use.* New Haven, CT: Yale University Press.

10

MEDIA REPRESENTATIONS, STIGMA, AND NEIGHBOURHOOD IDENTITY

Amanda Haynes, Eoin Devereux, and Martin J. Power

Introduction

This chapter relates the results of a study of print and broadcast coverage of one of the seven case study neighbourhoods – Moyross, in Limerick city. Our work takes place in the context of a wider debate about the ways in which mass media can contribute towards the stigmatising of the socially excluded and the places in which they live (see Devereux, Haynes, and Power, 2011a, 2011b; Golding and Middleton 1982; Lens 2002, p. 144; Bullock, Fraser Wyche, and Williams, 2001, pp. 229–230; Hayward and Yar, 2006, pp. 11–12). Previous research on these themes has examined how mass media and other social forces contribute to the creation of negative stereotypes, which damage the reputations of the neighbourhoods in which the 'underclass' or poor reside (see Greer and Jewkes, 2005; Bauder, 2002; Blokland, 2008; Hastings, 2004). Negative and sensationalist media coverage of poor neighbourhoods is consistently referred to in studies that attempt to explain how neighbourhoods come to suffer from endogenous stigmatisation (see Warr, 2006; Oresjo, Andersson, and Holmquist, 2004; Gourlay, 2007; Wassenberg, 2004). The existing research literature demonstrates that negative reputations of such places can, in themselves, have a profound effect upon the life chances, experiences, and self-image of those who live in neighbourhoods that carry a stigma (Permentier, van Ham, and Bolt, 2008, 2009). Our analysis of this issue is guided by two overarching and inter-connected conceptual frameworks, namely social exclusion and political economy (see Levitas, 2000; Byrne, 1999). Through this research, we have sought to address a number of key issues:

1   to establish how Moyross is depicted in media representations;
2   to establish how the material and social conditions in Moyross are explained in media representations;

3   to establish which actors have a role in constructing Moyross in media representations.

We argue that, for the most part, media coverage is stigmatising, highlighting the very real challenges that the neighbourhood faces with regard to crime and social order at the expense of any significant engagement with the positive characteristics of the locale, its residents, their community, and achievements. We argue that this depiction can be best understood within the context of the commercial realities, which progressively impact upon media production, increasing the pressure to absorb rather than just inform and reducing the time available to media professionals to directly connect with the people and places upon which they report (see Ryfe, 2009). In acknowledging these realities, we do not seek to legitimise the stigmatised identity of Moyross, neither do we want to deny the very real problems facing the residents in this neighbourhood, which result from both a combination of long-term state neglect, poor planning, and criminality. Nonetheless, the routinely negative media portrayal of Moyross, in common with other social housing neighbourhoods in Limerick city (such as Southill and St Mary's Park), has very real and significant malign consequences for its residents and their inter-actions with non-residents in particular. Barnes (2010), for example, found that students in a middle-class Limerick school replicated the themes that this chapter identifies in media coverage of Moyross, associating the neighbourhood with crime, disorder, and social unrest (Fitzgerald, 2007, p. 7 cited in Devereux, Haynes, and Power, 2011b, p. 126). Negative media portrayals have, according to the Limerick Regeneration Agency, contributed significantly to the poor image of these neighbourhoods as well as to the city as a whole (Limerick Regeneration Agency, 2008) and have stymied attempts to regenerate these areas in social and economic terms.

A tripartite methodological approach

Following the Glasgow University Media Group (Philo, 1990), the methodology employed here adopts a tripartite approach to media analysis, incorporating content, production, and reception. Specifically, we have undertaken a qualitative content analysis of print media and broadcast texts, interviews with media professionals, and focus groups with residents and grassroots activists in Moyross itself. The tripartite approach to media analysis allows us to give equal weighting to all three aspects of media coverage, namely, an understanding of the dynamics that shape the initial making of media texts; their discursive content and their reception by audiences. In the context of this chapter, this allows us to investigate how media texts about Moyross are constructed; their assumptions about Moyross and their likely influence in shaping public beliefs and perceptions about the neighbourhood.

Media content: Print media content was sampled from four newspapers, which were chosen for their diversity of audiences and styles. Specifically, we selected our sample from a national broadsheet (*Irish Independent*), two national tabloids (*Irish Mirror* and the *Irish News*), and a local imprint (*Limerick Leader*). The time period within which we selected articles was 1 January 2006 to 31 December 2007.[1] We selected this timeframe in order to examine media coverage of the regeneration project and of a specific case of an arson attack on two young children. In September 2006, Millie Murray and her five-year-old brother Gavin were severely burned in an arson attack on their mother's car in Moyross. Three teenagers from Moyross were subsequently convicted of the petrol bomb attack on the children. The arson attack on these two young children was the final catalyst for state intervention in Moyross. The cabinet asked the former head of Dublin City Council – John FitzGerald – to carry out an immediate assessment of the issues prevailing in the neighbourhood. Fitzgerald reported back on the scale of social exclusion in March 2007 and the Cabinet's Committee on Social Inclusion agreed to the creation of two regeneration companies to oversee the redevelopment of four social housing neighbourhoods in Limerick city including Moyross (Fitzgerald, 2007).

The articles selected were subjected to qualitative content analysis. Content analysis can be defined as 'a research technique for making valid and replicable inferences from texts ... to the contexts of their use' (Krippendorf, 2004, p. 18). Content analysis involves identifying themes, concepts, and patterns thereof within the data. We infer meaning through interpreting these patterns. Themes and concepts may emerge from the data as a result of close reading and constant comparison, a process facilitated by sensitivity to:

1   the relationship between the research question and the text;
2   the relationship between the texts and the context to which meaning will be inferred.

Such knowledge can be acquired through existing theoretical and empirical literature, as well as access to key informants and expertise. Existing theory can also be used to develop an initial list of themes and concepts in advance of analysis. In the case of this analysis both approaches have been adopted. A literature review informed the development of a series of analytical constructs whose relevance to our data is investigated through theory-driven coding. However, we have not permitted these analytical constructs to confine our coding to confirming initial propositions. We have specifically sought to look for other themes that may provide alternative findings to those suggested by the literature.

Television broadcasts were selected from the Irish national, public broadcaster RTE's *Six One News* and *9 O'Clock News* programmes from 1 September 2006 to 31 December 2006 and using RTE's proprietary news archive. These programmes were selected on the basis of audience share. In instances where the same report was broadcast by both programmes, only one was included in our sample. We also included a radio documentary in our analysis made by the local licensed radio station Live 95fm. The documentary, broadcast in November 2006, was based upon a composite of radio broadcasts concerning the Millie and Gavin Murray story.

The strategy of triangulation is employed to enhance the credibility (Lincoln and Guba, 1985) of our interpretation. Specifically, we seek to triangulate the findings of our content analysis with those generated from primary data gathered through research with residents of Moyross and with media professionals.

Reception analysis: Two focus groups were conducted in Moyross following preliminary analysis of the print and broadcast media content. Each involved six participants, most of whom were residents of Moyross. In each focus group, one non-resident grassroots activist also participated. Participants were sourced through the Moyross Community Forum and, as such, many of the residents to whom we spoke were active in their community.

Production analysis: What has come to be known as the production research paradigm places the spotlight on the initial 'making' of media texts or messages. Drawing on a range of ethnographic research methods including interviews and participant observation, it investigates the culture of media organisations, the dynamics involved in 'gate-keeping', and the activities, experiences, and ideologies of journalists and other media professionals (Gitlin, 1994; Philo, 2008; Devereux, Haynes, and Power, 2011b). The paradigm seeks to explain how and why particular discourses, ideologies, templates, or frames come to predominate within media coverage. Influenced, in the main, by organisational sociology and by theories of political economy (Fenton, 2007; Mosco and Wasko, 1988) in particular, the production research paradigm carries with it the promise of revealing more about the realities of doing media work, the constraints within which journalists and other media professionals operate, and the intended meanings that are encoded into media texts (Hall, 1974). Semi-structured interviews were undertaken with five media professionals who work in the print and broadcast media sectors. All but one of the media professionals to whom we spoke have a broad remit with regard to covering events in the Limerick region. One is primarily a crime and court reporter, but also has a secondary broader remit.

Image is everything? Themes in evidence

We begin this discussion of our findings with an overview of the primary themes apparent in the print media data. In addition to the stigmatising and 'othering' of members of the underclass or poor, a growing number of researchers have sought to understand how the places in which these groups live come to be stigmatised (Greer and Jewkes, 2005; Bauder, 2002; Blokland, 2008; Hastings, 2004). Influenced largely by Goffman's (1963) classic sociological treatise, which understood stigma as 'spoiled identity', this important body of work has examined how mass media and other social forces contribute to the creation of negative stereotypes, which damage the reputations of the places in which the underclass or poor reside (Devereux,

Haynes, and Power, 2011a, p. 125). In establishing the existence of a stigmatised identity, Nauta, Tulner, and van Soomeran (2001), in writing about the Dutch experience, focus on the balance of stories about crime and safety; policy, housing, and the environment; urban renewal; and 'social items' regarding such issues as employment and education. In our analysis we have classified both the primary theme of the content and the precipitating event.

Of the 420 articles in our sample, 298 or 70 per cent were about crime. The period of our study incorporates the arson attack on Gavin and Millie Murray. As such, one would anticipate that many of these reports focus on that event. Indeed, 84 of the articles do focus either specifically on the attack, on the arrests and trial following the attack, or on related demonstrations or TV appearances. However, this does not negate the predominance of crime-related articles in our sample. Even excluding those reports that focus on Gavin and Millie Murray, crime is by far the largest category of stories.

There was general agreement among the media professionals whom we interviewed that bad news sells, in this vein one interviewee told us:

> When it bleeds it leads. If something negative happens in Moyross it's on the nationals . . . if it's a negative story it is closer to getting to the front page than a happy clappy story in relation to Moyross. . . . but I think that's across the board in the local media.

The Moyross residents who we interviewed also placed economics at the centre of the equation stating variously that the media report negatively on Moyross 'to sell papers' or 'because we don't have the money to sue them'.

Of the remaining articles, whose primary theme we categorised as crime, the majority relate to specific incidents of violent crime, such as murders, shootings, armed robbery, and arson (on homes). A smaller number of articles relate to the availability of drugs and drug seizures. Among these articles there are examples of single incidents resulting in multiple articles in the same publication, sometimes over a period of weeks as the precipitating incident, investigation, and trial are reported upon. For example, the murder of Brian Fitzgerald, a nightclub security guard from a middle-class suburb of Limerick, received large amounts of coverage. The *Limerick Leader* provided daily reports on the resulting trial, for example, repeating in each report the association of one of the accused with Moyross. Such reports were sometimes very factually oriented making little comment on Moyross. Nonetheless, the constant association between the neighbourhood and the murder contributes to its stigmatisation. Although we hold that the role of the sub-editor in the construction of stories cannot be underestimated, it is noteworthy that while all the articles make specific mention of Moyross, only nine of the 298 articles on crime do so in their headlines. Of these nine, two were published in the national press and seven in the local newspaper, the *Limerick Leader*. Nonetheless, articles that were categorised as primarily focused on crime represented only 52 per cent of the *Limerick Leader*'s total coverage of Moyross, compared to 77 per cent of the *Irish Independent*'s, 88 per cent of the *Irish Mirror*'s, and 90 per cent of *Irish News* articles.

Next to crime, regeneration was the next most common primary theme of the articles in our sample, representing 10 per cent of all articles. Articles on politics, published primarily in the *Limerick Leader*, represented 5 per cent of our sample. Ten articles were categorised as focusing primarily on community spirit within Moyross.

Normalising versus pathologising discourses

Hastings (2004) classifies discourses regarding stigmatised neighbourhoods as either normalising or pathologising. Normalising discourses are critical, even dismissive, of a neighbourhood's stigmatised image. They reject the idea that the behaviour of residents as a group exceeds the limits of expected deviance or differentiates them from residents of other neighbourhoods. They depict anti-social behaviour as the actions of a small minority. They explain the neighbourhood's stigmatisation and problems in terms of structural causes. Based on her analysis of resident and non-resident perceptions of three UK neighbourhoods, Hastings (2004) found that in some cases, an attempt was made to normalise an area by pathologising other neighbourhoods.

In contrast, pathologising discourses focus on behavioural explanations for the neighbourhood's stigmatised images and problems. They regard residents as possessing deviant norms and values, which represent a threat to mainstream culture, and might be transmitted to and reproduced by their children. Such 'culture of poverty' and 'cycle of deprivation' explanations are a feature of pathologising discourses. Residents may be among those who pathologise their neighbourhood (Hastings, 2004). Indeed, Costa Pinto (2000, cited in Gourlay 2007, p. 4) clarifies that residents may internalise the stigmatised image of their neighbourhood, impacting their self-image in turn.[2]

Following Hastings (2004), we seek to establish whether pathologising and normalising discourses are evident in the print media coverage of Moyross. Drawing on Hastings' (2004) work we conceptualise normalising discourses as:

1   critical of stigmatised images of the neighbourhood;
2   critical of behavioural explanations for problems within or the image of the neighbourhood;
3   favouring structural explanations for problems within or the image of the neighbourhood;
4   depicting deviant behaviour within the neighbourhood as exceptional;
5   depicting deviant behaviour within the neighbourhood as within normal parameters;
6   depicting residents of Moyross as the same as residents of other neighbourhoods;
7   or comparing Moyross favourably to other neighbourhoods.

Pathologising discourses as:

1   accepting of stigmatised images of the neighbourhood;
2   favouring behavioural explanations for problems within or the image of the neighbourhood;
3   characterising residents as possessing deviant norms and values;
4   characterising residents or the neighbourhood as pathological, integrally flawed, or abnormal;[3]
5   comparing Moyross unfavourably to other neighbourhoods.[4]

Having already evidenced the excessive coverage of crime in relation to Moyross, the print media articles on the subject of regeneration provide a useful alternative focus for such an analysis. First, we find that of the 44 articles that are categorised as focusing primarily on regeneration only three can be regarded as engaging in any meaningful way with the causes of Moyross' problems. A *Limerick Leader* editorial (2006, 29 May), a feature from the same newspaper (2007, 26 May), and an editorial from the *Irish Independent* (2006, 30 October) offer the reader an analysis of the causes of the neighbourhood's difficulties. While the *Limerick Leader* focuses on political neglect, the *Independent* focuses on the impact of illegal drugs. The remaining articles cite perceived problems or proposed solutions without analysis or critique.

Reflecting the concerns of Professor François Heinderyckx who 'worries that news comes immediately but in little pieces – gone is a media which gathered facts, views and evidence to present its readers with a complete, considered analysis' (cited in White, 2008, p. 68), most of the articles on regeneration rely on brief direct or indirect quotations for this purpose, rather than on their own analysis. As such, the explanations provided to the reader are dictated by the source – mostly official, for example the Fitzgerald report, a local councillor, or the manager of the Moyross Community Enterprise Centre. Indeed, the influence of the former source is apparent in the number of articles that identically repeat the challenges of crime, disorder, and social exclusion listed in the Fitzgerald report, without further comment, and focus on physical regeneration as the solution. As Shoemaker and Reese (1996) convincingly argue, the sources used by media professionals play a determining role in highlighting (or not) the salience of particular issues.

Depictions of Moyross and its residents, with the exception of headlines and the three articles cited above, likewise depend on direct and indirect quotes. Although there was frequent reference to the challenge of crime, alternatives were provided by sources such as a group of Roman Catholic monks who live in Moyross and the manager of the Community and Enterprise Centre highlighting the excellent character of the majority of Moyross residents. However, sources that are less positive in their depictions are also reproduced unquestioningly. For example, one article uncritically cites a source who describes Moyross as a battlefield (*Limerick Leader*, 2007, 21 April). Other articles uncritically cite official sources who depict Moyross as 'living in fear of tearaway tots' (*Irish Mirror*, 2007, 9 November). It is notable that most of the articles on regeneration are episodic and as such the selection of sources is informed by the event that precipitated the article, e.g. a residents' meeting or the publication of a report.

A number of the regeneration article headlines stand out as particular examples of the role of sub-editors in the stigmatisation of a neighbourhood. For example, in their headlines national newspapers refer to Moyross as 'troubled city suburb' (*Irish Independent*, 2006, 25 October), 'feud estate' (*Irish Independent*, 2006, 30 October), 'crime ridden housing estate' (*Irish Independent*, 2007, 31 March), and a 'gangland' (*Irish News*, 2007, 11 September), while the *Mirror* calls (in capitals) to 'TEAR DOWN MOYROSS' (*Irish Mirror*, 2007, 11 September). Sub-editors play a very significant role in the location of and reshaping of stories. They will also write the story's headline and select the accompanying image(s).

Media professionals interviewed shared an understanding of Moyross that focused on the structural causes of the exclusion experienced there. One stated 'There's a massive social divide in Limerick more than any other city in this country . . . actually it's massive'. Yet, with some notable exceptions, we found that these articles evidenced a focus on the factual reporting of episodic events, rather than a focus on the provision of analysis, context, or critique that seem to be reserved for editorials and features. Structural explanations are largely confined to brief excerpts from sources' comments, often presented only as lists of named causal factors. Even such articles, in legitimating the need for regeneration, accept the stigmatised image of Moyross. The phrase 'social exclusion' is generally accompanied by reference to crime and/or disorder. For example one article cites a source who describes Moyross as 'plagued by social exclusion, crime and disorder despite a number of community based initiatives' but the author also refers to the neighbourhood as 'one of Ireland's worst estates' (*The Mirror*, 2006, 30 October). Where they occur, normalising discourses commonly refer to the problems challenging the neighbourhood as generated by a minority of pathological residents.

Contextualising positive stories

While articles on regeneration would seem to require some reference to the challenges faced by Moyross, articles focusing on community spirit might be expected to forgo such associations. However, we find that even stories on these positive themes are contextualised by reference to stigmatising images (see Dean and Hastings, 2000, p. 21). In this instance, we take as our example the ten stories that were categorised as focused on community spirit. Through this means we seek to further our understanding of the impact of valuing 'bad news' on positive coverage (Dean and Hastings, 2000, p. 21).

Only three of the ten stories categorised as focusing on community spirit were published in the national press, including one in a tabloid paper. Of the ten stories, four focused on a Nativity play organised by the monks located in Moyross. Two of the stories focused on the community's welcome to a child returning from hospital. It is notable that seven of these stories were published in one local newspaper, the *Limerick Leader*.

Even within this category there was evidence of a tendency to contextualise positive stories by reference to a stigmatised image of the neighbourhood. For example, a good news story about a production of the Nativity story in Moyross was foregrounded by the information that the locale was 'ONE of the country's most socially deprived areas, which has suffered extensively from feuding criminal gangs, anti-social behaviour and drug dealing ...' (*Irish Independent*, 2007, 15 December). A second national story regarding the return of the hospitalised child described Moyross as 'plagued by petrol-bombings, shootings, murders and increasing bursts of gang violence over the past three weeks' (*Irish Mirror*, 2006, 28 September). The third national story in this category bears the headline 'Sports stars tog out for troubled estates' children' (*Irish Independent*, 2007, 8 August) and states that the 'event was welcomed locally, in view of the negative publicity some communities have had as a result of violent incidents'. It can be argued that the newsworthiness of these stories printed in the news section of national papers was derived not from the event reported but from the juxtaposition of a positive event with the stigmatised image of the neighbourhood.

The concept of newsworthiness is pivotal to understanding the practice of journalism (Clayman and Reisner, 1998; Shoemaker, Hyuk Lee, Han, and Cohen, 2007). It was clear from speaking to media professionals that Moyross' association with criminality and deprivation in the public mind (and more recently the resulting regeneration project) is the primary source of its interest for the media. Thus, one participant claimed:

> [P]eople have a kind of a morbid interest in this family feud, the gang feud that goes on in Limerick. I think because it's almost like something out of the Sopranos. So from that point of view it is interesting, I mean, people are watching *CSI*, watching programmes like *The Wire* and so they see a lot of that happening in Moyross. And it's true up like, up till very recently that definitely was the case. I think that Moyross does have that appeal. Unfortunately it's a negative appeal ...

Although one of our media professional participants specifically cited educational developments as the source of their interest in Moyross, this is still framed in relation to the principal newsworthiness of the neighbourhood's association with criminality: 'I've considered it [Moyross] newsworthy because I have in my time attempted to do other news stories in Moyross, apart from the ones that would oblige me to be there, in terms of crime and anti-social behaviour'. We argue that media organisations tend to view the audience as located outside of Moyross, and the media as providing a window into this place from which the audience themselves are socially distant (Devereux *et al.*, 2011a, p. 130).

It is worth noting that the tendency to juxtapose the positive with a negative is not as evident in the locally published articles on the theme of community spirit.

One such article does reference external negative perceptions of Moyross and another references violence in the neighbourhood, but in both cases these references rely on the direct quotes from the individuals who are the central focus of the pieces rather than the reporter's own formulation or additional sources.

Nonetheless, of all the articles in this category, only one, which relates to the presentation of the Gaisce (president of Ireland's) award to Moyross residents, communicates local achievements (in terms of civic participation, also mentioning the Corpus Christi Pipe and Drums Band, as well as local involvement in boxing and carpentry) (*Limerick Leader*, 2007, 10 November).

The residents who participated in our focus groups felt strongly that there are very positive aspects to Moyross, which are seriously neglected in media coverage and impact upon external perceptions of the neighbourhood. Residents hold that:

> They haven't seen what we have … There's such beautiful places out here. These are the good things: the schools, our Church, our library, the activity, the adult education classes, our pipe band. I mean, they're never shown like that … But if there is a shooting or a mugging or a robbery – Moyross, Moyross, Moyross.

> When our pipe band win these big competitions, where are they then? You never hear of our band or how good the school is. They didn't report on the television last week or two weeks ago about the girl from Cosgrave … she became a guard. … I mean, she's from Moyross and as far as I know, I think we have ten guards from Moyross.

Like our focus group participants, residents interviewed by Dean and Hastings (2000) perceived that the media coverage of their neighbourhoods was not representative of their lived experience. They held that coverage focused disproportionately on the negative and media professionals regarded positive events as lacking news value. They contended that the newsworthiness of negative events occurring locally was fuelled by the neighbourhood's stigmatised image. Significantly the participants believed that even stories about positive events were accompanied by references to the stigmatised image that they held to be the source of the neighbourhood's media interest.

Uncritical repetition of Moyross' stigmatised identity

In commending the continuing importance of professional journalism, in an age of citizen journalists, White (2008, p. 69) argues that

> communities need more than point to point and point to multi-point communication if they are to understand better the political, social and economic tumult around them. They need access to reliable information and they need analysis, context and perspective about what that information means.

Yet, it was not uncommon for the articles that we analysed to uncritically reproduce Moyross' stigmatised identity.

The *Limerick Leader* (2006, 21 September), Moyross's local newspaper, acknowledges (uncritically) the stigmatised image of the neighbourhood citing the target areas of Limerick's regeneration project, 'the deprived estates whose names are synonymous with crime, anti-social behaviour and neglect'. The *Mirror* (2007, 8 November) acknowledges that: 'The decent people of troubled Moyross and Southill in Limerick must be sick to the back teeth of their area being constantly dragged through the mud' and extends the impact of what they regard as a pathological minority to the 'blackening of a city's name'. The author of an article in the *Irish Independent* (2007, 26 August) specifically states that 'The stigma of having Southill or Moyross as an address is also a cause of discrimination by employers and there are extraordinarily high levels of unemployment at a time when Limerick is undergoing an economic boom'. Despite these acknowledgements, there is a dearth of critical commentary on the neighbourhoods' stigmatised image, with the exception of a *Limerick Leader* editorial of 21 September 2006, in which the editors states that 'Moyross is not a jungle or an area people should be ashamed to say they are from'.

Indeed, 38 articles define Moyross as troubled ('troubled estate', 'troubled Limerick suburb', and 'troubled area' being common descriptions), sometimes grouping Moyross and Southill in doing so. A further two articles refer specifically to Pineview Gardens, Moyross in this fashion. Notably, the term 'troubled' is one employed routinely by journalists and sub-editors rather than by their sources.

All 592 references to Moyross specifically were analysed for descriptors other than 'troubled'. Aside from geographical qualifiers such as 'area', 'estate', or 'Limerick's Moyross', the most common descriptor was 'notorious'. There were a small number of references to the neighbourhood as a 'blackspot', a site of 'endemic problems', or a 'time-bomb'. Positive descriptors were in a tiny minority and consisted of three references to Moyross as a community. One article referred to the locale as 'formerly a tight-knit, caring community'. In another ambiguous description, one small part of the neighbourhood was referred to, in inverted commas, as 'respectable' in contrast to the remainder (*Irish Independent*, 2007, 26 August). As we will see in a later section in this chapter, it is not inevitable that the media use the epithets 'troubled' or 'troubled estate' in reference to Moyross. Live 95fm's documentary on Millie and Gavin Murray successfully managed to narrate a tragic story about the arson attack and its aftermath without ever once referring to Moyross in this fashion.

A number of articles employ the metaphor of a war-zone to describe the neighbourhood. The media professionals to whom we spoke accepted that much media coverage serves to pathologise Moyross (and by extension Limerick). For example, one of our interviewees spoke of being introduced recently on radio as 'We now have [...] from the Gaza Strip' echoing the war-zone discourses evident in our content analysis.

The residents interviewed are acutely aware of the kind of labelling that we have documented through our research:

> [N]o matter what story that comes up you will find the 'troubled estate', 'the ghetto', it is categorised, it is stigmatised, and no matter what story, if they are giving a story about something that happened, if it's from Moyross they will always make sure that it is known that this is a stigmatised area.

Sources – internal and external

Wassenberg (2004) clarifies that the media's impact is upon external images, i.e. those held by people who are not residents and may have little or no direct experience of the neighbourhood in question. In turn, in research conducted in Scotland, Gourlay (2007) found that external images, including those shaped by the mass media, were particularly influential in perpetuating the stigmatised image of disadvantaged neighbourhoods. Residents to whom we spoke were conscious of external perceptions of their locality. One resident suggested that those living outside Moyross misperceive it as a 'Total disgrace' and a 'No-go area'.

We have previously noted the importance of sources, particularly official sources, to defining the manner in which regeneration was presented to the audience. A strong reliance on official sources is mirrored across our sample as a whole, in particular, a dependence on councillors and other political figures, clergy, Gardaí, and legal professionals. Relations and friends of crime victims were also employed as sources. Of concern was the significant number of anonymous sources used, particularly anonymous Garda sources. About a quarter of the articles, predominantly national in origin, lacked any reference to a source.

With regard to televisual reports, while grassroots activists were used as sources, national and local politicians dominate in terms of those who are asked to comment on events in the neighbourhood.

The low levels of reference to Moyross residents or even community representatives suggest a reliance on external sources to define and characterise life in the neighbourhood and limited opportunities for residents to challenge misrepresentations in the mainstream media. Nonetheless, it should be noted that residents used as sources by the press, particularly when they comment anonymously, do not always reflect well on their experiences of living in Moyross. A resident who participated in our focus groups suggested that residents are more likely to be used as sources where their comments are negative:

> [T]hey don't want to listen to the people like us that's willing to say the positive side of Moyross. If I can say something bad I'll have a reporter down to me and I'm great and I'll be on the television, I'll be on the radio and everything. And if they go to Mary and she has something good to say, well you're not going to put Mary on you're going to put me on, because I am the one that's running the place down. And even after all these years, I mean

> I never had a problem, thank God, out here. Never did now. So, they're not actually targeting the good parts – the good parts of Moyross, the good people of Moyross.

Overall, residents were critical of the limited range of sources used by the media.

Homogenising the neighbourhood

Media professionals' understandings can themselves be conceptualised as external:

> Unless a journalist is living in the area, something that hardly ever happens, media images are externally set. As the lines in the newspaper and the minutes on television are short; they opt for stereotypes and leave out the nuances that scientists are used to making. A stereotype, once set, is hard to change.
>
> *(Wassenberg, 2004, p. 275)*

The national media's distance from events in Moyross (and Limerick) suggests to us that proximity (see Shoemaker *et al.*, 2007) is also of significance in explaining the shape of media coverage (Devereux *et al.*, 2011a, p. 133). Participants in our focus groups were conscious of journalists' sometimes limited experience of the neighbourhood or local issues on which they are reporting. Commenting on national media, one resident stated that:

> Some of them report, like what I call, from a distance and they don't actually come down. Like I said they don't see the area. So they get the wind of a story. They run with the story and they might make one or two phone calls and write it up and sometimes its actually inaccurate – their information.

Media professionals, too, were conscious of the less-nuanced understanding of Moyross held by more geographically removed colleagues and emphasised that a dearth of local knowledge is not restricted to journalists. Some sub-editors may conflate social housing neighbourhoods that are in fact geographically distant from one another, e.g. confusing Moyross and Southill, which is on the opposite periphery of Limerick, as a result of insufficient local knowledge.

One of the complaints made by focus group participants was that the media fail to differentiate between parks within Moyross. The continuing existence of distinctions among the 12 parks is supported by the work of Eileen Humphreys (2011). Her analysis draws on two studies, one conducted with the general population of Moyross and a second conducted with older residents, whose residences were concentrated in '"more settled" areas of Moyross'. She finds that this latter sub-population of residents are more likely to perceive the neighbourhood as a good place to live (73 per cent), as a place where people watch out for neighbours (84 per cent), as forming a close community (50 per cent), and report higher levels of trust in their neighbours (44 per cent) than the general population of Moyross.

The media professionals to whom we spoke were agreed that 'Moyross' and 'the troubled estate of Moyross' is used as a form of shorthand in communicating with audiences. While accepting the implications of writing about Moyross (as if it were a single entity) one of these media professionals asserted:

> [E]verybody is tainted with the one brush ... if you say Pine View Gardens Moyross, people hear Moyross. If you are from Sarsfield Gardens ... it's still Sarsfield Gardens Moyross so people will still know ... if somebody said Westbury Corbally you'd still hear the Corbally bit.

Our media participants explained that Moyross is a geographical identifier to which the audience can relate and the provision of more nuanced geographical descriptors was not seen to be of interest to national audiences: '[T]he splitting up of Moyross into its constituent elements or of Southill into its constituent elements isn't something that ... trying to imagine myself living in Wexford, that I'd be particularly interested in.

It is worth noting that all the media professionals we interviewed believed that local print and broadcast coverage of Moyross was more positive and balanced than their national counterparts. This was explained in terms of proximity and familiarity with the issues on the ground as well as market realities. However, our content analysis does not depict such a clear-cut distinction between the national and local media. Residents too were divided on this issue. One stated that 'The *[Limerick] Leader* is quite good because it has a space for different little parts of the county. . . . Moyross news is one of them'. But others disagreed and even felt somewhat let down by the coverage of local events, such as a ball celebrating 30 years of Moyross: '[I]t wasn't as big as I thought. I thought for 30 years in Moyross they were going to come in and blow it up, you know, and do all the positive. And you had a few photos of us that was there . . .'.

The role of the editor

In previous sections we have emphasised that the role of media production in reproducing pathologising discourses cannot be understood without consideration of the role of the editor and sub-editor. One of the journalists to whom we spoke emphasised that the pieces they write can be altered by sub-editors and editors to the point that they will not permit their name to be associated with the work. A journalist who contributed to tabloid newspapers found this relationship most problematic:

> I have sources know me and trust me but you know it's still very hard to explain to people that there's a sub at work here or you know who's writing headlines and stuff. . . . there are times when I am filing copy I'll say and I'll know myself now at this stage what they're going to change and I'll say if

you're changing that take my name off it or don't use my stuff you know. It's very difficult because it is, it's what I do and it's my wages as well but at the same time I want and I have to be able to stand over what I write.

However, print journalists in general talked about having to 'push' good news stories:

> I think Moyross definitely does have that appeal [criminality] unfortunately that's a negative appeal and I know from even my own point of view if something positive happens and I try to push it to our news editor I'd have a way better chance if there was some major crime out there about that making it to the front page than a positive story from Moyross making it to the front page.

Editorial resistance to good news stories about Moyross can be understood in the context of intensifying commercial pressures, but may also be grounded in fundamental assumptions that editors make about places and people. In this vein one media professional told us:

> I rang up the news editor one morning giving him a news list and I said there was nothing from Moyross last night and he joked and said that's probably an even bigger story – there was no shootings in Moyross last night.

Broadcast media and Moyross

We now turn to examining how the local and national broadcast media portray Moyross. We focus on a radio documentary about the Millie and Gavin Murray story produced by Live 95fm and on RTE's television news coverage in the period of September to December 2006.

In stark contrast to the pathologising discourses evident within much of the print media coverage, the radio documentary narrates the story of the September 2006 arson attack and its aftermath in a sensitive way. Based on an amalgamation of archive news coverage and interviews, what emerges is a consciously balanced account in this human interest documentary. The programme interviews the children's mother and father, their Godmother, and the children themselves. It also draws upon the views of a grassroots activist, a senior Garda, as well as the then prime minister, Bertie Aherne, and the president of Ireland, Mary McAleese. Normalising discourses are to the fore. Moyross is portrayed as being no different than the rest of the nation. It emerges as a place united in its anger and grief. There are no references at all to Moyross as 'troubled'. There is one striking difference in how the story is told. Live 95fm's own news service makes specific reference to the event as happening in Pineview Gardens, whilst the nationally syndicated INN news talks of the 'Moyross area' in its report. The Millie and Gavin documentary is exemplary in that it seeks to balance the viewpoints of those most affected by this horrific attack with the perspectives of grassroots and national leaders. Crucially, it narrates a catastrophic story without ever once pathologising Moyross or its residents.

Seeing the world for real?

Residents interviewed by Dean and Hastings (2000, p. 21) were sensitive to the manner in which media professionals construct the neighbourhood for the audience. In particular, they raised the selection of unrepresentative visual images (still and moving) and negative descriptors. Our analysis of televisual media images relates to this question. Changes in work practices (and cost considerations) have resulted in a greater reliance on archived images. Images can have a significant impact on the meanings readers associate with an article (Andén-Papadopoulos, 2008). They are part of the text with which the audience engages.

In comparison to the print media, a far greater proportion of television news stories were concerned with crime; 22 of 24 television news reports examined had crime as their primary theme. All reports were *episodic* rather than *thematic* in orientation – in other words they focused on a precipitating event (such as a shooting or an arrest) rather than examining a general theme such as social exclusion or marginalisation. Eleven stories were concerned with or made reference to the arson attack on Gavin and Millie Murray. We again found a strong tendency towards reporting on Moyross as if it were an homogenous entity. The locus of the incident is referred to as the 'troubled estate of Moyross', the 'Moyross area', and the 'Moyross estate', rather than Pineview Gardens for example. As in the case of print articles, the convention of constructing Moyross as a 'troubled estate' extends beyond the reporting styles of individual reporters. The epithet is used by newscasters in introducing reports about Moyross and even as a descriptor within RTE's news archive itself.[5] By contrast, a discussion on Moyross broadcast by RTE's *Prime Time* on 12 September 2006 managed to convey the complexities of the many issues facing the residents of Moyross from contrasting ideological positions without once using this phrase. Within television news the underlying causal reasons for Moyross' marginalised status are largely invisible. The makers of television news might argue that in a 90-second report there is no room to refer to the background reasons for poverty and exclusion yet ironically there is space for assertions that pathologise neighbourhoods like Moyross.

At a visual level the imagery used within the television news reports convey a strong message about a place that is in its entirety beyond the pale, out of control, and in the grip of lawlessness and criminality. As well as crime scenes, we repeatedly witness images of boarded up and burnt out houses, wandering horses, and hooded youths. Given the focus on crime in the reports on Moyross at this time we also see a preponderance of images concerned with policing, crime scenes, surveillance, and the courts. In spite of the homogenising tendencies of this media coverage, it is interesting to note that footage of the neighbourhood – which stops at the entrance to parks such as Pineview Gardens or Delmege Park – are used numerous times giving, we argue, a sense of a place cut off from mainstream society, as a place that the imagined viewer cannot/will not go.[6] Houses and roads in and out of the neighbourhood are also used, we argue, to signify exclusion and desolation. Moyross is also conflated with other working-class neigh-bourhoods in Limerick and beyond such as O'Malley Park, Thomondgate, and Clondalkin. Residents we interviewed were sensitive to such limited visual representations of their locale:

> All I see emphasised is a horse and big stones and burnt out houses. There isn't a burnt out house in Cliona Park ... There's one burnt out house in Cosgrove Park. They haven't gone down there. . . . spotless clean. There's one or two areas and there's a handful of young undesirables who are holding us all to ransom.

Our examination of television news coverage during September–December 2006 also found a dependency on the use of archival footage in reporting on Moyross. This included the aforementioned burnt out and boarded up houses; the scorched ground in the aftermath of the September arson attack as well as wandering horses. There may be practical[7] (and economic) reasons for repeatedly using the same images of the place but their repeated use cannot be without its impact on audience perceptions and (mis)understandings of Moyross. Indeed, in recognising the profes-sional codes (see Hall, 1974) used by some media professionals one of the residents who participated in our focus group felt that she could recite the likely footage to be used at will:

> If the camera comes in here in the morning ... you'll see the school – a quick shot – and the Church, and it just goes up the hill and then you'll have the burnt out houses. Then it goes down over Hartigan's Hill and you have the burnt out houses down there.

She holds that media professionals choose not to film better areas. As with the textual juxtaposition of the positive and the negative in print media content, visual images may be used to juxtapose the positive and the negative in televised content. As with print media coverage, this can have the effect of negating the positive impact of the story, while adding to its perceived news value. Participants in our focus groups cited an example of such an occurrence in a recent episode of RTE's *Nationwide* news programme regarding a positive story about a successful local project that looked after the horses that once wondered loose around parts of the neighbourhood: 'And it was very positive I have to say ... But the images they showed with it was just horrendous ... for something that was such a positive story ... all the boarded up houses'.

Some of the participants in our focus group indicate that the use of archival footage may also lead to inaccuracy. For instance one resident claimed: 'There is certain things shown on TV that do not exist in Moyross. There was a hill there and I know for a fact it is Southill. .... It wasn't Moyross'. Another suggested:

> It's the same photograph going down Hartigan's Hill, going down Sarsfield Gardens. .... and all the houses are gone – the majority of them are gone. So, I mean, why don't they come out and take photographs now? You know, when the fields are green again. .... and come around the other parts? I mean there's more than the drugs and the guns in Moyross. I mean there is good people out here and we are all targeted with the same brush because we live in Moyross.

In the print media articles, pathologising discourses often focused on the visual appearance of Moyross.[8] Some are balanced in their depiction of the physical conditions in the neighbourhood. For example an article by David Hurley accompanies reference to the existence of burnt out houses in Moyross with a quote from a senior official within Limerick City Council who emphasises the selectivity of a focus solely upon damaged housing stock:

> I'm heartily sickened at constantly seeing photographs and video footage in the national media of houses with bits missing off them. I know those things exist but there are also very nice parts in places such as Moyross and O'Malley Park.
>
> *(Limerick Leader, 2007, 2 June)*

However, more make exclusive reference to burnt out and otherwise damaged housing. One article describes 'hundreds of derelict and badly damaged houses' (*Irish News*, 12 September 2007) while another reports that 'Of the 1,000 houses in Moyross, more than a third are unoccupied' (*Irish Independent*, 13 October 2007). Another article in the *Irish Independent* describes the neighbourhood as follows:

> Graffiti, including slogans such as 'scum' and 'rats out', adorns the shattered homes and burned waste scars the roads. Hooded teenagers roam the streets, suspiciously eyeing strangers, even driving alongside cars so they can check out the occupants for their bosses. Anyone who has opposed the gangs has been forced out. Towards the rear of Moyross the scene is apocalyptic. Delmege Park is a wasteland, its houses destroyed and completely uninhabitable.

These articles conceal more than they reveal. Of the original 1,130 houses in Moyross, 878 (77. per cent) were occupied as of February 2009.[9] There is also significant variation within Moyross as to the location of houses that are boarded up or previously demolished. At the time of writing, Dalgaish Park, for example, has had no houses demolished or boarded up. Cosgrave Park, likewise, has had no houses demolished and just one boarded up by the local council. Pineview and Whitecross Gardens, by contrast, have had significant levels of demolition or decommissioning of housing stock.[10]

Paraphrasing a source, one article makes a distinction between Moyross in general, which is depicted as 'violence-scarred', and a smaller area within the locality that is characterised as apparently comparable to other neighbourhoods: 'At this end of the neighbourhood, Moyross seems like any other respectable working-class estate in Ireland'. Clearly image matters.

Tarring the neighbourhood with the one brush

Dean and Hastings (2000) find that stigma has real impacts on the lives of residents. Of over 200 residents of stigmatised neighbourhoods whom they interviewed, all reported that their lives were impacted by stigma:

> They report that they are economically disadvantaged by living on the estate, that their relationships with non-residents are coloured by prejudice, and that they receive lower quality services from both the public and private sector than others in the wider area. In addition, the estate's reputation has an emotional impact felt by virtually all the residents, who are angry, hurt and upset by the expressions of stigma that they live with.
>
> *(Dean and Hastings, 2000, p. vii)*

These findings are confirmed by a number of other studies that document the economic and emotional impact of living in a stigmatised neighbourhood in particular (see Gourlay 2007, for confirmatory findings and a useful review of other studies drawing similar conclusions).

Our resident participants were acutely aware of the media image of their neighbourhood and made direct connections between this source of representation and the public perception of the area. While many vocally resisted stigmatising constructions, they also related ongoing impacts on their emotional and material wellbeing (Devereux *et al.*, 2011a, p. 136). In addition to a general acknowledgement of the stigma associated with their address, they cited specific examples of how the stigmatised identity of their neighbourhood translates into prejudice and differential treatment. With regard to the former, one resident cited the following example:

> If you go to Caherdavin [adjacent middle-class neighbourhood], you can see the gangs hanging around in Caherdavin the same as they are hanging around here. But if you talk to somebody from Caherdavin and you say 'God did you see the gangs up around the Church last night?' [the response would be] 'Ah sure, they're all from Moyross'. [Group laughs] I went up and I saw three different gangs and I didn't know one person in them. So, they weren't from Moyross.

With regard to the latter, participants cited the refusal of full service from companies that engage in delivery in general and highlighted taxi services in particular:

> One lady in particular she was in her seventies and she ordered a taxi from town with her groceries and she said Moyross. That man pulled up outside Watchhouse Cross [on the outskirts]. That lady was living up in the very top of Moyross. She had to walk with six bags.

More generally, the stigmatised identity of Moyross contributes to residents' sense of exclusion:

> I know there's a lot of people who won't go into Moyross because they are probably nervous. But it's like us if we read a paper and see something in Dublin . . . Do you know what I mean it's all down to the papers like?

Conclusions

The tripartite analysis of media coverage, on which this chapter reports, reveals a neighbourhood subject to stigmatising processes (Goffman, 1963). During the period 2006–7 Moyross was regularly constructed as an abnormal entity, a pathological place – 'troubled' and crime-ridden. Failures to distinguish between minority and majority actions and experiences served to homogenise the neighbourhood and its residents, tarring all with the same stereotype.

As with all stigmatising identities, Moyross' media image is constructed externally, by journalists, sub-editors, and editors, some of whom have developed a relationship with residents, but many of whom lack any intimate knowledge of the place. What are now cultural stereotypes of Moyross inform their knowledge of the neighbourhood and are reproduced in their cultural products.

The media professionals, who cooperated with this research, explain stigmatising constructions as the unintended consequences of self-interested practises on the part of media professionals and organisations struggling for survival in an ever-more competitive commercial environment. A political economy approach illuminates the role of commercial pressures in the stigmatisation of Moyross, drawing our attention to the impacts of rationalisation on the time and resources to which journalists have access in developing more nuanced familiarities with the places and people whom they report on. The same perspective also illuminates the commercial pressures that encourage editors and sub-editors to sensationalise for the sake of circulation figures (Devereux et al., 2011b). Such insights should not, however, be taken as an acceptance of the status quo; as is demonstrated by the radio documentary analysed as part of this research, alternative representations are possible should the will exist.

Whether intentional or not, the consequences of stigmatisation are very real for the residents of Moyross and other pathologised places (Dean and Hastings, 2000, p. viii; see also Permentier et al., 2008, 2009). Stigmatisation is nothing less than an exercise of power (Goffman, 1963). The unintended effects of rationalisation and competition can, we argue, also be read as latent manifestations of the place of mainstream media in Ireland's existing class structure. They draw our attention to the classed politics of representation. Stigmatising identities limit access to resources. The stigmatisation of disadvantaged neighbourhoods contributes to perpetuating their residents' inequitable social location.

Beyond the unbalanced nature of news coverage, the failure of mainstream news media (with a small number of laudable exceptions) to address the structural causes of the social problems on which their reporting concentrates serves to perpetuate the systems that, at a minimum, have permitted them to persist. Relaying selected 'facts' without analysis presents the challenges that face Moyross as occurring within a political vacuum and lend themselves to pathologising behavioural explanations. The unintended consequences of current mainstream news media depictions of Moyross is thus to support the status quo.

Indeed, many mainstream news media professionals, most of whom are themselves drawn from the middle classes (Bardoel and D'Haenens, 2004) do not, we assert, think of neighbourhoods such as Moyross when they imagine their audience. Disadvantaged neighbourhoods are of interest as the object of (commercially viable) constructions, to be explained and interpreted to the consumers of media products. Those media professionals who have worked to build trusting relationships with the residents of pathologised places find themselves caught between the interests of the neighbourhoods whose stories they seek to tell and the commercial concerns of the organisations for whom they work.

Although the residents to whom we spoke expressed a sense of frustration and powerlessness in the face of their external construction, we conclude this chapter by positing some possibilities for resistance. Erving Goffman (1963), author of the seminal work on stigmatised identities, conceptualised the possibilities for resistance as lying in the capacity of stigmatised individuals to insulate themselves from the impacts of their pathologisation. Informed by a critical theory perspective, we propose, rather, a process of empowerment that facilitates neighbourhood residents to take a more active role in their own representation, through knowledgeable engagement with the mainstream media and through the dissemination of their own discourses through community media. As of yet there have been only limited avenues made in this regard.

Wassenberg (2004) emphasises that attention to image is ineffectual without actual improvements in the lived experiences of residents. Regeneration in Limerick seeks to redress some of the factors that have contributed to Moyross' poor public image. Through physical regeneration they can address the environmental conditions that are used to pathologise the neighbourhood and its constituent areas. Social regeneration is equally required to address underlying issues such as unemployment and early school leaving.

Part of that social regeneration might involve directly addressing the stigmatised image of Moyross and the relationship of its residents and representatives with the media. Even where physical, social, and managerial issues are addressed, stigma may be intransigent (Wassenberg, 2004; Gourlay, 2007; Permentier *et al.*, 2008) and where stigma persists despite real improvements residents continue to suffer its effects in their interactions with those external to the neighbourhood and the neighbourhood itself remains a destination of last resort – in itself sufficient to produce a desire to leave on the part of residents (Dean and Hastings 2000). Image is worthy of our attention in seeking to understand the causes of decline and the challenges faced by regeneration. Indeed, Gourlay (2007, p. 1) holds that

> stigma should be approached as a distinct entity rather than as one of many neighbourhood problems and that placing stigma as a central focus of regeneration activity is beneficial for maintaining the quality of residential life and the long-term vitality of stigmatised urban neighbourhoods.

The media are, of course, only one of many actors involved in constructing neighbourhood identity. Dean and Hastings (2000, p. 24) conceptualise involvement in image construction in terms of shaping (generally unintentional contributions to the neighbourhood's image), responding ('reactions'), and challenging (purposeful attempts to influence the neighbourhood's image), and list the following actors: residents, grassroots activists, residents of neighbouring areas, regeneration initiatives, public services, private services (e.g. estate agents, supermarkets), employees working in the neighbourhood, other local employers, commercial media, and community-based media. Significantly, they do not regard commercial media as involved in challenging images of disadvantaged neighbourhoods. Indeed, they argue that this function is the primary remit only of community media and grassroots activists (Dean and Hastings, 2000, p. 24).

Community media initiatives: Community media provide groups with an opportunity for self-construction in the public mind. As well as initiatives using photography and video, Moyross has a regular newsletter – *Moywrites*. Moyross is also the home of the *Changing Ireland* publication, which has given extensive coverage to community development issues and challenges in the locality and in other communities. In 2009, a local newspaper, *The Moyross Voice*, was produced by students of journalism at the University of Limerick; the newspaper – distributed to all households in the neighbourhood – focused on positive stories of community engagement in Moyross. It now continues in an online format. These are positive developments. Community media are important to constructing a positive self-image, however, local people must also be empowered to challenge mainstream media, which are accessed by a much wider public.

Community media literacy: Scholars such as Howley (2005, 2009) have demonstrated in a convincing fashion the range of possibilities that exist in terms of the development of community-based media. In an Irish context, Conway, Cahill, and Corcoran (2009) document that media coverage of Fatima Mansions has undergone a striking alteration, with largely negative coverage of the neighbourhood in the 1990s being replaced by more positive coverage over the last number of years (see also Chapter 3). Fatima Mansions is particularly interesting because of the role its residents played in managing its media image. The community challenged the dominant negative storylines about their neighbourhood by emphasising positive stories, the strong social bonds, and locally based initiatives to address the neighbourhood's social problems. Media training helped the neighbourhoods' residents acquire resources to challenge their neighbourhood's 'spoiled identity' and residents became more proficient and refined in their offerings to the media (Conway *et al.*, 2009).

New media technology like the internet has an important role to play in opening up access to the media. The emergence of such technology offers everyone the opportunity to construct media content and communicate with local, national, and international audiences. With information, knowledge, and equipment everyone has the potential to become a citizen journalist, which impacts significantly on the power differentials between media producers and those that they portray (Howley, 2005).

The Fatima United Group also stressed the importance of empirical research in endorsing their endeavours and in gaining media coverage of them (Donohue and Dorman, 2006, p. 16). In effect, they argue that successful regeneration revolves on 'the community's ability to relate in an effective way to internal and external audiences and to exercise strategic control over how it is represented in media spaces' (Conway *et al.*, 2009). Media training and citizen journalism equally offers the residents of Moyross a chance to have a greater say in the construction of their own image.

Communities seeking to influence media content can capitalise on the pressures to which journalists are currently subject by providing their perspective in a media-ready format. We argue that in order to be effective, both of these strategies require sustainable and significant resourcing. Further locally based media training would contribute towards social regeneration. Even more importantly it would allow locals to challenge mainstream media representations of their neighbourhood. Given that community groups are in direct competition with a range of other and often better resourced interest groups, in attempting to shape the mainstream media's agendas it is imperative that such an initiative would be properly resourced. The repair of the neighbourhood's damaged reputation must be approached as a long-term project and as a pivotal aspect of social regeneration.

Power to the people? Finally, it is worth reminding ourselves that if people refuse to purchase media products that they perceive as portraying people or places in an unfair manner, it could successfully work as a strategy in challenging how Moyross is portrayed in the media. In 1989, for example, the *Sun* newspaper published a front-page article about the Hillsborough disaster. A boycott of the *Sun* was launched on Merseyside, which continues to this day. Sales of the paper plummeted (BBC, 2005). In 2004, while the paper sold 3.3 million copies throughout the UK, it sold only 12,000 in Liverpool, resulting in approximately £55 million of lost revenue over a 15-year period (Smith, 2004). Billy Butler, of Radio Merseyside, believes 'it's a marvellous way that ordinary people have to show their power, and this city used it' (Brown, 2009). Moreover, journalist Robin Brown argues the boycott 'sends an important signal to news media that smear journalism against honest, decent people has repercussions' (Brown, 2009). As audience members we should therefore reflect critically on our own practices and ask whether we can create a market for alternative representations.

Notes

1 In order to select a complete sample we began by searching both Nexis Lexis and the newspapers' proprietary archives for the term 'Moyross'. We later searched for the names of the 12 parks within Moyross, those being 'Delmege Park', 'Glenagross', 'Cosgrove Park', 'Pineview Gardens'/'Pine View Gardens', 'Daglish', 'College Park', 'Cliona Park', 'Creaval Park', 'Hartigan Villas', 'White Cross Gardens', 'Sarsfield Gardens', and 'Castle Park'. After all of the search terms had been used a number of duplicate articles were identified and consequently eliminated. Our sampling strategy returned a final total of 420 articles (*Irish Independent* – 82; *Irish News* – 21; *Limerick Leader* – 179; *Irish Mirror* – 138).
2 The frustration experienced by local community representatives with the negative image of Moyross and other social housing neighbourhoods was noted by Fitzgerald (2007). The Fitzgerald report, which was a precursor to the setting up of the Limerick Regeneration Agency, notes the 'intense negative publicity' (2007, p. 7) received by Moyross in 2006 as well as the wider implications for Limerick city as a whole resulting from its negative (media) image. This theme is repeatedly discussed in the Limerick Regeneration Agency's (2008) report *Limerick Regeneration: A Vision for Moyross, Southill/ Ballinacurra Weston and St. Mary's Park*. It recognises the implications of this negative image for the residents and also stresses the wider implications in terms of investment in the city.
3 The assertions of participants in Dean and Hastings' (2000) study regarding the negativity of descriptors used to characterise stigmatised estates are analysed in this fashion.
4 Wassenberg (2004, p. 274) notes that 'Whereas inhabitants look at satisfaction and a good dwelling, external actors define neighbourhoods in relation to each other and give them a place in the local neighbourhood hierarchy'. We will examine media content for the existence and characteristics of comparisons between Moyross and other neighbourhoods. Wassenberg draws our attention to the use of labels that signify such comparsions, such as 'working-class district, a slum, a middle-class area and the gold coast' (Wassenberg, 2004, p. 275).
5 Nonetheless, it should be noted that television journalists, unlike print journalists, have much more control over the editing and packing of the stories they produce.
6 Nonetheless, one of our interviewees explains that difficult relationships with the communities on whom they report can in some instances prevent media professionals from acquiring footage beyond entrances to the parks.
7 Including lack of access.
8 Although an article by the *Mirror* (8 November 2007) incorporates reference to the perceived intergenerational transmission of deviant values and norms from a criminal minority to the children of Moyross and Southill, 'These scum are passing on their poison to a new generation. Impressionable kids they may be and bravado they may spout but in a few years they could carry through their threats'.
9 Source – communication to the authors from the Northside Regeneration Agency, February 2009.
10 Of the 67 houses originally built in Whitecross Gardens 15 have been demolished and 14 boarded up.

References

Andén-Papadopoulos, K. (2008) The AbuGhraib torture photographs: News frames, visual culture and the power of images. *Journalism*, 9(1), 5–30.

Bardoel, J. and D'Haenens, L. (2004) Media accountability and responsibility: New conceptualisations and practises. *Communications: The European Journal of Communications Research*, 29(1), 5–25.

Barnes, C. (2010) *Young masculinities, class and community: A comparative perspective across local boundaries*, Irish Social Sciences Platform Project Report 2008–10. Limerick: ISKS, University of Limerick.

Bauder, H. (2002) Neighbourhood effects and cultural exclusion. *Urban Studies*, 39(1), 85–93.

BBC (2005) *'Sorry' Sun tries to woo Scousers: Asking for forgiveness is not usually the Sun's style.* http://news.bbc.co.uk/2/hi/uk_news/magazine/4258455.stm (accessed 5 September 2009).

Blokland, T. (2008) You got to remember you live in public housing: Place-making in an American housing project. *Housing, Theory and Society*, 25(1), 31–46.

Brown, R. (2009) *Why does Liverpool boycot the Sun? Liverpool culture blog.* www.liverpoolcultureblog.co.uk/2009/03/why-does-liverpool-boycott-the-sun/ (accessed 5 September 2009).

Bullock, H., Fraser Wyche, K., and Williams, W. (2001) Media images of the poor. *Journal of Social Issues*, 57(2), 229–46.

Byrne, D. (1999) *Social exclusion.* Buckingham: Open University Press.

Clayman, S.E. and Reisner, A. (1998) Gatekeeping in action: Editorial conferences and assessments of newsworthiness. *American Sociological Review*, 63(2), 178–99.

Conway, B., Cahill, L., and Corcoran, M. (2009) *The 'miracle' of Fatima: media framing and the regeneration of a Dublin housing estate.* Maynooth: NIRSA Working Paper Series No. 47.

Dean, J. and Hastings, A. (2000) *Challenging images: Housing estates, stigma and regeneration.* Bristol: Polity Press/Joseph Rowntree Foundation.

Devereux, E., Haynes, A., and Power, M. (2011a) At the edge: media constructions of a stigmatised housing estate. *Journal of Housing and the Built Environment*, 26(2), 123–42.

— (2011b) Tarring everyone with the same shorthand: Journalists, stigmatisation and social exclusion. *Journalism: Theory, Practice and Criticism*, 13(4), 500–17.

Donohue, J. and Dorman, P. (2006) *Dream/Dare/Do.* Dublin: Fatima Groups United.

Fenton, N. (2007) Bridging the mythical divide: Political economy and cultural studies approaches to the analysis of media. In E. Devereux (ed.) *Media studies: Key issues and debates* (pp. 8–31). London: Sage.

Fitzgerald, J. (2007) *Addressing issues of social exclusion in Moyross and other disadvantaged areas of Limerick city.* Limerick: Limerick City Council.

Gitlin, T. (1994) *Inside prime time.* London: Routledge.

Goffman, E. (1963) *Stigma.* London: Penguin.

Golding, P. and Middleton, S. (1982) *Images of welfare: Press and public attitudes to poverty.* Oxford: Martin Robertson.

Gourlay, G. (2007) *'It's got a bad name and it sticks . . .' Approaching stigma as a distinct focus of neighbourhood regeneration initiatives.* Paper presented to the EURA Conference, September, The Vital City, Berlin.

Greer, C. and Jewkes, Y. (2005) Extremes of otherness: Media images of social exclusion. *Social Justice*, 32(1), 20–31.

Hall, S. (1974) The television discourse: encoding and decoding. *Education and Culture*, 25, 8–14.

Hastings, A. (2004) Stigma and social housing estates: Beyond pathological explanations. *Journal of Housing and the Built Environment*, 19(3), 233–54.

Hayward, K. and Yar, M. (2006) The 'chav' phenomenon: Consumption, media and the construction of a new underclass. *Crime Media Culture*, 2(1), 9–28.

Howley, K. (2005) *Community media: People, places and communications technologies*. Cambridge: Cambridge University Press.

Howley, K. (ed.) (2009) *Understanding community media*. London: Sage.

Humphreys, E. (2011) Social capital, health and inequality: what's the problem in the neighbourhoods? In N. Hourigan (ed.) *Understanding Limerick* (pp. 185–210). Cork: Cork University Press.

Krippendorf, K. (2004) *Content analysis: An introduction to its methodology*, second edition. Thousand Oaks, CA: Sage.

Lens, V. (2002) Public voices and public policy: Changing the societal discourse on welfare. *Journal of Sociology and Social Welfare*, 29(1), 137–54.

Levitas, R. (2000) What is social exclusion? In D. Gordon and P. Townsend (eds) *Breadline Europe* (pp. 357–64). Bristol: The Policy Press.

Limerick Regeneration Agency (2008) *Limerick regeneration: A vision for Moyross, Southill/Ballinacurra Weston and St. Mary's Park*. Limerick: Limerick Regeneration Agency.

Lincoln, Y.S. and Guba, E.G. (1985) *Naturalistic inquiry*. Beverly Hills, CA: Sage.

Mosco, V. and Wasko, J. (eds) (1988) *The political economy of information*. Madison: University of Wisconsin Press.

Nauta, O., Tulner, H., and van Soomeran, P. (2001) *De Bijlmer Monitor 2000*. Amsterdam: Van Dijk and Van Sommeren en Partners.

Oresjo, E., Andersson, R., and Holmquist, E. (2004) *Large housing estates in Sweden: Policies and practices*. Utrecht: Faculty of Geosciences, Utrecht University.

Permentier, M., van Ham, M., and Bolt, G. (2009) Neighbourhood reputation and the intention to leave the neighbourhood. *Environment and Planning*, 41(9), 2162–80.

— (2008) Same neighbourhood . . . different views? A confrontation of internal and external neighbourhood reputations. *Housing Studies*, 23(6), 833–55.

Philo, G. (2008) News content studies, media group methods and discourse analysis: A comparison of approaches. In E. Devereux (ed.) *Media studies: Key issues and debates* (pp. 101–33). London: Sage.

— (1990) *Seeing and believing*. London: Routledge.

Ryfe, D.M. (2009) Broader and deeper: A study of newsroom culture in a time of change. *Journalism*, 10(2), 197–216.

Shoemaker, P. and Reese, S. (1996) *Mediating the message: Theories of influences on mass media content*, second edition. Boston, MA: Longman.

Shoemaker, P. J., Hyuk Lee, J., Han, G., and Cohen, A.A. (2007) Proximity and scope as news values. In E. Devereux (ed.) *Media studies: Key issues and debates* (pp. 231–48). London: Sage.

Smith, D. (2004) The city that eclipsed the *Sun*. *The Observer*, 11 July, www.guardian.co.uk/media/2004/jul/11/pressandpublishing.football (accessed 5 September 2009).

Warr, D.J. (2006) There goes the neighbourhood: The malign effects of stigma. *Social City*, 19, 1–11.

Wassenberg, F. (2004) Renewing stigmatised estates in the Netherlands: A framework for image renewal strategies. *Journal of Housing and the Built Environment*, 19(3), 271–92.

White, A. (2008) *To tell you the truth: The ethical journalism initiative*. Brussels: International Federation of Journalists.

Print media articles cited

Irish Independent (2006, 25 October) Help at hand for troubled city suburb.

Irish Independent (2006, 30 October a) Gang buster's tough job.

Irish Independent (2006, 30 October b) Ex-city manager drafted into feud estate.

Irish Independent (2007, 31 March) Radical plan to clean up city's crime-ridden housing estates.

Irish Independent (2007, 8 August) Sports stars tog out for troubled estates' children.

Irish Independent (2007, 26 August) A voice crying in the wilderness of crime, dereliction and neglect.

Irish Independent (2007, 13 October) Wealthy, modern Ireland and gang culture live side by side.

Irish Independent (2007, 15 December) City's wise monks recreate Bethlehem.

Irish Mirror (2006, 28 September) OUR BABY OF HOPE; HEART TOT OP DELIGHT FOR ESTATE FROM HELL.

Irish Mirror (2007, 11 September) TEAR DOWN MOYROSS.

Irish News (2007, 11 September) Regeneration work starts on city's gangland estates.

Irish News (2007, 12 September) Children hurt in fire-bomb recovering.

Limerick Leader (2006, 29 May) County types.

Limerick Leader (2006, 21 September) Editorial.

Limerick Leader (2007, 21 April) Councillors are disappointed at not being told of Fitzgerald plans.

Limerick Leader (2007, 26 May) The dispossessed.

Limerick Leader (2007, 2 June) IN WITH THE NEW AS CITY CHANGES FOR THE BETTER.

Limerick Leader (2007, 10 November) Gaisce chief meets the Moyross youth achievers.

The Mirror (2006, 30 October) CRIME TSAR FOR MOYROSS.

The Mirror (2007, 8 November) IRISH DAILY MIRROR COMMENT: THREATS TO KILL ARE NOT CHILD'S PLAY.

11

CONCLUSIONS

Michelle Norris and Tony Fahey

Ten years of change in seven social-housing neighbourhoods

This book has employed evidence from two rounds of research on seven urban neighbourhoods in Ireland to examine social change and the local impact of public policies for the ten-year period between 1997–8 and 2007–9. Much of the original round of research has already been reported on (Fahey, 1999). In the present study we add both a ten-year follow-up on the seven neighbourhoods, along with some further reflection on both the original and the follow-up findings viewed together. All of the seven neighbourhoods examined here were originally constructed by local authorities for letting as social housing, but due to the longstanding policy of sale of social-rented dwellings to tenants in Ireland, most now contain large proportions of homeowner households and many include some dwellings let by private landlords and other social landlords such as housing associations. However, the neighbourhoods continue to draw much of their identity and character from their origins in the social housing system and from the continuing relationship that many residents have with local authorities as landlords. Furthermore, they share an important socioeconomic characteristic with the wider social-rented tenure in Ireland – all seven suffer high levels of disadvantage relative to the Irish population at large and, as explained in Chapter 2, three of the case study neighbourhoods are among the 5 per cent of the most disadvantaged in Ireland.

Two main inter-related themes run through both the initial study and the ten-year follow-up. One is the concern to recognise the internal differentiation of the social housing sector in Ireland as a key feature, in place of a common tendency to regard social housing as uniformly problematic. Some social housing fails and provides poor living environments for residents but most of it succeeds and blends into the general housing stock. Even within individual neighbourhoods, there are often startling contrasts between settled, well-integrated streets or roads and clearly unsettled counterparts within minutes' walking distance. Our research on the neighbourhoods paid a great deal of attention to this diversity and sought both to highlight and understand it.

Our second and closely related concern was to focus on the *liveability* of the neighbourhoods (particularly their *social* liveability) as a feature that needed to be kept conceptually separate from their level of social disadvantage and seen as a distinct dimension of differentiation. By liveability we mean the extent to which neighbourhoods succeed in attracting and retaining residents and giving them environments they like to live in as opposed to becoming so rundown and unpopular that they undermine residents' quality of life and, at the extreme, require regeneration through radical and costly programmes of demolition and rebuilding. Because social housing is targeted on low-income families, social housing neighbourhoods typically originate in broadly similar conditions of relative disadvantage but that is not to say that they produce social environments of broadly similar levels of liveability. Rather, it is the differentiation of liveability in spite of the similarity of profiles of disadvantage that is the striking feature of social housing neighbourhoods. While we recognise that many factors affect liveability, we point here to locally variable instances of social order problems as a key influence and in that sense point to the social element in liveability as a central issue.

In addition to these two concerns running through both the original and the follow-up studies, there were two further concerns that gave additional prompt to the follow-up and gave it much of its direction. One derived from the economic boom that was underway more or less until the end of the ten-year period of the study. The concern here was to ask whether and in what ways the effects of the boom filtered into the study neighbourhoods and affected the patterns of differentiation they revealed. The second concern related to the upsurge in Ireland of area-based interventions – programmes specially targeted on disadvantaged areas – as a means to tackle the problems of poor urban neighbourhoods. Activities arising from these interventions were abundantly in evidence in our study neighbourhoods (though in some more than others) and it seemed useful to try to get a better picture of their extent and significance on the ground.

Liveability of the seven neighbourhoods

The themes of differentiation in the social housing sector and its relative disconnect from levels of social disadvantage that had emerged from our original study were borne out by the contrasting developments that occurred in our study neighbourhoods by the time we revisited them ten years later. One of the most illustrative contrasts is that between Fettercairn (located in Tallaght in southwest Dublin, an area with large tracts of newly developed social housing) and Moyross (on the edge of Limerick city). In 1997–8, these neighbourhoods were in broadly similar condition: neither was the worst of the seven estates but both had similar high levels of social disadvantage and had a mixed record in coping with the strains of accommodating large numbers of newly settled social housing residents. If anything,

Moyross seemed to have the more promising outlook as it had a strong community development movement and had the benefit of what seemed a newly activist and creative approach to estate management by the housing department in Limerick City Council. Since then, however, the two neighbourhoods have evolved in sharply different directions. Following an eruption of inter-gang feuding in Moyross in the early 2000s, conditions in the area deteriorated sharply and lead to the deluge of adverse media coverage reported on in Chapter 10. Soon after our fieldwork was completed, a government commissioned report on Moyross and certain other local authority neighbourhoods in Limerick (the Fitzgerald report – Fitzgerald, 2007), was sharply critical of social conditions in these areas and condemned the failure of public policy to take effective remedial action. Moyross had thus quickly become a classic instance of a failed local authority housing area. There soon followed a hugely ambitious €3 billion plan to regenerate the areas involved. Although considerable demolition of dwellings and resettlement of residents has taken place, most elements of the regeneration plan have floundered under the impact of spending cuts caused by the newly arrived recession. The future of Moyross is now uncertain. Fettercairn, by contrast, as has been outlined earlier, showed considerable improvement and embarked on what still seems a long steady process of estate maturation. Most significantly, the rhetoric of failure that has resounded around Moyross and certain other areas in Limerick has been absent in Fettercairn and indeed in the wider Tallaght area. Fettercairn thus far has experienced the welcome fading from public view that is the standard sign of the reasonably successful development of a settled social housing neighbourhood.

Another striking instance of change is offered by the experience of Fatima Mansions. This Dublin inner-city complex of balcony flats emerged from our original study as the worst living environment of any of the seven estates, primarily because of an out-of-control heroin problem. The sense of crisis surrounding the area led to a radical regeneration plan by the early 2000s. This was implemented through a complete demolition and rebuild of the housing, along with a dense and well-organised provision of new and creative support services. The result was a positive transformation of the locality – a striking instance of successful regeneration.

Other neighbourhoods followed relatively static liveability trajectories. In the eyes of residents, Deanrock was the most liveable of the case study neighbourhoods in 1997–8. Despite a mediocre built environment, it experienced very high demand for tenancies among social housing applicants and our interviews with residents revealed high levels of satisfaction. By 2007–9 Deanrock had retained high levels of satisfaction among residents, the community remained vibrant, and privatised houses there were selling for close to the norm for adjacent private neighbourhoods. In 1997–8 Muirhevnamore in Dundalk and Cranmore in Sligo were positively evaluated by many residents, but some enclaves within these neighbourhoods were characterised by lower liveability, therefore our fieldwork indicated that they were less uniformly successful than Deanrock, but were closer to the high end of the liveability continuum than, for instance, Fettercairn. Over the decade since then both neighbourhoods have benefited from piecemeal refurbishments and social interventions, rather than more comprehensive programmes of regeneration, but they appear to have stabilised over time. Despite some continuing difficulties, they remained towards the more relatively successful end of the liveability continuum in 2007–9.

Parts of Finglas South were closer to the 'moderate to low' end of the liveability continuum in 1997–8 due to problems of anti-social behaviour and criminality that impacted negatively on these neighbourhoods. Most dwellings in Finglas South have been privatised, market demand for these was strong in 2007–9, and many additional community facilities were provided there during the preceding decade. Despite this, our fieldwork found dissatisfaction among residents of some districts within the neighbourhood, weak community structures, and extensive anti-social behaviour. In this regard in this neighbourhood liveability remained mixed during the decade under review. Our 1997–8 fieldwork revealed similar problems in Moyross, coupled with weaker housing demand and more dereliction, but we were more optimistic about its future because of strong community activism and good housing management standards there. This proved erroneous as by 2007–9 demand for housing had declined to the extent that dwellings were selling for a quarter of the regional average, voids were widespread and criminality and anti-social behaviour were more extensive than in Finglas South. Thus we found that the liveability of this neighbourhood had declined further – a judgement that is substantiated by a recent housing ministry report (Fitzgerald, 2007).

This complex picture of diversity *between* the seven neighbourhoods in terms of liveability is further complicated by significant variation *within* these same areas. For instance, neighbourhoods were rarely found to be uniformly improving or declining across all of the various dimensions of liveability under examination. In both 1997–8 and 2007–9 we found that all of the seven neighbourhoods were characterised by strong place attachment and supportive relationships between neighbours and mutual aid to an extent that would be unusual in wealthier districts (Burns and Taylor, 1998, make the same point). In addition, our 1997–8 fieldwork revealed marked variations in the liveability of different small areas within the neighbourhoods that were much stronger than liveability variations between the neighbourhoods (Rowlands, Musterd, and Van Kempen, 2009, reach a similar finding). Some parts of individual neighbourhoods were in high demand among applicants for housing and prospective purchasers and were well-kept and settled while other parts were unpopular, had high turnover, and were in varying degrees of dereliction. In 1997–8 this internal diversity was particularly marked in Cranmore, Fatima Mansions, and Moyross. Some of the variations within these neighbourhoods have since been modified by regeneration programmes – this was most ambitious and successful in Fatima Mansions, but the more modest refurbishment of Banks Drive in Cranmore nevertheless improved the relative position of that area within the neighbourhood, while the demolition of the blocks of flats in Deanrock removed the most precarious segment of what generally was (and remains) a settled, stable neighbourhood. Today, internal diversity remains significant in South Finglas and also in Moyross, where a new wave of decline since the early 2000s has affected much of the neighbourhood, but stable, liveable areas remain.

Drivers of declining and improving liveability

The analysis presented in this book also sheds light on the drivers of liveability changes in the case study neighbourhoods and, by extension, on the relevance of the existing literature on neighbourhood decline to these cases.

In Chapter 3 Mary Corcoran highlights three factors that contributed to an improvement in liveability across time. These are: a generalised raising of aspirations among residents; sustained engagement by residents in attempts to improve quality of life in some neighbourhoods, much of it focused on the arts and sports; and enhanced capacity on the part of these communities to act collectively in their own interests, as evidenced by their efforts to establish and shape regeneration programmes and their involvement in community development activities. On the other hand she argues that the ongoing problems of stigmatisation and marginalisation of parts of some neighbourhoods and the communities that reside there continue to weaken the overall liveability of the neighbourhood. A proportion of residents also suffer from multiple problems but are alienated from their neighbours and key service providers so they remain a 'hard-to-reach group'. Furthermore, there is also evidence of a deeper institutionalisation of an intergenerational dependency culture among some members of this alienated minority, characterised by the internalisation of norms and values that militate against individual capacity building and self-actualisation.

Corcoran's analysis of the factors that undermine neighbourhood liveability is reinforced by the investigation of drugs and drug markets and crime and social (dis) order presented by Aileen O'Gorman in Chapters 8 and 9 respectively. These chapters point to a marked coincidence between the prevalence of serious social order problems (often related to the operation of drugs markets) and low liveability. This is because these social order problems are often caused by the alienated minority identified by Corcoran.

Notably, there is no similarly strong coincidence between trends in the liveability and two of the other most prominent and longstanding themes in the literature on neighbourhood decline – social disadvantage and the quality of the built environment, although these issues appear to have exerted some influence in some neighbourhoods. Despite the marked inter-neighbourhood variations in liveability, in Chapter 2 Trutz Haase demonstrates that all of the seven neighbourhoods are in relative terms deprived, and Deanrock, which was consistently the most liveable neighbourhood examined here, experienced a marked increase in disadvantage during the decade under examination (from −8.8 in 1996 to −19.1 in 2006). The 1997–8 fieldwork revealed that most of the neighbourhoods suffered from either poor housing quality or a weak physical infrastructure, or a combination of both, irrespective of liveability levels. Some of these physical problems were eliminated during the decade since then but improvements in liveability have not occurred in parallel to improvements in the built environment. Housing conditions in Fatima Mansions improved dramatically between 1997–8 and 2007–9, while in Fettercairn they improved modestly but both neighbourhoods enjoyed a marked concurrent improvement in liveability. This said, the 1997–8 fieldwork in Fatima Mansions indicates that the design of common areas did facilitate the social disorder that undermined its liveability, and its demolition and reconstruction did help to avert these social order problems (see Chapter 9). Thus the evidence presented in this book indicates that neighbourhood liveability is driven primarily by the strength and cohesion of the communities and the life-ability of the individuals who live there, and the built environment and disadvantage exert only a secondary influence, albeit one that is significant in some cases.

Policy, services, and liveability of disadvantaged neighbourhoods

The analysis of variations in liveability and the drivers of these also has implications for the design and delivery of social and community services in the seven case study neighbourhoods and for policy on the regeneration of disadvantaged neighbourhoods and the area-based initiatives that target them. Michelle Norris' analysis in Chapter 6 indicates that area-based initiatives targeted at disadvantaged neighbourhoods have expanded significantly in recent decades in Ireland to the extent that they constituted a major area of public expenditure in 2007–9. Furthermore, both Norris' analysis of the operation of ABIs at the national level and Des McCafferty and Eileen Humphries' analysis of their impact at the neighbourhood level in Chapter 7 highlight a number of problems associated with their design and implementation, which indicates that despite many successful elements, collectively these schemes were less than the sum of their parts when our second round of fieldwork was conducted in the late 00s.

Targeting disadvantaged neighbourhoods: The first key lesson arising from this research relates to methods for targeting public investment on disadvantaged neighbourhoods. In Chapter 6 Michelle Norris points out that the rationale behind decisions to target this investment on particular neighbourhoods was often not explicit and, even when it is, targeting decisions were rarely linked to any empirical evidence, such as the location of spatial concentrations of disadvantaged house-holds. In addition, the spatial units to be targeted by ABIs are often defined only loosely, if at all, and the tendency over time was to extend the spatial scope of programmes, thus reducing the intended benefits of targeting since there was then no effective means of ensuring that programmes reach the neediest groups. The latter weakness – failing to reach the neediest – is difficult to overcome because of the particularly wide geographical dispersion of social disadvantage in Ireland (Watson, Whelan, Williams, and Blackwell, 2005). The low density of population and the small number of large urban centres means large spatial concentrations of disadvantaged households are less common in Ireland than, for instance, the United States, the United Kingdom, or the Netherlands (Dorling *et al.,* 2007; Glasmeier, 2005; Musterd, de Vos, Das, and Latten, 2012).

The scale of public spending on ABIs coupled with the difficulties in accurately targeting this investment indicate that spatial targeting have become an over-used element of social policy in Ireland by 2007–9 and should be scaled back to instances where there is a clear rationale and effective methodology for employing this approach. This is not to say that expenditure currently devoted to these schemes should be cut proportionately, but rather that the case for targeting it spatially rather than on disadvantaged groups within the population needs to be made in all cases, and where that case is weak, the adoption of more traditional distribution mechanisms should be considered.

Furthermore, if spending is spatially targeted the methodology used to select target neighbourhoods should take account of variations in liveability. In the Irish context this would require the extension of the Pobal HP Deprivation Index to include indicators of neighbourhood liveability as well as deprivation. Indexes of this type (albeit not explicitly linked to liveability) are employed in a number of countries (e.g. Department for Communities and Local Government, 2011) and the methodology used to assess liveability in this volume, and the discussion of how it is manifested in the seven case study neighbourhoods, could inform the design of a similar index for Ireland that, if supplemented by additional information on for instance neighbourhood satisfaction, would enable the more effective targeting of ABIs.

Implementing policies which target disadvantaged neighbourhoods: during the 2007–9 tranche of fieldwork in particular we came across many instances of good practice among the ABIs in the case study neighbourhoods and several of these projects and the national programmes that fund them have been shown in independent evaluations to be effective in their own terms. However, we found that the valuable work carried out by ABI staff and volunteers in the case study neighbourhoods was not supported effectively by national arrangements for their funding, monitoring, and governance.

Chapters 6 and 7 highlight a confusing proliferation of ABI funding programmes and schemes in Ireland, overall responsibility was fragmented, and funding streams and local governance arrangements were overly complex. The multiplicity of programmes hindered their coherent integration into national anti-poverty strategies and created significant challenges for service providers in disadvantaged neighbourhoods who are forced to seek contributions from a number of funding programmes in order to finance their services. While in theory area-based interventions are said to facilitate local empowerment, adaptation to local circumstances, and community development, in practice they were often rigidly controlled by centrally defined eligibility criteria and accountability regulations. This means that the ABI programmes had largely failed to achieve their objectives in relation to deliberative democracy, while at the same time the existence of this alternative system of local governance had tended to weaken the status of the formal local government sector in Ireland. The management of ABI programmes nationally was also excessively oriented to inputs and associated accounting controls with little systematic orientation to outcomes or to assessments of impacts. This placed an excessive bureaucratic burden on managers of the local projects funded by the ABIs while generating limited information relevant to monitoring achievements and therefore improving project design. In addition, the funding principles that underpin the design of ABI funding schemes nationally (for example, in regard to the balance between capital and current funding) seemed to be *ad hoc* and dependent on larger national budgetary priorities rather than on the problems of the neighbourhoods they seek to help.

Many of these problems have been identified in reviews and evaluations of area-based initiatives conducted since the late 1990s (see Chapter 6 for a summary). It is disquieting to note that while these programmes continued to grow for much of the 2000s, only limited progress was made in tackling the problems identified. Some of the attempted solutions, such as the establishment of County Enterprise and Development Boards as a means to integrate local development activities, seem simply to have added an additional pillar of complexity to an already over-complex system. A major review of public spending, initiated at the beginning of Ireland's current economic crisis, recommended extensive consolidation of programmes and streamlining of delivery systems in the community development field (Special Group on Public Service Numbers and Expenditure Programmes, 2009). The evidence presented in this book supports these recommendations (and some progress had been made in their implementation at the time of writing) and the growing need for supportive interventions in disadvantaged neighbourhoods as a result of the ongoing economic crisis also indicates that these types of efficiency gains are urgently required if ABI expenditure cuts are to avoid undermining vital supports on the ground.

The analysis presented in Chapters 6 and 7 indicates that structure and governance of area-based initiatives in Ireland could be simplified and greater responsibility could be given to local authorities in the local coordination and management of programmes. At national level the large number of individual funding programmes currently in existence should be amalgamated into a smaller number of more generalist schemes, the focus of which reflects the most critical interventions required in poor neighbourhoods that are outlined below. At local level, responsibility for the distribution and monitoring of this funding should be undertaken within the structures of local government and governance arrangements should be simplified. These changes could reduce the rigidities that arise from existing centralised controls and ease the pressure to 'chase' funding from central sources. Increased powers of decision making at local level could thus enhance the potential for genuine participation of local civil society.

Designing policies that target disadvantaged neighbourhoods: While the targeting of services for the disadvantaged on an area basis should be less widely used in Ireland, efforts to combat disadvantage that are focused on the neighbourhood level, such as estate regeneration schemes, are necessary and useful in many cases. However, in addition to the reforms to implementation arrangements outlined above, the focus of ABIs needs to be reconsidered to improve their effectiveness in reversing low and declining liveability.

ABIs should focus on acutely disadvantaged and multi-problem households, in which deprivation (low incomes, lack of access to jobs, low education, inadequate housing) is compounded by a range of additional problems such as poor mental health, drug or alcohol addiction, family disruption, poor capacity for parenting, and conflict with neighbours. These households should be given high priority in the design of area-based interventions and in social inclusion policy more broadly, primarily because they are in extreme need and are therefore entitled to support on welfare grounds, but also because their problems often have spill-over effects at neighbourhood level in the form of various kinds of anti-social behaviour that reduces the quality of life for those who live around them. These types of 'neighbourhood effects' are often the single most important source of collective disadvantage in poor neighbourhoods, over and above disadvantages that arise for residents at household level. Progress made to date in the provision of intensive, high-quality support services for these acutely disadvantaged households is one of the most positive developments of the past decade in the seven case study neighbourhoods under examination here. This progress should be sustained and further developed with a particular focus on the following core areas:

1. Health and family support: particularly in regard to services such as parenting supports, mental health, and addiction treatment (in view of the high rates of occurrence of these problems among acutely disadvantaged households).

2. Education: services targeted at those suffering multiple deprivation that should be less classroom based and school bound than is currently the case in Ireland and more effective in reaching out to involve parents, other relatives, and the wider community as well as children themselves. In addition it is desirable that interventions in this area be able to draw on a wider range of skills in dealing with extreme disadvantage than are available within the largely pedagogical focus of current school-based programmes.

3. Criminal justice: especially for effective methods of community policing, with a focus on creative responses to young people at risk of running into trouble with the criminal justice system (though in some cases the requirement extends to problems of serious crime). These would include the capacity to offer more intensive services over a longer period of time where necessary, and more attention to, and capacity to engage in, preventive action (e.g. by identifying children at risk earlier, structuring interventions around families, etc.).

This focus on the provision of intensive ongoing supports for acutely disadvantaged households in turn highlights the need to avoid excessive focus on capital programmes (refurbishment or replacement of dwellings, rehabilitation of the physical environment, provision of community buildings) to the neglect of services. The experience of the seven neighbourhoods examined in this book demonstrates that public funding agencies are often more willing to provide one-off capital grants (which may be quite large) rather than commit to long-term annual services expenditure even where the latter is what is required to address key problems in disadvantaged areas. The balance between capital and current expenditure in area-based interventions schemes should be based on a well-informed diagnosis of what is needed in those areas rather than on *a priori* preference for capital over current expenditure.

References

Burns, D. and Taylor, M. (1998) *Mutual aid and self-help: coping strategies for excluded communities*, Bristol: Policy Press.

Corcoran, M. (1998) *Making Fatima a better place to live*, Dublin: Fatima Groups United.

Department for Communities and Local Government (2011) *The English indices of deprivation 2010*, London: HMSO.

Dorling, D., Rigby, J., Wheeler, B., Ballas, D., Thomas, B., Fahmy, E., Gordon, D., and Lupton, R. (2007) *Poverty, wealth and place in Britain, 1968 to 2005*, Bristol: Policy Press.

Fahey, T. (ed.) (1999) *Social housing in Ireland: A study of success, failure and lessons learned*, Dublin: Oak Tree Press.

Fitzgerald, J. (2007) *Addressing issues of social exclusion in Moyross and other disadvantaged areas of Limerick city*, Limerick: Limerick City Council.

Glasmeier, A.K. (2005) *An atlas of poverty in America: One nation, pulling apart, 1960–2003*, London: Taylor and Francis.

Musterd, S., de Vos, S., Das, M., and Latten, J.J. (2012) 'Neighbourhood composition and economic prospects: A longitudinal study in the Netherlands', *Tijdschrift voor Economische en Sociale Geografie*, 103(1), 85–100.

Rowlands, R., Musterd, S., and Van Kempen, R. (eds) (2009) *Mass housing in Europe: Multiple faces of development, change and response*, Basingstoke: Palgrave Macmillan.

Special Group on Public Service Numbers and Expenditure Programmes (2009) *Vol I. & Vol II. Detailed papers*, Dublin: Government Publications Office.

Watson, D., Whelan, C., Williams, J., and Blackwell, S. (2005) *Mapping poverty: National regional and county patterns*, Dublin: Institute of Public Administration and the Combat Poverty Agency.

INDEX

References in **bold** indicate tables and in *italic* indicate figures.